INTRODUCTION
TO THE
STUDY and PRACTICE OF LAW
IN A NUTSHELL
THIRD EDITION

By
KENNEY HEGLAND
James E. Rogers Professor of Law
University of Arizona

WEST
GROUP

ST. PAUL, MINN.
2000

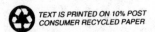

In memory of

> Arthur Leff and Grant Gilmore
> Hall of Famers

And dedicated to lawyers

> In good times, great jokes;
> In bad, great friends

*

PREFACE

This book will make you a better law student and, down the road, a better lawyer. I'm thrilled to play a part in your professional development. Thanks.

On the shore, about to embark on one of life's greatest journeys, you have dreams . . . and fears.

"Is law school the right choice? Will I survive; will I prosper?"

"Will law be my life's work? Will I make a difference? Will I be happy?"

"This book seems pretty long. Do I have to read the *whole* thing?"

No matter how lofty our dreams, no matter how distant our vision, we live in the present moment. No, you don't have to read the whole thing, at least not now. A crib sheet will follow.

But maybe I've been talking to the wrong person. Maybe you aren't planning to be a lawyer but simply picked up this book in hopes of learning something about the law and about the profession. Good for you. Law is the neglected Humanity. How does our society resolve conflict? How is power checked? How does the law change to reflect, or lead, societal changes? What is legal reasoning? How does the adversary system work and what are its premises? How are lawyers trained, and how do judges decide?

As to style, I'll crack jokes. While law deals with serious matters, it needn't be pompous, tedious nor laborious. That's my view and, I hope, will become yours as well. At the end of the day, you should *enjoy* the law.

This isn't a sit back and read book. I'll ask you to throw pots. I will describe and illustrate the key skills: legal analysis, legal argument and, oh yes, taking exams. Then I will give you an opportunity to develop and practice those skills: cases to analyze, arguments to construct, and exams to take.

Throw pots and you will soon be "thinking like a lawyer" (but, I hope, not mixing metaphors like one). The more you put into your pottery, the more you will teach yourself about the art of lawyering. As for me, I'll stick around, offering encouragement and advice.

So, where's the crib sheet?

Part One: Legal Analysis Made Simple.

Both law students and academic voyeurs should read this part first. It explains the operation of the common law system and simply is key to understanding such doctrines as *stare decisis* and the *case method* of legal education. Law students should *reread* it toward the end of the first semester. You will understand it at a deeper level and will be amazed at how much you have learned. Some students have told me that they reread this part before taking the Bar Exam and it helped clear up areas they never fully understood during their three years in law school.

Part Two: Study Skills

Law students should read this right away. It deals with very critical matters: how to read and brief cases and how to take law exams. The sooner you read this material, the better. And, just when you have convinced yourself that you are the dumbest one in your entire class, read Chapter 14, "Fear and Loathing in the First Year."

General readers, if they want a hands on experience of law school, should read Chapters 8 and 9. You will read, and get to play with, two appellate court opinions, the "cases" of the case method. Finally, if you want to try your hand at all of this, there is practice law exam in Chapter 11.

Part Three: Litigation

Law students and general readers should take this walk through the litigation process, from late night television advertising to closing argument. You'll see a Complaint, read a deposition, hear jury instructions, and finally visualize yourself waxing poetic, bringing tears from the jurors and a knowing nod from the judge. This overview will prove invaluable in understanding one of your first year courses, Civil Procedure. More importantly, seeing how legal doctrine plays out in a jury trial will deepen your understanding of all your courses.

This Part gives you a good understanding of how courts, as opposed to philosophers and scientists, attempt to answer the question, *"What is the truth?"*

So you don't have to read this whole book, right now; only Parts 1, 2 and 3, and, of course, the spiffy Prologue. The rest of the book awaits your leisure.

Part Four: Legal Writing and Oral Advocacy: The Essential Skills

Law students should read the chapters on legal writing as a supplement to their writing course and read the chapters on appellate argument when they have to make an oral argument. Chapter 21 on Legal Argument will interest the general reader as it lays out a theory of how judges decide cases.

Part Five: The Great Hereafter

Chapters 23 and 24 deal with choices confronting law students in their second and third years and can be skipped for now. Chapters 25 and 26 deal with career choices, the latter being a collection of short essays by lawyers in varying kinds of practices. General readers will enjoy these chapters. For law students, I recommend reading them sometime during the first semester when anxiety and self-doubt begin to overwhelm you. You need to remind yourself that you came to law school, not to be a great law student, but to become a great lawyer.

———

Alas, I have many debts.

PREFACE

First, my students, at Arizona, Harvard and U.C.L.A. Their insightful questions (and blank stares) have forced me time and again to think more deeply about matters I thought I understood. Thanks.

As to this edition, lot of people helped: Charles Ares, Carol Denis, Stanley Feldman, Alex Lane, Anna Medico-Stevens, Amy Wilkens, Laura McKinny and, as always, Barbara Sattler.

I want to particularly thank my mentor George Gross, who not only helped with this draft but taught me, long ago, the joys of writing. I also thank my son, Caleb Hegland, for refusing to believe in this book when I did.

Previous editions had their helpers too: Mohyeddin Abdulaziz, Barbara Atwood, Bill Boyd, Dan Dobbs, Carol Eliot, Toni Massaro, Andy Silverman, Karen Waterman, David Wexler and Winton Woods.

Kay Kavanagh read the entire manuscript, made great suggestions and was marvelously supportive. (Struggling authors, send her your stuff.)

My sister, Sherina Cadmun, as always, played the tough, constructive critic. My parents, Edwina Kenney and "Heg", taught me so much about writing that, even though they are now gone, I know what they would say. My wife Barbara and my three older sons, Robert, Alex and Caleb, read chapters, made wise cracks, and offered advice and encouragement.

As to Little Ben, frankly, he helps simply by being him.

I wish to thank the author and publisher who have given permission to reprint copyrighted material:

Turow, *One L.* Excerpts reprinted with permission of G. G. Putman's Sons.

Finally, as to my two dear friends at U.C.L.A., David Binder and Paul Bergman, *Lawyers as Counselors* is a terrific book and I recommend it strongly. Had there been a Chapter 24, it would have been perfect.

OUTLINE

*

INTRODUCTION
TO THE
STUDY AND PRACTICE OF LAW
IN A NUTSHELL
THIRD EDITION

*

PROLOGUE
LAW SCHOOL

It is the best of schools, it is the worst of schools.

And it won't be the same old stuff.

As an undergraduate you sat and took notes while the professor lectured. You left, often inspired, occasionally depressed, but with the feeling that your life had advanced, that you had actually *learned* something, such as:

"Sartre believed that essence precedes existence" (or vice versa—I'll look it up for the final).

"The Second Law of Thermodynamics suggests that entropy (a measure of disorder) will continue to increase until the universe becomes a mush of completely undifferentiated chaos."

"Sartre, had he known of the Second Law of Thermodynamics, would have been even more depressed."

Naturally, when you get to law school, you expect to go to class, sit back and *learn* the law.

"Murder is the unlawful killing of a human being."

"Minors don't have contractual capacity."

"Torts are not English muffins."

It is not to be. Law professors seldom lecture, rehashing last night's Chapter 22 and offering additional insights to be noted and memorized. In fact, in law school you don't read chapters at all; you read "cases." What's a case?

When a court case is appealed to a higher court, such as a state supreme court or the United States Supreme Court, the appellate judges decide the matter and then write an *opinion* justifying their decision. Opinions generally begin by reciting the facts of the controversy, then move on to discuss, and resolve, the legal issues raised by those facts. These opinions are the cases you will read in order to get ready for class.

When you get to class, professors will assume you have a fairly good grasp of the cases assigned for that day; their job is to put you to work, using the cases as starting points. You don't passively mull over interesting points; with your classmates, you actively analyze the cases you have read, testing their coherence, exposing their assumptions, and pondering their implications: "Let's change the facts of the case and see if it comes out the same way."

Classes are never boring; but they can be exhausting and confusing.

Often you leave class convinced that you lost ground: "Before class, I worked real hard on that first case and finally learned what 'murder' is. I felt good about myself. Then came class—people to the left of me, people to the right of me ... getting called on ... and questions, questions, questions.

Never any answers! Just confusion. When the person next to me answered, was she right or wrong? The professor only turned and called on someone else. What was the professor getting at? I no longer know what murder is.... Frankly, I don't think I even know what a human being is, much less an English muffin."

Preparing for class isn't a cakewalk either. You don't skim text looking for central ideas, nor do you sit long hours attempting to memorize key points. In law school you struggle with the ideas—expect, at first, to be whipped by a two-page case.

You think that's hype? Okay, try out this case; it's only a paragraph:

Nichols v. Raynbred

Nichols brought an assumpsit against Raynbred, declaring that in consideration, that Nichols promised to deliver the defendant to his own use a cow, the defendant promised to deliver him 50 shillings: adjudged for the plaintiff in both Counts, that the plaintiff need not to aver the delivery of the cow, because it is a promise for a promise. Note here the promises must be at one instant, for else they will be both nuda pactum.

That's the entire case.

Yes, it does has something to do with a cow. Good for you.

Stop trying to figure it out. It drives seasoned law students bonkers. But I have given it to you to illustrate an important point.

Much of your first year is not (optimistically) "learning how to think like a lawyer," nor (pessimistically) exposing yourself as the simpleton you know, deep down, you are. Much of the first year is simply vocabulary building, just like grade school:

"Marie, stand up and spell 'assumpsit.' "

"Good. Now, Tommie use 'assumpsit' in a sentence."

Don't beat yourself when you find yourself bewildered the first several weeks. You are not dumb; you just speak the wrong language. Picture yourself on a Greek island, in a crowded restaurant. People are talking, apparently about events of great moment, and you don't understand a word.

"Oh, no ... I'm an idiot. I should never have come. I'm going to flunk out of Greece."

Law exams are different, too. You won't be asked to recite what you have learned ("Define murder.") nor will you be given broad essay questions such as, "Is Law Just?" Law exams will require you to apply the law you have learned to new situations. You will be given little short stories filled with the stuff of human conflict: neighbors arguing over the location of a fence, business people arguing over the meaning a contract, and criminal defendants claiming "The Devil made me do it." It will be your job is to "discuss" the case. What legal issues does it raise? What factors might a court use to resolve them? This is, by the way, exactly what lawyers do in real life.

Law exams are great fun to *take,* and you will be surprised at how much you have learned and how competent you are becoming. (Admittedly, law exams, particularly in the wee hours, are not great fun to *worry* about.)

The differences you are to encounter in law school are bewildering, threatening, challenging and exhilarating. It is the worst of schools, it is the best of schools.

You will read of real murders, of real scoundrels and of real heroes: of five-year-olds who pull chairs out from their aged aunts, of neighbors who fight over water wells, of New York executives who manipulate stock prices, of old fogies cutting off ungrateful kids (hopefully, the chair pranksters) and of lawyers standing tall in the fight against injustice. And you will share this dizzy ride through human experience with marvelous classmates and professors, folks with different lives and different outlooks. Like you, they are bright and challenging.

You will learn to read carefully—more carefully than ever before—and you will become sensitive to the ambiguities of language (almost to the point of losing old friends, friends who prefer the familiar sloth, their *"Can* you pass the salt?" to your *"Will* you pass the salt *to me?"*) You will come to suspect the rush to judgment (it seems there is nothing so sweet to humans as condemning others on the basis of thirdhand gossip, overheard in crowded lunch rooms). You will come to appreciate that even the most despised among us have things that can be said on their behalf. In fact, you will get so good at seeing the other side that eventually you'll have a hard time even getting mad at the plumber (all to the chagrin of your friends and family).

You'll learn "*Yes, but . . . .*" reasoning. In the heat of class discussion, you will find that for all good points, there are always competing points and always other ways of characterizing the conflict. You will learn, in your bones, to suspect that somewhere, out there, lurks the Ultimate Rejoinder. Perhaps thinking like a lawyer is no more than training your Little Voice to whisper "Yes, but have you considered the other side?" every time your Big Voice waxes profound.

Yes, learning to challenge your own ideas is no doubt a good thing, *but* being too critical early on might shut down a creative train of thought.

Finally, and perhaps most exhilarating, in law school you will discuss and debate things that *matter*. You will grapple with the problems of free will and autonomy; with the quest to predict and control the future (the stuff of Greek tragedy); with the nature of knowledge and the precision of language; with the deep human need to have rules and to be free of rules; with questions of justice and fairness and economic efficiency; and, at the end of the day, with the question that motivates all the others: what should we *do* in this particular case? Will *this* accident victim recover? Will *this* contract be enforced? Will *this* defendant walk free?

Law, and law students, muck around in the wonderful chaos of human existence.

Exciting stuff. It is the best of schools!

Welcome.

All good law schools are alike. Go to any law school in the country, and, once inside, you could be anywhere. Same cases, same books, same questions, and, thankfully, same Nutshells. This uniformity should solace those who didn't get in to their "first choice"; it should (but probably won't) humble those who did. But this is not a book of therapy.

Almost all law classes employ the "Socratic method," where students read cases before class and, under the questioning of the professor, extract from those cases the relevant rules of law. This is a very cumbersome way of getting at them. Wouldn't it be a whole lot easier to assign a text which simply comes out and tell you what you need to know, that, for example, torts are not English muffins? In short, what does the case method of legal education, what does the daily exhausting struggle, have to do with the practice of law?

Everything!

Day in, day out, trying murder cases, negotiating widget contracts, and counseling divorce clients, lawyers focus on the *interplay of law and fact*. Legal rules gain meaning only in relation to specific factual patterns. Conversely, the facts of a given dispute are only relevant to the degree that they trigger the application of specific legal rules. Staying up late struggling to understand the assigned cases, being battered around in the class with new fact patterns and competing legal rules, you are focusing on the interplay of law and fact, learning how to apply legal principles to the new situations and how to evaluate the legal significance of various real life events. In short, you are lawyering.

The uniformity of American legal education means something else as well. All lawyers have gone through what you are about to. I don't care if your hero is Earl Warren, William Rehnquist, Thurgood Marshall, or Sandra Day O'Connor; I don't care if your hero prosecutes vicious criminals or defends the downtrodden; I don't care if your hero advises the President or advertises on the late show.

All of them once sat where you will sit; all of them read many of the cases you will read; all of them occasionally cursed the profs; all of them longed for clear rules; and, ultimately, all of them realized, "By Jove, I think I've got it ... really got it!"

You are now one of them; you are now part of a great tradition. And, despite all the jokes and calls for reform, it is a great tradition: that our country is as free and open as it is is due in significant part to the hard and often gutsy work of lawyers and judges. Don't you forget it!

And don't forget one other thing. You have come to law school to become a lawyer. In the hurly-burly of law school, it is possible to get distracted and come to think that what matters most is being a successful law *student*. Some students, not getting the grades they wished for, grow despondent. Don't. Keep your eye on the prize. Every now and then look at Chapter 25, on career choices and Chapter 26, where lawyers talk about what they do all day. Remember why you are here. You are here to be a lawyer. Even if you get straight C's, you can still become a great lawyer. The harder you work, the better lawyer you will be.

From now on it is no longer about you and how well you do; from now on it is about your clients and how well you will do for them.

Let's get started.

*

PART ONE

LEGAL ANALYSIS MADE SIMPLE

First year students complain that their professors "hide the ball."

This Part *is* the ball. Legal analysis.

Chapter 1 involves you in your very first case. You will be given the hands-on experience of considering the three questions which lie at the heart of our common law system: Should judges follow the rules announced in prior cases or should they decide each case anew? Assuming we have a doctrine of *stare decisis*, how will lawyers argue and distinguish prior cases? And, if there are no prior cases, how should a judge decide a case?

Chapter 2 continues this analysis by showing you how "cases" come to be. It shows you how judicial opinions are written and offers some tips on how to understand them better. It then gives you further opportunity to practice the essential lawyering skill: *arguing* and *distinguishing* cases.

Chapter 3 describes the mechanics of *stare decisis* and then the process of *case synthesis*. While *case analysis* takes cases apart, *case synthesis* is the process of taking two or more cases and trying to

11

find a rule that explains what at first may look like inconsistent results. We'll see how this works and note that it responds to the deep human need to impose order on an unruly universe.

Chapter 4 continues the discussion of legal analysis by looking at "cases of first impression" (those where there is no controlling prior authority) and how courts decide them. Chapter 5 discusses statutory construction and introduces *arguments that eat Pittsburgh*.

In Chapter 6 we return to the topic of why courts follow precedent and discuss a central problem in law: the general and the specific. Here we'll meet Carl and his druggist. Let's go!

CHAPTER 1

YOUR VERY FIRST CASE

In law school, there is only one game worth playing: I call it the "Second-Case-in-the-World." It is the key to your legal education; indeed, it may be the key to everything!

(There you have it, you have learned something profound in the very first paragraph! You're going to love this book.)

"Is it enough for us to know that the Second-Case-in-the-World *is* the only game worth playing or must we know *why* it is the only game worth playing?" Alas, a typical student question.

Alas, a typical professorial response:

"Knowing why is knowing what."

("Wow, an incomprehensible, Zen-like sentence on the first page! This is gonna be great!")

The *what* of your legal education is the "law," a body of legal rules and doctrines. How you will learn them, however, is not by sitting down and memorizing them. The way you will learn them is by struggling with their *whys* ("Why did the court adopt this rule? What are its implications?"). By engaging in this struggle, you will learn the rules and doctrines at a much deeper level than by simply

13

closing your eyes and memorizing them. That's the key to legal education; indeed *knowing why is knowing what.*

So why is the Second-Case-in-the-World the only game worth playing? Because once you learn how to play it, once you know its rules and appreciate its deep structure, you will know everything you need to know about law. It shouldn't take more than an hour. As to the remainder of your first year, indeed, as to the next three years, it is simply review ... and some necessary filler.

Playing the game, you will be asked to think hard about three essential matters:

1. *Should courts follow "precedent"?* This will allow you to explore the pros and cons of a central tenet of our judicial system.

2. *How can you "distinguish" one case from another?* This leads to an understanding of how to analyze the judicial opinions you will read in law school.

3. *How can you argue a case of "first impression"?* This will allow you to explore one of the basic dilemmas of the law and, surprisingly, will teach you something about how to interpret statutes.

Precedent

At the core of our jurisprudence is the concept of *precedent* or *stare decisis.* The root idea is that, in reaching decisions, courts should follow the rules laid down by judges in prior cases. If the first judge ruled, "Negligent drivers should pay, in addition to their victim's medical bills, compensation for their pain and suffering," then, the second judge, when faced with a case of a negligent driver, should apply the same rule and allow compensation for pain and suffering. It would be improper for the judge to say, "Well, I don't think victims should get compensated for pain and suffering, so I'm going to have my own rule and follow it."

Given that our courts have adopted the doctrine of precedent, why revisit the issue?

Because. . . .

Never, not once, assume that the status quo makes sense, that a group of wise folks sat down and planned things out and that they had "their reasons" and that we live in the best of all possible worlds. A lot of what we live is simply historical accident. Is law school three years because once a lot of professors and lawyers got together and after much study and debate decided three years was the time needed to educate a lawyer properly? No! Law schools are three years because the first law school was three years. That's the long and short of it.

It is only by questioning the "wise lessons of the past" that we can either embrace them or reject them. Learning today's Wisdom, don't just accept it, challenge it. Maybe there are better ways.

One way to challenge the status quo is to envision a different system and then compare it to what we have. To sharpen our inquiry as to whether judges should follow the rules laid down in prior cases, consider an alternative. We could have a system where, when folks got into a dispute, they'd go to the designated Wise One and tell their stories. Then the Wise One would decide, free from the obligation to decide as did other Wise Ones. What would the costs and benefits be of such a system? What are the costs and benefits of a system that requires the Wise One to decide the same way as previous Wise Ones?

A Note on Learning

Often it is helpful, in approaching an issue, to assume a point of view. If one takes the position, say, that following precedent is a great idea, one is likely to get more involved in the issue, to see more of its ramifications, than if one hikes up the mountain, assumes the Lotus Position, and muses, "I will now think about whether precedent is a good idea. Ooommm."

Taking sides is the root notion of the Adversary System (the clash of mad dogs) as opposed to the Inquisitorial System (one very nice dog, sniffing). The idea is that truth is more likely to emerge from conflicting positions than from the most well-meaning of neutral investigations.

Do the mad dogs of the adversary system lead to truth, or simply to a lot of mauled and dismembered chickens? A good question, one to consider throughout your legal career. For now, just know that taking sides is a great way to explore and thus learn legal doctrine. Put yourself either in the position of the person advancing the doctrine *or* in that of the person resisting it.

Here's the rub. *Always consider what your opponent will argue and how your opponent will respond to your points.* Remember *"Yes, but...."* There are always good points on both sides, and we must, to understand our own position, test it in the hot fire of competing positions.

As indicated in the Prologue, *yes,* learning to challenge your own ideas is a good thing, *but* being too critical early on can shut down a creative train of thought. *Yes*, being too critical of ideas may harm creativity, *but* noting the importance of playfulness in generating ideas may counteract this danger.

Another device that will help you to think through your positions and to develop their complexity is to *write them out*. I will repeat this again and again and again, and some of you might actually try it once, probably sometime in November. I am a person of few illusions. But I know this because I have lived this: *Writing out your thoughts slows the mind, highlights gaps and inconsistencies, and deepens analysis.*

Finally, think concretely. Legal analysis falters when it gets too abstract. "Precedent: Yes or No?" Concrete examples, perhaps from your own experiences, help. Following past cases is a familiar concept, no doubt employed by your parents ... sometimes ..., and no doubt employed by yourself ... sometimes. Take an example from your past. "Last week, faced with the same situation, I did X. Should I do X now, merely because I did X last week?"

Analyzing and Distinguishing Cases

Assume that we decide, as we have, that courts should follow prior cases. Assume now that we have two cases. In Case One, the judge announced Rule X. Under the doctrine of precedent, the judge in Case Two must apply Rule X but *only if* Case Two is sufficiently *like* Case One that it would make sense to follow the rule of Case One.

As lawyers state the question, "Does Case One (and the rule of law it laid down) *control* Case Two?" This question introduces the art of legal analysis and legal argument. In a moment you will have the opportunity to practice this art. Its importance cannot be overstated; you will spend much of your first year perfecting this skill.

To say a case is *distinguishable* is like saying someone is quoting something out of context:

"Sure, in the Prologue, I did say that it was possible to be a great lawyer even if one didn't do well in law school, but I said it in the context of urging students who were disappointed with their grades to continue to work hard so as to serve their clients better. You are misquoting me when you say I suggested that law school isn't important to being a great lawyer."

Cases of First Impression

Sometimes a judge is faced with a case where there is *no* controlling law and thus must decide it as a matter of *first impression*. This can happen if there have been *no* prior cases ruling on the issue or, if there have been, they are all *distinguishable* and thus do not *control*. (This also assumes that there are no controlling statutes on the subject, but we haven't gotten to statutes yet.)

What kinds of arguments should a judge consider in deciding a matter of first impression? What goals should be sought? We will focus on a particular controversy: should a court, for public policy reasons, refuse to enforce a specific contract clause? I selected this issue because it raises a question that lurks in the shadows of every law school discussion: *where should the line fall between personal autonomy and freedom, on the one hand, and the well-being of others and community welfare on the other?*

The Second–Case–In–The–World

Of course, to play "Second Case," we need a First Case.

Assume Paradise. People mind their own business, and everyone is happy. No one sues anyone, not for anything. Then, alas, Trouble in Paradise. Someone sues. It results in the FIRST CASE in Paradise. Here is a "brief" of that case:

Globe v. Credit Bureau,

1 Paradise Reporter 1

Facts: *Plaintiff Globe hired defendant Credit Bureau to run a credit check on a man named Jones who wished to borrow money from plaintiff. Due* *to defendant's neglect, it failed to find a mortgage that was on Jones' property; it reported that Jones' credit was good. Had it found the outstanding mortgage, it would have labeled Jones a bad credit risk. Based on this favorable yet erroneous report, plaintiff lent Jones money which was not repaid.*

Plaintiff sued defendant for negligence, arguing, "If it weren't for your negligence, I would not have lent the money, and thus, I would not have lost the money."

Defendant moved to dismiss plaintiff's case based on a clause in the contract between plaintiff and defendant wherein plaintiff agreed not to sue defendant for negligence. In response, plaintiff argued that the **agreement not to sue** *should not be enforced by a court because it would violate* **public policy** *to do so. The court rejected plaintiff's argument, enforced the clause, and threw plaintiff out of court. (Ouch!)*

Rule: *In Paradise, exculpatory clauses do not offend public policy and are enforceable.*

Rationale: *The court stressed the importance of freedom of contract. The court wrote that if parties who make contracts cannot agree to limit the extent of liability, it is difficult to see where such a ruling would lead.*

Alas, we are now on the verge of the First Litigation Explosion in history (bad for our friends and neighbors, great for us lawyers). The SECOND CASE in Paradise involves a Ms. K who falls down the back stairway in her apartment house and is severely injured. She sues Landlord for negligence in maintaining the stairs (allegedly there was a defective step). In the lease Ms. K signed, we find an exculpatory clause:

> *Tenant hereby agrees, covenants, and promises not to sue Landlord for any or all injuries received due to Landlord's neglect.*

At court, Landlord will argue:

> *"Tenant cannot bring this case because she signed a lease agreeing not to sue me for negligence."*

Tenant will respond:

> *"Agreements not to sue should be unenforceable as a matter of public policy."*

Landlord will answer:

> *"Your Honor, the* Globe *case held that exculpatory clauses are not against public policy."*

At this point, the odds are heavily in Landlord's favor. But Ms. K is not down for the count. She will make three arguments.

First, she will argue that the rule laid down in *Globe*, that these clauses are enforceable, shouldn't matter because the courts in Paradise should decide controversies on the basis on fairness and not on the basis of precedent. (Note, because this is only the second case in the world, there is no current rule about following precedent; the court must decide it as a matter of first impression.)

Second, she will argue that, even if the court decides to adopt the doctrine of precedent, whatever the *Globe* case had to say about exculpatory clauses does not matter because *Globe* involved a very different kind of case and thus is *distinguishable*. It does not *control*.

Third, she will argue that the courts should not enforce exculpatory clauses in cases like hers. Note that even if she has convinced the judge not to *automatically* enforce her promise based on the *Globe* decision, she still has not won. All she has done is to make her case a *case of first impression*, and she now must win on the merits. The judge could say, for example,

> *"I do not feel obligated to follow the rule laid down by Globe. However, it strikes me that if Ms. K agreed in her lease not to sue, that agreement should be enforced. Goodbye."*

On the Need to See the Relationship Between Arguments

Legal arguments get complicated. A lawyer (or judicial opinion) may make four basic points: it is essential that you not only understand the points but the *relationship* between them. Does the lawyer need to win all four points to win the case? Or will one victorious point carry the day?

To prey upon your math anxiety, let's say a lawyer makes four basic points as to why her client should win. There are several possibilities:

$1 + 2 + 3 + 4 = \text{VICTORY}$

Here the lawyer must prevail on all four points in order to win; lose one and it's back to late-night advertising.

$(1 + 2)$ or $(3 + 4)$ = VICTORY

Here the lawyer doesn't have to win all the points, only either (1 and 2) *or* (3 and 4).

1 or 2 or 3 or 4 = VICTORY

Here, Hog Heaven. She wins if she prevails on only one point.

There are several other combinations, such as $(1 + 2 + 3)$ or 4 = VICTORY. In our case, Ms. K makes three points:

1. Precedent shouldn't matter.

2. *Globe* is distinguishable.

3. As a matter of public policy, agreements not to sue should be rejected.

For her to win, fill in the blanks:

1 __ 2 __ 3 = VICTORY

When reading cases, it is not enough to understand each specific point; you must understand the *relationships* between the points.

A Review and an Assignment

To review the issues:

First Issue: Should the courts of Paradise follow "precedent," or should they decide each case as if it were a matter of *first impression*?

Pick a side and write out your argument. Writing deepens thought (Repetition Number 2). Be sure, in developing your own arguments, to anticipate those of your opponent (Repetition Number 3).

Of course, you need not do this. You can keep on reading, confident in the knowledge that eventually I will discuss the issue. When I do, you will learn something ... but realize that the knowledge you get from others is a tad lifeless and dead, something to be memorized and forgotten. The knowledge you develop yourself, is, well, a triumph. Besides, it will be fun to compare answers.

Second Issue: Assume that the judge in Case Two, after argument, decides that she will follow "precedent" and "treat like cases alike." Does the rule of the first case, *Globe*, ("exculpatory clauses do not offend public policy") *control* Case Two? It would, under the doctrine of precedent, *if* the cases are "alike." But are they?

Here, take the position of Ms. K. Prepare what you will say when you stand before the judge, swallow once, and argue:

"Your Honor, the Globe *case is distinguishable on its facts from this case. Hence, this court need not apply the rule it laid down, that exculpatory clauses are enforceable. The reasons* Globe *is distinguishable, the reasons it is not 'alike,' are as follows...."* (Fill in the blanks; that's the crucial part.)

To distinguish a case, it is not enough to point to factual differences in the two cases. You must also tell the judge why these factual differences should make a *difference in the rule of law to be applied.* There will always be factual differences between cases. For example, the names of the parties are different, but *so what*? There is no rational reason why a court would apply a different rule simply because the names of the parties were different.

Thinking like a lawyer is more complicated than I indicated in the Prologue: in addition to *"Yes, but ...,"* your little voice must be trained to repeat, and repeat, *"So what?"* whenever your big voice comes up with something it takes as quite profound.

"Your Honor," booms your Big Voice, "In *Globe* there was merely a financial loss; here we have a physical injury!"

All together now: *"So WHAT? Why should a court treat a case involving physical injury differently from one involving financial loss?"*

Third Issue: Assume that the judge is free to decide the Second Case as if it were the First Case, either because she rejects the notion of following precedent or because, accepting the notion of precedent, she finds *Globe* "distinguishable," or not sufficiently "alike" Tenant's case to control it. (Reread that last sentence—particularly if you didn't do your math assignment. Don't just underline and think you "got" it.)

The math of it is:

(1 or 2) + 3 = VICTORY

Should courts disregard what the parties agreed to and hold that it is unenforceable? What are the pros and cons of complete "freedom of contract"?

At this point, **STOP!!!** Don't read the next chapter until you have written on the three issues. Looking ahead is cheating and, as you full well know, you won't be cheating me ... unless, of course, you stole this book.

CHAPTER 2

THE CASE METHOD

Judicial argument is quite somber and grown-up: the judges fearsome in black, the audience nervous with anticipation, a lawyer opening with "May it please the Court," and a little old bailiff, whispering "Hush."

Best analogy to all this sober fare is Ping–Pong.

One lawyer serves what he thinks will be a winner but his opponent fends it off, returning a crushing forehand which she believes will end the matter, but, with a quick turn of phrase, the first returns a deep one to her backhand, and on and on it goes until finally the judges yell, "Hold, enough!" and then scurry off to discuss and decide the case.

Let's do a play-by-play of the case we considered in the first chapter, *K v. Landlord*:

Landlord: You can't sue me because, in the lease you signed, you promised not to sue me.

Tenant: *Yes,* I made that promise, *but* it should not be enforced because it violates public policy.

Landlord: *Yes,* that argument can be made, *but* the court rejected it in *Globe*.

Tenant: *Yes,* the court held that such clauses do not violate public policy, *but* the case of *Globe* is distinguishable because it involved a financial loss and not a personal injury, and second, *Globe* involved a contract signed by two business people while our case involves a landlord and a tenant.

Landlord: *Yes,* there are factual differences between the two cases, *but* the rule of *Globe* should apply, no matter the kind of injuries or the kind of contract, because the *rationale* of *Globe* applies. It stands for the proposition that parties have freedom of contract and can make whatever agreements they please. The court in *Globe* stated, "The parties must be free to make their own contracts and once the courts start rewriting them there will be no end to it in sight."

Tenant: *Yes,* the Court said that, *but* those words were used in a particular factual context. The kinds of injuries do matter. It is one thing to agree not to sue for financial harm, but quite another to agree not to sue for doctors' bills and lost earnings. There is a great public interest in freedom of contract, but there is also a great public interest in preventing physical injury. Allowing landlords to exempt themselves from liability will encourage them to be negligent, thus leading to more injuries.

Further, as to the rationale of *Globe, yes*, freedom of contract is important, *but* freedom of contract is premised on the notion of equal bargaining power, which assures both sides are making free choices. Who the parties are *does* matter. It is one thing to say that parties of equal bargaining power should be allowed to agree to what they will; it is quite another to allow a strong party to force a weak party into accepting his terms. And that's what we have in this case. Enforcing this term against Ms. K will violate her freedom of contract.

Judge Flintstone: (in desperation) *Hold, enough!*

Now, when lawyers actually argue a case, they don't go back and forth like this; usually they get up and make all their points at one time. Not to worry—there is a chapter on Legal Argument later.

So what happens? The judges leave, discuss the case, and, probably several months later, a written opinion appears:

K v. Landlord

1 Paradise Reporter 2

*Flintstone, J. This case involves the validity of an exculpatory clause in an apartment lease where the tenant is suing for personal injuries caused by the alleged neglect of the landlord. **While it is true** that this court, in **Globe**, upheld an exculpatory clause, we note that was in the context of a commercial contract and involved only financial loss. **Even though** we quite properly give contracting parties great freedom to fashion their own agreements, and **despite the fact** that we are fearful of where voiding such agreements will lead us, we feel we must invalidate this agreement. We note that there is inherent unequal bargaining* *strength between landlords and tenants and that, in this case, the tenant is seeking recovery for personal injuries. A landlord, under traditional doctrine, has a duty to take reasonable steps to keep common areas safe; if we allow landlords to escape this duty by the simple expedient of a standard lease term, physical injuries that could be avoided will not be.*

Note that legal writing is marked by *words of contrast* which you should begin using:

On the one hand . . . .

Although this is so, that is so

Even though . . . .

However . . . .

While X is true, so is Y.

Judges write "down the middle." They collapse the competing arguments, and the case reads as if the judges made it all up themselves. They didn't. Judges are like the character in Gilbert and Sullivan, the "Ruler of The Queen's Navy," who sings:

"I never thought of thinking for myself at all."

Every case they cite, every point they make, the judges stole from one of the lawyers!

It is a good thing, not a bad thing, that judges rest their decisions on points stolen from the lawyers. This is a manifestation of the adversary system and its commitment to have all positions considered in the heat of battle.

Say that Judge Flintstone decided K on the basis of a point not argued by counsel. Assume that K's lawyer argued only the personal injury aspect and did not bring up the matter of unequal bargaining. Now, if Flintstone, on her own, after the case was submitted, thought up that point and decided the case upon it, it would not be fair to the landlord. The landlord would not have had the opportunity to argue against it. And it might lead to a bad decision because, without its being tested in adversarial fires, we don't really know how good the point actually is.

Yes, but, on the other hand, if judges rely *only* on the arguments developed by counsel, injustice can result. What if Ms. K hired a dullard as a lawyer who overlooks key arguments? Should she lose a substantial case simply because she hired an incompetent?

Tough call. Respected judges go both ways on it.

A great device to help you understand a court decision is to *restage the game*. Figure out which party raised which point and why. To get a feel for this, recall that Judge Flintstone mentioned three points in the opinion:

> *Globe*
>
> commercial loss
>
> freedom of contract

Which side brought up *Globe* and why? Which side brought up "commercial loss" and why? Which side argued "freedom of contract" and why?

Some beginners playing this game answer only the "who brought it up?" question and not the "why?" question. Yes, Ms. K did bring up the matter of "commercial loss." But why? Some arguments are punches, going for the win, and others are counterpunches, warding off punches thrown by the other side (it is permissible, by the way, to mix metaphors as long as they are in the same category, say sports). Landlord brought up *Globe* as a knockout blow; he thought he would win with it. Tenant counterpunched with *commercial loss,* as a way of deflecting *Globe* by distinguishing it. Tenant knew that if she prevailed on the "commercial loss" point, all she would had done is avoided Landlord's knockout punch; there is no way that she could win the entire case with that particular jab.

Landlord brought up "freedom of contract." But why? Think a minute; there are two possibilities.

Landlord, in bringing up *freedom of contract,* could have been counterpunching to Tenant's "commercial loss" argument ("No, *Globe* is *not* distinguishable because freedom of contract is involved in both cases"), or he could have been using it as another knockout blow ("Even if *Globe* does not control this case, Your Honor, you should enforce the lease as written due to the value we attach to freedom of contract.").

Admittedly, very seldom will a professor ask you, "Which side raised that point?" So what's the value of replaying the game?

To understand it.

Sometimes cases get very complicated. A diagram will help:

I. Plaintiff's main contention

A. Defendant's response to defeat that contention

1. Plaintiff's response to defendant's attack, arguing that defendant's attack in fact falls short.

   a. Defendant's answer to this response, which, if correct, would defeat the response.

Often a case will focus solely on the issue raised in (a) and go on at great lengths about it. You may well understand that the court has decided that the defendant wins point (a) but, without Ping–Ponging, you may not understand how this impacts the ultimate outcome: "If the defendant wins (a), then plaintiff's argument in (1) fails, which means that defendant's argument in (A) is valid, and thus plaintiff's main contention fails."

Returning to the case of *K v. Landlord*, note that Judge Flintstone *distinguished* the case of *Globe*; she did not *overrule* it. Judges can do this. Flintstone could have said:

"The case of *Globe* is simply not well thought-out. It is overruled. All exculpatory clauses are invalid as being against public policy."

That Flintstone chose not to do this tells us a lot about our case system.

On Overruling and the Appearance of Permanence

Sometimes courts *overrule* prior cases—come out and admit that they (or, more likely, their predecessors)—got it wrong. The most famous overruling was in *Brown v. Board of Education,* which overruled the "separate but equal" doctrine of *Plessy v. Ferguson* and held segregated schools to be unconstitutional.

Once a case is overruled, it can't even come to the party. *Plessy v. Ferguson* is no longer good law: it has been overruled. Lawyers cannot use that case in their legal arguments. Had Flintstone overruled *Globe,* then, in a very real sense, we would be back to having only one case in Paradise. The next case would be resolved by looking only at *K. v. Landlord,* with no reference to *Globe.*

Courts are very reluctant to overrule prior decisions. To do so presents a major theoretical problem. Judges, in reaching their decisions, are supposed to follow the law. If law comes from prior cases, where do they get the law to overturn a case? In addition, overruling tears at the notion of predictability. How can you ever rely on a case if a later court can overrule it? Take *Globe.* Even if the second case was on all fours, indeed involved the same parties and the same contract, a lawyer couldn't confidently advise, "The exculpatory clause will be enforced." This is because maybe the next judge would simply overrule *Globe.*

For these reasons, courts prefer to "distinguish" prior cases.

This preference has an interesting side effect. Law appears to be above history. Had Flintstone overruled *Globe,* we could see that things had changed. The world of *Globe* was likely a world where giants walked the earth and stern judges let the chips fall where they might. The world of *K* is likely the world of judges committed less to freedom of contract and more to judicial intervention in the name of fairness. These are radically different worlds, but to read the opinion in *K*, which merely distinguished *Globe*, no one would know it. The seamless web of distinguished cases conceals great changes in society.

Change, of course, is inevitable, except from a vending machine.

Now, because Flintstone distinguished *Globe* rather than overruled it, it is still *good law*. We now have two cases in Paradise, and we are well on our way to the first litigation explosion in history (and some smart Norwegian in St. Paul is off to incorporate the West Publishing Company).

An Opportunity to Practice:
Cases Three and Four

Because *K* did not overrule *Globe*, both are still good law. To play the Next-Case-in-the-World, I give you two new cases:

Case Three

Once upon a time, a resident of Paradise awoke with a start: "This ain't Paradise! Sure, winter doesn't come until December, and summer lingers until September. And yes, the rain never falls before sundown, and by eight the morning fog disappears. But you know what we ain't got?

You know damn well. We ain't got politicians!"
(It is permissible, by the way, to mix literary
allusions as long as they are in the same category,
say show tunes.)

Thus it came to pass that Paradise created a
legislature. One of the first things it did was to
pass a law (a *statute)* that provided tenants must
be given a 30–day notice before they could be
evicted. Joe, a single father earning a low wage,
moved into an apartment house with his two
children. He signed a lease waiving his right to a
30–day notice. The landlord has brought an eviction action which could not be brought under the
Paradise Statute. The landlord asserts that the
protection was waived.

Under *K* and *Globe*, who wins?

Case Four

At a tyrannosaurus riding stable (this gets boring for me too), a rider (a lawyer) is eaten (alas,
bringing great joy to the residents of Paradise).
Nonetheless, the lawyer's heirs bring suit based
on the owners' negligence (they forgot to feed it).
Needless to say, as part of the riding agreement
the lawyer signed on that fateful day, there was a
clause providing, "Riders cannot sue for negligence."

Under *K* and *Globe*, who wins?

Discussion of Practice Cases

Hopefully, with pencil in hand or with computer running, you took advantage of the two problems to begin to develop your skills in case analysis. If not, it's still not too late.

Both cases raise basically the same issue: will the court enforce the exculpatory clause? Both also raise the issue whether, to avoid the clause, you need *both* unequal bargaining power and personal injury (as you had in *K v. Landlord*) *or* is it enough if you have only one of the two?

Hopefully, when you read the problems and began to think about them, these issues more or less jumped out at you. This illustrates the first of several points I want to make about the exercise.

You learn the law by struggling with it, not by closing your eyes and memorizing it. As you worked your way through *Globe* and *K v. Landlord* you were not trying to learn contract law; you were struggling to understand the cases and why they were decided the way they were. Your knowledge of contract law, your ability to spot contract issues, came as *a by-product of that struggle.*

The struggle is hard work and will involve late evenings and even moments of despair. You will be tempted to throw in the towel and buy a commercial outline. They are in the bookstores, and they will tell you what the law is: "Courts have refused to enforce exculpatory clauses in cases where there has been unequal bargaining power and personal injury has resulted." Avoid that temptation. Legal knowledge comes not from highlighting but from struggle. If you continue to struggle, even when you are unsure you are getting it "right," you will be learning the law at such a deep level that you might not even be aware you know it until it matters, when you face the issue on a test or with a client.

Second, this exercise underscores the need to focus on the relationship between elements. Is the relationship between unequal bargaining and personal injury an *"and* relationship" or is it an *"or* relationship"? In other words, must there be both unequal bargaining strength *and* personal injury before the court will throw out the exculpatory clause, or is one enough? If it is an *"and* relationship" then both Joe and the lawyer's heirs would be out of luck. While Joe did not have equal bargaining power, there was no personal injury; while the lawyer suffered personal injury, she had oodles of bargaining power (not only was she a lawyer, but, unlike a tenant who needs a place to live, she did not need to go riding and could therefore easily walk away if she didn't like the contract).

To figure out the relationship between the elements, let's review what Judge Flintstone said in *K v. Landlord*:

> *We note that there is inherent unequal bargaining strength between landlords and tenants and that, in this case, the tenant is seeking recovery for personal injuries. A landlord, under traditional doctrine, has a duty to take reasonable steps to keep common areas safe; if we allow*

> *landlords to escape this duty by the simple*
> *expedient of a standard lease term, physical*
> *injuries that could be avoided will not be.*

This raises yet another point. Judges often take the easy way out. In *K v. Landlord,* we had both elements and Judge Flintstone did not have to decide between them. Note that she does not tell us the relationship between the two; she just mentions them and then decides. It will be up to the judges deciding the next cases, like those of Joe and the lawyer's heirs, to decide the issue.

Rather than being faulted for "taking the easy way out," Judge Flintstone could be praised for following the judicial tradition of deciding *only* the case before the court. Because the case had both elements, Judge Flintstone did not have to decide whether one would be enough. We follow prior decisions because we believe that the prior judges thought real hard about them before coming to their decision—because Judge Flintstone did not *have to* decide the issue in *K v. Landlord*, she would not have thought real hard on the issue so it was better for her to just keep quiet.

Finally, legal analysis is more than simply spotting the issues. They give a framework for analysis. To illustrate this, in the case of Joe, one might write:

> While Joe lacked equal bargaining power, there
> was no personal injury. *While it is true* that
> courts have refused to enforce exculpatory
> clauses if they might lead to personal injury,

and this is not the case here, *a case might be made* that the requirement to give a 30–day notice before eviction also protects public safety in that it allows individuals like Joe to find a new place to move his family before he is thrown out in the street.

Always remember *yes, but ... Yes,* there are no personal injuries here, *but* maybe I can make the possible harm to Joe like personal injury.

Don't be upset if you didn't "get" this point in your answer. You probably got some I didn't. In any event, I will have more to say on this subject in later chapters. You will be given another opportunity to practice, and then I will give you model answers to work with.

This has been a long chapter. Goodnight.

CHAPTER 3

STARE DECISIS, CASE SYNTHESIS, AND LAW AS A SCIENCE

Several years ago a juvenile court judge in Florida was asked to decide the right of a surrogate mother to retain custody of her child. Paid to carry the father's baby to term, the surrogate mother changed her mind and wished to keep the child. The father filed an action to gain custody based on her promise to give the child to him and on the fact that he was the biological father. It was the first such case ever, the ultimate case of first impression.

The press wrote as if the trial judge's decision would conclusively establish the respective rights of surrogate mothers nationally and for all time.

Not so.

Under the doctrine of *stare decisis*, courts are *obligated* to follow *only* the law set down by higher courts in their *own* state and those of the United States Supreme Court. These cases are known as "*controlling authority*." Trial courts in, say, Iowa *must* follow the law laid down by the Iowa Supreme Court; they are not obligated to follow the law as laid down by the California Supreme Court or any other state courts. Note that, even in Florida, the judge in the next courtroom could ignore his neighbor's surrogate decision. He would be bound only by the decision of a higher court, a Florida appellate court.

This does not mean the Florida decision would have no impact elsewhere. If a judge were faced with a similar case in Montana, the Florida decision could be cited as *"persuasive"* (as opposed to *"controlling"*) authority. It is significant, but not conclusive, that a judge in Florida came to a particular decision. There are several sources of "persuasive authority" (things that lawyers can cite to judges in support of their positions). They include decisions from other states, statutes from other states, Restatements, law review articles, and state bar journal articles.

There are two other terms you will come across that may cause confusion: *primary authority* and *secondary authority*. Primary authorities are the cases and statutes themselves; secondary authority is what commentators say about them, perhaps in law reviews, or in legal reference books.

Finally, in terms of definitions, be aware that lawyers use the word "control" in two different senses, a status sense and an application sense. If we are in a Missouri trial courtroom, all Missouri State Supreme Court decisions "control" legal controversies in that courtroom in the status sense of that word: the trial court judge must follow them if they apply to the case before him. Cases from the Supreme Court of, say, Maine, do not "control" in this status sense; the Missouri trial court judge can ignore them even though they address the exact same issue that he must decide.

All of this is straightforward enough, but lawyers muddy the waters by arguing that a case that clearly controls in the status sense, say a case from the Missouri Supreme Court, does not "control" the particular decision the trial judge must make if that case is "distinguishable." So in our little corner of the world, you can have a "controlling" case which doesn't "control."

Case Synthesis

In our prior chapter, we spent a lot of time tearing apart *Globe* and *K v. Landlord*. This is known as *case analysis*. The process of putting two or more cases together is known as *case synthesis*. You can expect to do a lot of it during your first year. A casebook will have a couple of cases, usually from different jurisdictions, which face the same general issue but which come to apparently different results.

"Consistent or inconsistent?" puffs your professor.

You will long to make them consistent, and this longing is a manifestation of a deep human need to reduce the "bloomin' confusion" of our world to patterns that we can understand and, eventually, control. We need to understand the apparent randomness of things. If every event in our lives were a specific instance reflecting no underlying cause or theme, we could never learn from our experiences, for there would be nothing to learn. If sickness, floods, and famines had no causes we could understand, we would huddle in our caves fearing vicious and irrational gods (which are an explanation in their own right but not much of one).

William James wrote of "our pleasure at finding that a chaos of facts is the expression of a single underlying fact" and that, in our chaotic world, "each item is the same old friend with a slightly altered dress." He continued:

Who does not feel the charm of thinking that the moon and the apple are, as far as their relation to the earth goes, identical; of knowing respiration and combustion to be one; of understanding that the balloon rises by the same law whereby the stone sinks....

How does a scientist reduce the world's complexity? By finding a "law" that explains apparently different phenomena. An apple falls and the moon circles the earth: at first blush, these seem to be very different kinds of phenomena, but, wait, both are but different manifestations of the law of gravity. How do lawyers reduce complexity? By stating a rule of law that explains what appear to be inconsistent cases.

That science and law are similar is not a fanciful suggestion. In fact, the father of modern American legal education and the first dean of the Harvard Law School in 1870, Christopher Columbus Langdell, claimed that law *is* a science. Just as botanists go to botanical gardens to study and compare specific plants in order to discover the laws of nature, lawyers and law students go to the law library to study and compare judicial opinions to discover the basic principles underlying law. According to the law-as-science thesis, while there may be a great number of cases, careful analysis of them will lead to the realization that they are really specific manifestations of a relatively small number of basic legal principles, with each case then becoming the same old friend, in slightly altered dress.

Let me show you how this works. You will learn in your first-year Contracts class that gift promises are unenforceable. If I promise to give you $50 tomorrow, if I do, fine, but if I don't, the courts will not enforce my promise. To explain this result, the courts came up with the doctrine of consideration: to be enforceable the person making the promise must "get something" for the promise. For example, if a father asks a stranger to care for his sick adult son and promises to compensate the stranger for his expenses, the father's promise would be enforceable: he "got something" for it, the care of his son.

But what happens if the father's promise comes *after* the stranger cared for his son? Then it looks like the father *"got nothing"* for it and hence is unenforceable. This is the case *Mills v. Wyman*, a case you're likely to read in your Contracts class. Wyman, the father, heard that Mills had played the part of a Good Samaritan in caring for his son during his last illness. He wrote Mills promising to pay his expenses but thereafter refused to do so. Mills filed suit.

"My promise," argued the father, "is not enforceable because I got nothing for it. When I made it, Mills had already cared for my son."

At this point, Mills brought to the court's attention a series of cases where the courts enforced promises even though, like the father, the promisors had "got nothing" for them. The cases were of two types:

Bankruptcy Cases.

1. A owes B $1000 pursuant to a previous transaction.

2. A goes to bankruptcy court and has his debt to B discharged; he is now under no legal obligation to pay B.

3. Thereafter, A promises to pay B $1000.

In this kind of case, the courts had enforced A's promise even though he didn't seem to get anything for it (anything that he didn't already have.)

Statute of Limitations Cases

1. A owes B $1000 pursuant to a previous transaction.

2. Under the *Statute of Limitations,* B has only four years in which to file suit on the debt. Thereafter it is barred.

3. B allows the four years to pass without filing suit; A is now under no legal obligation to pay B.

4.   Thereafter, A promises to pay B $1000.

In this kind of case, the courts had enforced A's promise even though he didn't get anything for it (anything he didn't already have).

Of course, neither of these kinds of cases involved fathers promising to pay for past services rendered. What the judge must do to rule on the father's case is to find a rule that explains those cases, and then apply it to the father's case.

The judge puts on a white coat, assumes a somewhat crazed look, and weird background music comes up: what is the underlying legal principle that explains the Bankruptcy and Statute of Limitations cases? The judge studies the cases and notes that, in both kinds of cases, the person making the promise to pay the debt once had a legal obligation to pay it. *Eureka*! The underlying legal principle:

> *Even if the promisor did not get something for the promise to pay a debt, the promise is enforceable if the promisor previously had a legal obligation to pay the debt.*

This principle neatly explains the prior cases. Now, if we were to apply this newly discovered legal principle to the case at hand, the father *wins* as he *never had a previous obligation* to pay Mills.

But not so fast there! Maybe there is a different principle to explain the Bankruptcy and Statute of Limitations cases. Studying those cases, we could conclude that in all of them the promisor had a *moral* obligation to pay the debt. We could come up with an alternative explanatory legal principle.

> *Even if the promisor did not get something for the promise to pay a debt, the promise is enforceable if the promisor has a moral obligation to pay the debt.*

If this is the correct rule of law one extracts from the prior cases, then the father would likely *lose* his case as most would agree he had a moral obligation to pay Mills' expenses. Obviously, a great deal is at stake in how we characterize the prior cases.

How is the judge to choose between these competing theories? Alas, there are no set rules. Sometimes there will be language in the prior cases that points in a certain direction. Often, however, the decision turns on what the judge thinks, for reasons of policy, the best rule would be.

Note, however, that the result is not dictated by the "science of law" because the science of law has produced two equally logical explanations of the prior cases. As Oliver Wendell Holmes once wrote:

> *The life of the law has not been logic: it has been experience. The felt necessities of the time, the prevalent moral and political theories, intuitions of public policy, avowed or unconscious, even the prejudices which judges share with their fellow men, have had a good deal more to do than the syllogism in determining the rules by which men should be governed.*

For a fascinating look at how scientists decide between competing scientific theories, see Kuhn's *The Structure of Scientific Revolutions*. His basic argument is that the choice is *not* a scientific one, in that the competing theories usually come out pretty much the same in terms of explaining the observed data. He argues that the choice is often based on aesthetics: on which theory is more elegant.

One of the fun things to note about judicial reasoning, indeed human thought, is what can be called *historical doctrinal revisionism*. Faced with a tough decision, a judge will cite several previous cases and say, "These cases were all decided upon Principle X." But in the case the judge must decide, Principle X will do no good at all. However, Principle Y will do loads of good. So the judge simply rewrites the historical record: "While these judges in these cases may have justified their decision upon Principle X, they could have justified them by Principle Y and, indeed, Principle Y explains them better. Now, applying Principle Y to the case before us. . . ."

An Opportunity to Practice Case Synthesis

Recall the case of *Globe* and *K*. At the level of rule, *Globe* (exculpatory clauses are *valid*) is inconsistent with *K* (exculpatory clauses are *invalid*). One's an apple falling to earth, the other's the moon orbiting the earth. Take a few moments to try to articulate a legal doctrine that makes them consistent. "*Globe* and *K* seem to be inconsistent with

one another, but really they are just different manifestations of one underlying rule, which is . . ."

I'll give you my answer in a minute. This will be
more helpful to you if you stop reading now and try
to come up with your own.

Two alternative theories come to mind which
make *Globe* and *K* consistent:

> *Exculpatory clauses are **valid** unless they re-
> lieve liability for physical injury liability and
> (or?) are signed by a party of unequal bargain-
> ing strength.*

> or

> *Exculpatory clauses are **invalid** unless they are
> signed by parties of equal bargaining strength
> and involve matters of financial, as opposed to
> physical, loss.*

Neat. *Globe* and *K* are no longer specific instanc-
es; just as the falling apple and the circling moon
are different manifestations of the same underlying
physical law, these two cases are different manifestations of the same underlying rule of law. We have
explained both cases in that we were able to fashion
rules which explain both. Good for us.

Note that, although both rules explain both decisions, they point to radically different outcomes
downstream: under the first rule, most exculpatory
clauses would be valid, while under the second,

most would be invalid. Which is the correct rule? Again we leave logic and turn to "felt necessities."

Today no one believes law is a science in the sense that all of the cases can be explained by a series of underlying basic principles. Langdell himself might have had his doubts: when he came across a case that he couldn't fit into his scheme, one he couldn't make consistent with other cases, he would simply label that case as "wrong" and move on. No scientist could make this move: "This tree doesn't seem to be growing the way my theory says it should. This tree is wrong."

In any event, a lot of good lawyering goes into trying to make cases consistent by discovering underlying legal principles, and a lot of good lawyering goes into arguing why one explanatory principle is better than another. It is great intellectual training to try to make cases consistent; work hard at it in your studies. But don't get comatose if you can't.

There are inconsistent cases out there. They raise a host of theoretical problems: just what *is* the law if it can be "X" in California but "Not X" in Arizona? Lawyers have a short fuse for theoretical problems; when they come across inconsistent cases, they label "X" the *majority rule* and "Not X" the *minority rule* and then go out for coffee.

———

Thus far we have looked at tearing cases apart (case analysis) and putting them back together (case synthesis). Legal analysis is more than that, however. Often it will deal with statutory interpretation (our topic in Chapter 5). It will also deal with all those arguments lawyers make when they aren't arguing over whether a certain case or statute applies. These arguments are the subject of our next chapter.

CHAPTER 4

FLOODGATES, SLIPPERY SLOPES, HYPOTHETICALS, ANALOGIES AND FREE RADICALS

Besides cases, what's to argue? As we have seen, a lot of legal argument is about whether prior cases "control" the current case or whether they are distinguishable. In this chapter, we will look at other kinds of arguments lawyers advance. What happens when there are no prior cases which have arguably decided the issue? These are known as cases of first impression. If there are no prior cases to guide the judge, how is the judge to decide?

Indeed, how was the *first* case decided?

We have something of a chicken-and-egg problem.

Actually, in practice, most cases that are appealed are of "first impression" in the sense that there is no prior controlling case (or statute) that is directly on point. If there were such a case or statute clearly stating what rule of law should be applied to the case, then the only argument the losing party would have is that the case should be overruled or, in the case of a statute, that it should be found unconstitutional. Most of the cases you will read are something of a mixed bag, with lawyers arguing and distinguishing "cases" and, in addition, making the kinds of arguments we will review in this chapter:

Policy arguments

Floodgate and slippery slope arguments

Arguments based on hypotheticals and analogies

We'll see how these work, and then look at typical responses to them.

Policy Arguments

Lawyers argue about justice and policy. No big surprise here. Take *Globe*. One of the lawyers no doubt waxed elegant about the importance of freedom of contract.

There are two ways to meet policy arguments; the first is to come up with your own.

> *There is a great public interest in freedom of contract, but there is also a great public interest in preventing physical injury. Allowing landlords to exempt themselves from liability will encourage them to be negligent, thus leading to more injuries.*

Note that there is no established pecking order that establishes which policies are preferred, such as:

> *Freedom of contract trumps public safety,* or

> *Public safety trumps freedom of contract.*

In cases of conflict between them, the judge will just have to choose. This is very much like the judicial choice we discussed in the last chapter, the choice between two competing explanations of a series of prior cases and, indeed, very much like the judicial choice involved in determining whether a prior case controls or is distinguishable.

The second response to a policy argument, and one which is great fun if you can carry it off, is to steal your opponent's argument and turn it around:

> *Yes, freedom of contract is important, but freedom of contract is premised on the notion of equal bargaining power, which assures both sides are making free choices. To allow a strong party to force a weak party into accepting his terms denies the weaker party freedom of contract.*

Of course you have known all about policy arguments, and the deep satisfaction that comes when you turn them on your opponent, ever since the day you first decided to become a lawyer, that day when you, with your razor wit, reduced your best grade-school friend to tears and heard, for the first time, that sweet refrain: "You should be a lawyer." Some policy arguments, however, will be new to you as they are premised not on what would be good for society, but rather on what would be good for the courts. Here we meet the *floodgate* argument and the *slippery slope* argument. In keeping with our poultry motif, both arguments look to, as their intellectual grandfather, Chicken Little.

Floodgates and Slippery Slopes

The *floodgate* argument is that if the court adopts the rule proposed by one's opponent, then the floodgates will open and the courts will be awash in lawsuits. It boils down to: "Your Honor, if you do justice in this case, all manner of ragamuffins will be pounding down your door asking for justice. You might as well kiss your golf game goodbye."

This argument, although quite popular, has always struck me as curious. One response is that justice isn't such a bad idea. The other, more solicitous to the golf industry, is to suggest to the court that the rule could be drawn quite narrowly so that most ragamuffins stay where they belong. We will see how this is done when we study *floodgate's* first cousin, *slippery slope*.

The *slippery slope* argument is a variation of the floodgate argument. "Your Honor, if you do what my opponent wants you to do, X, which may be a sensible thing to do, then in the next case the judge will have to do Y, which we all agree would be a bad thing, so don't do X." We saw a slippery slope argument in *Globe:* ("If we void this term, then we don't know where we would stop rewriting contracts").

There are *three* responses to slippery slope arguments.

1. Once you step onto the slope, you need not tumble to the bottom because there are things to grab on your way down. "Your Honor, if you void the exculpatory clause, this will not mean that in the next case you will have to rewrite a *rent term*, as there are obvious distinctions between the two. Exculpatory clauses affect public safely; rent terms

do not." What you are doing is inviting the judge to "distinguish" the opinion in advance, thus effectively slamming the door on those poor fools who are paying too much rent. In some opinions you will read, you will see judges doing exactly this: "We note that our decision merely goes to the narrow issue before us and would not apply to such things as. . . ."

2.   Another response to the slippery slope argument is that falling all the way down might not be such a bad idea. "Hey, that's not a bad idea. Given that many landlords take advantage of their tenants, courts should rewrite unfair leases."

3.   The final possible response to a slippery slope argument is to counter with your own. Whenever a judge is asked to make a decision, he stands on a sharp pinnacle with slippery slopes falling sharply on all sides. *All slippery slope arguments are reversible.*

> *Your Honor, if you **enforce** this clause because you don't want to get involved in rewriting contracts, then in the next case you will have to enforce a clause which requires the tenant, if one day late, to forfeit her first born.*

In short, meet slippery slope with slippery slope.

As slippery slope arguments are so common in legal argument, knowing these three responses is worth the price of this Nutshell.

There is one final response to the slippery slope argument which I don't recommend, at least not as strongly as the others. During an argument before a state supreme court, one of the judges, believing that he had trapped the lawyer in a deadly slippery slope situation, asked, "Counsel, but if we do what you ask us to do, won't you be back here in the next case, say on behalf of Acme Corporation, telling us that the rule requires us to sacrifice all first-born children?" The judge sat back, rather smugly.

The lawyer paused, looked him right in the eye. "No, Your Honor, I won't be making that argument. I don't represent Acme."

Hypotheticals and Analogies

Hypotheticals and arguments by *analogy* are quite popular in legal discourse. Here, too, we solve the chicken/egg problem.

Take *Globe*, where the issue is whether the court should refuse to enforce a certain contract provision. Never before has a court refused to enforce a contract term. The lawyer asking the court to throw out the provision would think of a hypothetical case where a court would do just that. The argument becomes,

> *Your Honor, in the situation I am about to describe, I am sure you will agree that no court would enforce the contract. Well, enforcing the exculpatory clause in this case would be basically the same thing.*

Can you think of a contract, or a provision in one, which *obviously* a court would refuse to enforce? Take your time. I am in no hurry.

My case of non-enforcement: A six-year-old promises to give his allowance, every week, to his big brother. No court is going to enforce that deal.

Of course, the attorney arguing for enforcement will make up her own hypothetical case, perhaps involving a contract signed by two major corporations after months of negotiation by competent lawyers.

Now we have two cases, neither of which happened, but so what? The next step is to decide whether our case, the one involving the exculpatory clause, looks more like the kid's contract or more like that of the corporations.

"Your Honor, this is basically like a case where a six-year-old agrees to give up his allowance; that agreement would not be enforced and neither should this one."

"No, Your Honor," replies the other side, "It's more like an agreement between two corporations, one we would surely enforce. You should enforce this one as well."

How do we decide which it is more like? By articulating why the hypothetical cases are easy ones. Why, exactly, is the six-year-old case an easy case? Once we understand that, then we can look and see if those reasons (policies) apply in the case at issue.

"We don't enforce kids' contracts because we don't think they know what they are agreeing to. Ms. K didn't know what she was agreeing to."

"No," replies the other side. "We don't enforce kids' contracts because we feel that they are not capable of understanding what they are agreeing to. Ms. K, as an adult, surely is capable of knowing what she agreed to; if she didn't take the trouble, that's not our concern."

What we have done is to make up easy cases and, by asking ourselves why they are easy, we have, in effect, written the supporting opinion. *We have created two new first cases, along with their supporting rationale. Presto, what was the first case now becomes the third, and we land safely on familiar ground.*

Neat trick!

As to the chicken/egg quandary, easy. The egg came first, created a hypothetical chicken, and the rest is history.

Okay, sure, it might have been the other way around. At least now we know how they pulled it off!

On Intuition and the Free Radical Problem

It is often thought that legal analysis and argument are matters of logic. Intuition plays a huge role. It is the engine that starts the whole process.

Split-brain research suggests that the two sides of the human brain have different roles. The right side is the intuitive side: it sees relationships, creates moments, and sings. Unfortunately, it has grunts for words. The left side is organized, logical, and has a brilliant vocabulary: alas, it has nothing much to say, pretty much limited to such things as "Pass the salt."

Whether the research is correct or not, I think it is helpful in understanding how we think. Prize both your intuitions and your logic.

Facing a new problem, our mind might throw out, "Gee, Ms. K's problem strikes me as the same as that of a six-year-old giving away his allowance." This is the brain's right side, grunting. Standing alone, it is a *free radical*.

Of course, those of us too squeamish to go to medical school have only the vaguest idea what a "free radical" is. But we know they are bad. They are bad in law, too. In law, free radicals are free-standing "good points" tied to no proposition of law. I knew a very talented lawyer who did prison-reform work. After several years she quit: "I am sick of trying to make filthy and dangerous jail conditions into 'cruel and unusual punishments.'" But courts have no power to do anything about filthy and dangerous conditions; they can only act to prevent "cruel and unusual punishments." Filthy and dangerous conditions are free radicals; they must be tied to legal requirements.

Free radicals are the product of the right side of our brain. They are often brilliant. But you must use the left side of your brain to tie them to the law. One device I have already mentioned to help you do just that: ask "So what?" of your insights.

Intuition is not the solution: it is an invitation to do the hard analysis needed to get to a solution.

CHAPTER 5

STATUTES, STATUTORY CONSTRUCTION, AND ARGUMENTS THAT EAT PITTSBURG

Thus far we have been dealing with judicial opinions as sources of law. Statutes are another source of law, and we have two questions:

1. If an irresistible statute meets an immovable judicial opinion, which wins?

2. If a statute is ambiguous, how do we figure out what it means?

Finally, we will discuss the question that may have led you to buy this book in the first place: just what is "an argument that eats Pittsburgh?"

On Statutes and Cases

Both statutes and case law are sources of law—judges must follow controlling statutes and controlling cases. As a general matter, statutes trump: legislatures can overrule the rules laid down in judicial opinions by simply passing a statute, unless the judicial rule rested on the United States Constitution, which trumps everything, or on the state constitution, which trumps state statutes. Judges can throw out statutes *only* if they contravene the Constitution.

To illustrate, if a court said, "Exculpatory clauses in leases are valid," the legislature could change that result by simply passing a statute saying they were void. On the other hand, if the legislature passed a statute saying, "Exculpatory clauses in leases are valid," a court *could not* change that rule unless it found it to be unconstitutional.

Bottom line, in terms of what you want to be when you grow up, if you want to change the world, become a legislator, not a judge. (This sentence entirely ignores the Civil Rights Movement and other great moments in our legal history, but Nutshell Writers have to make tough choices.)

On Statutory Construction

Statutory interpretation is a variation of the Second-Case-in-the-World (*everything* is).

Assume a statute in the following form: "No vehicles in the Park." Ben, age 4, drives his Big-Wheel in the Park. Has he violated the statute?

Obviously the question turns on the meaning we attribute to "vehicle." Much of your legal education (and much of your legal practice) will deal with the interpretation of language. You will face the issue in interpreting contracts, statutes, cases and even criminals' confessions. The question is always one of *intent*: when the person or parties used the word in question, what was their intent?

Often you don't have to go any further than the word itself. For example, if Ben's big brother, Caleb, was driving a large gasoline transport truck in the park, there is little doubt that he was running afoul of our rule about "vehicles" in the park. Unfortunately, few of your cases will be that easy. Those cases are never litigated. You will meet, daily, situations like the one raised by Ben's BigWheel, where it is unclear whether the chosen word was intended to cover such a case.

Unless the language has a plain meaning that applies to the case at hand (Caleb's gasoline truck), the first move in interpreting language is to put it in *context*. Now had "No vehicles in the Park" been announced in a judicial opinion, we would have the *facts* of the case to help guide us. Did the judges, in using the word "vehicle," intend to cover such things as BigWheels? If the rule had been announced in the context of a dispute over heavy trucks in the park, then we might conclude that the court, in using the word "vehicle," meant things of that ilk—things that could run people over and things which pollute the air and things that make loud noises. Ben's BigWheel does none of these things, and hence, the word "vehicle" should not be interpreted to include it.

Note that we were going through exactly the same process when we were distinguishing cases: "Yes, the Court said 'No vehicles in the park,' but that was in the context of discussing heavy trucks. Surely that rule should not be applied to a case involving a BigWheel; the case is distinguishable."

Further, if the rule "No vehicles in the Park," had been announced in a judicial opinion, we would have the court's *rationale or justification* to help guide us as to meaning. Assume the judges said:

"Public safety, noise abatement, and pollution control all require us to prohibit vehicles in the Park."

We would then have some sense of how the judge was using the word "vehicle" and whether it would include BigWheels.

Again, the first move in interpreting ambiguous language is to look to the *context* in which the language was used. In the case of judicial opinions, rules are announced in the context of specific facts and asserted rationales. What about statutes? Occasionally it is possible to put a statute into context as an aid to interpretation. For example:

1. Sometimes there will be *legislative history* in which the legislature writes out what it has in mind.

2. Sometimes what appears to be an isolated statute was in fact a part of a larger legislative package. Perhaps "No vehicles in the Park" was part of a "Clean Air Act" and, if it was, one could argue that, in using "vehicles," the legislature intended only those vehicles that pollute the air.

3. Sometimes statutes amend prior statutes. If the old statute read "No cars or trucks in the park," one could argue that, in substituting

the word "vehicle," the legislature intended an inclusive definition.

In your Legal Research class, you will learn how to check out all of these possibilities.

Unfortunately, most statutes come to us as simple declaratory sentences, with no description of the kinds of situations the legislators had in mind in passing the statute (the "facts" in a case) and with no rationale of why they adopted the statute. Statutes simply appear, like the ghost of Hamlet's father.

Let's assume all you have is a statute that reads, "No vehicles in the Park." Does it include Ben's BigWheel? How would we go about analyzing this problem?

We assume that the legislature must have had its reasons in passing such a law, and then we ask ourselves what that reason might have been. Once we have decided upon that reason, now we have a context in which to interpret the language.

"Your Honor, the legislature must have intended not only to abate noise and pollution in the park, but also to prevent clutter and to protect public safety. A park filled with BigWheels is not a pleasant place for adults to be, and BigWheels do in fact present a risk of injury."

Of course, the opposing lawyer would posit different legislative purposes.

Here too, lawyers put forth *hypotheticals* and *draw analogies*. Let's see how this works. The lawyer would first make up two easy cases: a gasoline transport truck would surely be a "vehicle" within the meaning of the statute, while a child's toy model truck would surely not be. Then the argument would be by analogy:

"Your Honor, a BigWheel is more like a gasoline transport truck than it is like a toy model car for the following reasons...."

To make these arguments by analogy, we are forced to tease out why our easy cases are in fact easy cases. Why is the gasoline transport case an easy one and does that reason apply to BigWheels?

Don't put this entire discussion down as an instance of bad legislative drafting. Let's say the legislature envisioned the problem and passed a statute reading:

No vehicles in the Park, and this includes Big-Wheels!

Ben drives his BigWheel in the Park and gets busted. Easy case? You don't know Ben.

He will argue: "My BigWheel was *on the road*, not *in the Park* and the purpose of the rule is to prevent damage to grass and flowers. The rule reads '*in* the Park' and not '*on* the road.' The very precision of the rule shows that the legislature was drafting very carefully. Besides, I had only *one* BigWheel. The rule specifically says 'BigWheels.' Probably the rule was aimed against vendors or people putting on races. So there!"

Let the legislature throw some more words at the problem; soon we will have an Internal Revenue Code—much too big to fit on a Yellow Sign. Park signs will read:

Warning: Certain rules may or may not apply. Read them!

No matter how carefully language is drafted, there will come a situation which will make that language ambiguous. That is the stuff of life; that is the stuff of law practice.

Turning briefly to a question of political science, it tells us a lot about courts and legislatures that courts must publicly justify their decisions while legislatures just vote. Judges have to write opinions, justifying the rules of law they lay down. This is because judges have limited power. Very few are elected. Their decisions should rest on reason, and that reasoning should be made public so as to prevent possible abuses. Legislators are elected, and if they misuse their power, they can be thrown out of office. Further, political decisions can be irrational as long as they are those of the majority.

Arguments That Eat Pittsburgh

Sometimes a word in a statute will be interpreted in such a fashion that it turns and devours the statute itself. Let's assume a burglary statute that requires, among others things, a "forced entry." Let's further assume a fact pattern where the culprit walked into the house though an open door.

If we were to interpret "forced entry" to include walking into a house, because walking requires "force," we have effectively defined that aspect of the statute out of the statute. All entries are now "forced entries," and the requirement vanishes. The response is, that cannot be a proper interpretation because the legislature, in requiring a "forced entry," must have wanted to distinguish some kinds of entries from others.

Be sensitive to these kinds of arguments. Would the proposed definition turn upon and consume the rule?

I call these arguments "arguments that eat Pittsburgh." I do not have any good reason to call them that. In fact, I have never been to Pittsburgh. But that kind of argument deserves a name and until you come up with a better one, I'll let mine stand.

CHAPTER 6

CARL AND THE DRUGGIST, STARE DECISIS AND THE LAW'S CENTRAL DILEMMA

In the first chapter, I asked you to consider whether courts should follow the doctrine of stare decisis. I hinted I would return to the topic, and here we go. We'll consider the main arguments for the doctrine and some of those in opposition. Along the way we will meet Carl and the druggist and discuss the central dilemma of law, the conflict between the general and the concrete. I will also introduce you to some "hot" jurisprudential debates that wage among law professors, debates that would no doubt put almost everyone else to sleep but, well, for us, they are the Worldwide Wrestling Federation.

An alternative system to one committed to precedent would be one where disputants tell the stories to a designated Wise One and that Wise One would decide the matter based on what is "fair." Before we look at the reasons advanced in support of the doctrine of precedent, it is well to remind ourselves that this is not simply an academic concern. There are very real costs in our system, which relies on prior cases to resolve current controversies.

Costs of Relying on Precedent

First, relying on prior case law makes dispute resolution vastly more expensive, and the only clear winners are the lawyers. Without a doctrine of precedent, folks would simply go to a Wise One. No lawyers. No need for the specialized knowledge on how to find and analyze the "prior cases." Alas, no Nutshells.

Second, the doctrine of precedent can produce injustice. Early cases can be wrong; recall the early Supreme Court decisions holding that racial segregation is permissible. Eventually many of the early errors are corrected; but before they are, we must realize that judges followed those bad precedents. Always remember this when you rejoice in reading a case that corrects a bad rule of law; hundreds, perhaps thousands, fell on that sword before it was corrected.

Third, to work at all, precedent must work at a general level. Yet it may very well be that justice resides in the details. We will return to this topic momentarily; note here, that if this is correct, the doctrine of precedent becomes something of a coin toss: sometimes the general rule produces justice; sometimes it doesn't.

Why do our courts follow precedent? There are four traditional justifications:

1. *Predictability*. The idea is that judges should follow the law in prior cases so that folks can plan their lives around what that law is. We'll examine the philosophic assumption that this

justification makes and then ask whether *stare decisis* can actually deliver what it promises: predictability.

2. *Universalization.* This justification goes to the effect of the doctrine on current decision-makers. Judges are, after all, only human. They may be tempted to decide cases on grounds we would all agree are improper, such as the politics of one of the parties or their race or sex. Because the judges will realize that they are not *only* deciding the case before them, but cases to come after, they will tend to think in terms of universals, rather than specifics. This mind set (and the fact that they must articulate and publish their decisions) helps factor out improper motives.

3. *Natural Law.* This is the tad old-fashioned view: we should follow prior cases because the first judges got it *right*. People used to believe in *natural law*, existing "out there," and that when judges made a decision, they were *finding* law, not *creating* it. A variation of "the first case is right" is that, while there might not be natural law out there, human reasoning is such that it will lead folks of good faith to similar conclusions. If this is correct, there is no need to retry the rule because the next judge would come to the same conclusion anyway.

4. *Efficiency.* It comes as a disappointment to many law students, who expect law to reflect the clash of policies and philosophies of great moment, to find that much of our law is of the "stay to your right" variety. That is, what the rule is, left or right, doesn't really matter; all that matters is that we have a rule. The argument is that, rather than have the parties argue what the rule should be each time, it is more efficient to have the judge simply look up a prior case and have everyone get on with their lives.

Let's take a closer look at these justifications.

Predictability

Today most folks justify stare decisis on the basis of predictability: unless judges follow prior case law, people will not know how to plan their lives.

Note the philosophic assumption: without a doctrine of precedent, judges would be all over the lot. Note that this assumption is opposite to the assumption made by those who believe in natural law or in the power of human reason to come to "like" decisions. If each judge (or Wise One), when faced with the enforcement or non-enforcement of exculpatory clauses in apartment leases, came to the same conclusion, there would be no need for precedent. Everyone would simply know how the issue would be resolved.

Whether there is natural law, or whether human reasoning can lead to similar conclusions, is beyond the scope of a Nutshell. It is not beyond my scope, however, to suggest that if one wants to argue against the doctrine of precedent, one need not argue that the Wise Ones would come to the same conclusion *every time*. This is because the doctrine of precedent does *not* guarantee predictable results *every time* either.

It surely didn't help Landlord!

We have already discussed how cases can be distinguished and how statutes can be interpreted. We have seen a considerable amount of play in the system. Given this play, may judges decide any case any way they want to? If so, then the whole house of cards comes crashing down: stare decisis cannot deliver on its promise of predictability (or on its promise to control arbitrary decision-making by judges).

The degree to which cases and statutes control judicial behavior is a central jurisprudential issue. On the academic side of things, there is a group of trouble-makers, known as *crits*, who write law review articles asserting that judicial rules are a sham and judges can do whatever they like. They draw on a literary interpretation argument method known as *deconstructionism*, which suggests that the meaning of a text resides in the reader and that all readings are equally valid. The upside to this argument is that you really need to buy only one book, sometimes reading it as *Huck Finn*, and other times reading it as *Cases and Materials on Civil Procedure*.

A brief aside. The crits are generally left-wing scholars pining for the 1960's. "In the opposite corner, wearing the expensive gold trunks," are the Law and Economics scholars, hankering for the 1870's. Both sides have important points to make, and I hope that sometime in your law-school career you have time to step back from the daily grind of cases and statutes to partake of the great academic debates about what the law is and what it should be.

Even with *stare decisis*, the law is uncertain, perhaps not as uncertain as the crits claim, but uncertain nonetheless. The practical aspect of legal uncertainty is that lawyers are hated. They can never give a clear answer. "Will this clause be upheld if we litigate?"

"Maybe."

Thanks to modern research techniques, the unpredictability of law may be getting even worse. When the common law system of precedent was being developed, there weren't that many cases. Stroll in your law library: that is no longer true today. When you had a few cases *on point*, the system worked; when you have hundreds, it starts to break down. A diligent researcher could find, somewhere, a case standing for about any possible proposition.

How to cope with this tidal wave of cases? *Restatement*s. These represent a kind of time-out, let's catch our breath effort. With too many cases pointing in too many directions threatening the case method, groups of law professors and leading practitioners sit down to distill the common law rules (case rules) of their subjects, add their own thinking and, when common law rules clashed, pick the one that makes the most sense to them. Uniform State Laws, such as the Uniform Commercial Code, fulfill a similar function by attempting to reduce the chaos produced by the case system. Written by professors and practitioners, they are adopted, modified or not, by state legislatures.

The basic idea of both movements is to allow more predictability in the law by allowing lawyers and judges to turn to a more certain set of rules than are found in the cases. Alas, old habits die hard. Now, like barnacles, scores and scores of judicial opinions hang on the Restatements and Uniform State Laws "interpreting" them.

Now, with computer retrieval systems, research becomes cheap and easy. Lawyers used to look for cases in their own state; it was just too hard to search nationally. Now, however, lawyers in San Diego can quickly access cases from Boston; the flood of relevant authority has expanded vastly. Who knows what eventual effect this will have on our system?

Before leaving the topic of predictability, let me say one kind word about unpredictability. When the law is uncertain, there is an incentive for the parties to compromise their dispute. If both the plaintiff's lawyer and the defendant's lawyer are telling their clients the same thing, "Gee, I don't really know if we will win or lose if we go to court," cooler heads are more likely to prevail and trigger serious negotiations.

Universalization

There is always the chance that judges may cheat. They may find for Ms. K, for example, not on the merits of her case but because they don't like the race, politics, or sexual orientation of the landlord. How can we prevent this from happening? We have already seen a couple of preventatives: the rule that requires judges to follow prior cases and the tradition that requires them to justify and publish their decisions. Universalization is another device.

The philosopher Kant urged us to universalize our decisions. When faced with a tough choice, I should ask how I would have everyone decide, not just myself. Should I claim a questionable deduction on my income tax? I'm leaning that way *because* I know what a good guy I am, and I know that, due to my general sloth, I probably forgot to take other legitimate deductions. To make an ethical decision, Kant advised, one must factor out all of these personal prejudices and decide the matter by asking: "Would I have all taxpayers claim questionable deductions?"

The problem with universalization is that it shores the problem of significant details. Can I ask the following? "Would I have all taxpayers claim questionable deductions provided that they are as good a guy as I am, and provided further that they are sloppy and no doubt forgot to take other legitimate deductions?''

The doctrine of precedent forced Judge Flintstone to decide the case not on the basis of whether he liked or disliked Ms. K or her opponent, but on the basis of what she thought would be fair to all tenants and all landlords.

Fine. But maybe that level is still too abstract.

Psychologists pose the following problem:

> *Carl's wife is dying. The druggist has a drug that will save her life but costs $1000. Carl doesn't have the money. One night he breaks into the drugstore and steals the medicine. He gives it to his wife, and she gets well. Did Carl do the right thing?*

Now, graduate students generally will answer this question at the level of "property rights" versus "human rights." But maybe this is wrongheaded. Younger kids, when asked the question, usually want to know a lot more before answering:

> *Does Carl love his wife? Did he try real hard to get the money? What's the druggist like? Does he kick puppies who accidentally wander into his store?*

Laugh as you will, but probably, when you actually make decisions (as opposed to discussing them in class), you probably consider any manner of specific details. Indeed, in fact we all treat those we love differently from the way we treat those we don't. Maybe fairness lives in the details and maybe there are no two cases that are really "alike" and it is simply a mistake to believe that there are.

The conflict between the general and specific is endemic to law. You cannot have a rule of law that reads:

> *It is okay to steal medicine, at least up to $1000 worth, if it is needed to save the life of your wife, as long as you love her and as long as you tried really hard to get the money and provided further that the druggist is a bad guy who kicks puppies for no good reason.*

You can't have such a law because it would do no work; it is too specific. Lawyers could not rely upon it to make predictions; judges could not rely on it to make decisions.

Note well the central dilemma of law. Legal rules must be somewhat general or they won't work at all; if they are somewhat general, they may be suppressing specific facts that should matter.

Natural Law, Right Answers

We hold these truths to be self-evident.

In discussions of stare decisis with countless law students, none, never, not once, said that courts should follow prior cases because those cases were "right." This is curious. We don't even consider the possibility of "natural law" or the possibility of human reasoning coming to correct solutions.

Ours is a world of relative value and power politics. We rejoice in debunking ideas and authorities and love to point to political or psychological factors as the "real" reasons behind decisions. As undergraduates, we analyzed Marx in terms of Freud and Freud in terms of Marx.

It is difficult for us to believe that judicial decisions are "right" in any strong sense of the word. But others have so believed.

Once, people believed in "natural law," that law somehow exists "out there," independent of us. Under this view, judges don't make law, they discover it. Scientists, after all, did not *invent* gravity. We don't buy natural law anymore. We believe that judges are not *discovering* the law; they are *creating* it.

This is not just some interesting (or boring) aside. Note what is at stake. Without some bedrock, how can we say any law or practice is unjust? Slavery? Dictatorship? Cruel and unusual punishment? Are these just matters of convention, or individual opinion, or whim?

This is getting us into heavy-duty philosophy. Here, two things. Never forget that just like those "fools" who believed in natural law, we are captives of our culture's assumptions. Second, when you are creating something, say writing a short story, how can you be sure you are creating it instead of discovering it? Mark Twain spoke of his books as "writing themselves." Did he create Huck Finn or did he somehow discover him?

Efficiency

The final argument in favor of the doctrine of precedent is that following old cases is a whole lot less expensive than retrying every issue. While this is surely the least grand of the justifications, in many situations it makes a great deal of sense. Much of law practice is routine. Many of the rules are clear. There are many more "Stay to your right" types of rules than there are "No vehicles in the Park" types. If there is a dispute about which side of the street to drive on, it makes more sense to have a lawyer reach for a dusty old law book to find the answer than it does to refer the disputants to a Wise One to fight it out.

So ends our discussion of the doctrine of precedent, how it works and why we use it. I will close by showing how your classroom experience teaches you to operate the doctrine and then, as is so typical of law professors, tack on some questions of ethics that we probably won't get to.

On Legal Education

In the Prologue I told you that law professors generally do not explain or supplement the assigned reading in class. Rather they put you to work in exploring the coherence, the assumptions, and the implications of the assigned readings. Now you will see why.

Assume the very first law school, the SNU College of Law (State of Nature University). Again, we have only one case, *Globe*. What the professor will do is to call on a student to recite the facts and law of the case. Now, rather than saying, "How about that?" the professor will veer off into insanity.

"Freedom of Contract? What does that mean? What assumptions about humans, about the good life, does it rest on?"

"This was a credit report. What if it were an X-ray report?"

"Why shouldn't courts rewrite contracts? We know better than these people. We did better on the LSAT. Besides, they live in caves!"

The professor will ask questions and the students will mumble responses and it will never be clear whether the student is right or wrong or what the answer is and then, wham, the class is over and it is 15 pages for tomorrow.

"I don't get it. Are exculpatory clauses valid or not? I knew before class but, frankly, now I couldn't tell an exculpatory clause from an English muffin."

Why do we do this to you? To teach you how to be a lawyer. Lawyers work with legal rules and doctrines: you must learn how to use them. Had you learned only the "law" of *Globe* and had Ms. K hired you, you would have given her incompetent advice: "Sorry, you signed an exculpatory clause, and they are valid. Go home."

Some Matters of Ethics

It may seem strange to end our discussion of legal analysis by raising questions of legal ethics. It isn't. Once you get the mechanics of legal analysis down, and you will, it becomes a lot easier. In practice, you will probably tend to specialize in a few areas of the law, such as criminal law, security law, elder law, or entertainment law. You will quickly learn the substantive doctrines in those areas.

The hard parts of legal practice are dealing with people (and I can't help you there) and resolving the tough ethical issues that seem to arise most every day. To get you thinking about such issues, consider the following ethical problems that could arise around the legal issue of exculpatory clauses.

1. If a landlord comes and asks you to draft a form lease, do you automatically include an exculpatory clause (assuming they are legal in your jurisdiction)? Should you discuss the issue with the landlord, expressing your feelings about the propriety of the clauses?

2. Assuming exculpatory clauses have been held unenforceable in your state, what if the landlord says, "Draft one anyway. Maybe the courts will change their minds; in any event, most of my tenants don't know the law and won't sue."

3. Assume that exculpatory clauses are valid in your state. A landlord who has been quite negligent and whose negligence has seriously injured a tenant seeks your representation. Reviewing the store-bought lease, you find an exculpatory clause buried on the second page. Would it be proper for you not to raise the defense? If you do raise it, should you tell your not-too-bright opponent that similar clauses have been found invalid in other states?

4. Should you decide these issues yourself or should you do whatever the official lawyer ethics dictate?

Someday, out there, you will have to resolve these issues. Best to think about them now, before the crush of phone calls and memos.

PART TWO

STUDY SKILLS

"What is it, exactly, that I'm supposed to be learning?"

You will be exposed to a bewildering set of materials: "cases" from different states and from different times, Restatements, law reviews, Uniform Codes, state and federal statutes and maybe even snippets of the United Nations Charter. What's going on? What are you to make of this mess? Should you memorize case names? Dates? The language of the Restatements? How a state statute differs from a Uniform Code provision?

What do lawyers do, day in, day out? Clients come, seeking help. When they explain their situation, their lawyers will spot the legal problems that must be resolved. Based on their training, these lawyers will know the law's general solutions to these problems and, based on that knowledge, will ask their clients to amplify certain portions of their stories in order to determine how the law's general solutions would play out in the clients' situations.

In law school, you are learning how to be a lawyer. You are learning:

1. To spot legal issues (problems) lurking in any fact pattern;

2. To know the general solutions the law has adopted to solve these problems; and

3. To apply these solutions to the case at hand.

This, and nothing more fancy, is what it is "to think like a lawyer." This is the essential format you will follow in your various tasks, from writing memos to taking exams. Law students, when I tell them that, have a hard time believing it. "Yeah, well, that's cool, but do I have to memorize dates?" Hopefully, as you work your way through this Part, you will get a hands-on sense of what I mean. Knowing what you are trying to learn will inform your understanding of how to learn it.

In Chapter 7, I expand on your educational goals and relate them to educational methods.

Most of your time will be spent reading and briefing cases. Chapter 8 gives you some tips on how to read cases and gives you one to work on. Chapter 9 goes into the matter of case-briefing, and it too gives you a case to work on. *Do the work*. Not only will you understand the general advice better, but also you will be getting a head start on your Contracts class: the two cases I use are classic first semester fare.

Chapter 10 offers general study tips on such topics as how to get the most out of your classes, the use and abuse of study aids, and "outlining" your courses (a grand law school tradition).

Read all of these chapters early as you will be reading and briefing cases, and attending class, from the get go. Chapters 11 and 12 can wait until mid-semester. They focus on law school exams and will make better sense once you have some law behind you. You will be given a test to take and two model answers to analyze.

The last chapter in this Part, "Fear and Loathing in the First Year," is basically therapy. Read it when you suddenly realize that you are the dumbest person in law school. Because this insight strikes different students at different times, there is no set time for that chapter.

CHAPTER 7

STUDYING LAW: ENGAGEMENT, NOT LOOKING BUSY

Once upon a midnight dreary,
*   while you ponder, weak and weary,*

Over many quaint and forgotten cases,

While you're nodding, nearly napping,
*   suddenly will come a tapping,*

As if some one gently rapping,
*   rapping at your chamber door.*

" 'Tis some professor," you will mutter,
*   'tapping at my chamber door–*

Quoth the professor,'Focus! Focus!
*   Evermore!' "*

Okay, it's not *entirely* original and, fine, the last lines don't *quite* scan. But my point is a good one. Many students believe that the way to study law is to put in long hours, nearly napping, and to look busy by highlighting cases, by copying over what the judges said, or by scanning material onto their computers.

Good news, "midnight drearies" are not required; bad news, a lot more is required than looking busy. You have to *engage* the materials. Law's difficult, sometimes boring. And there is a lot of it. The temptation to close up shop will be constant.

Let me rest! I'll just underline that passage even if I don't understand it; it seems important. I'll buy an outline. That should help. The person behind me has an outline. All these words. Where was I? How many more pages?

When I was a law student, I smoked. Once, after several hours at my desk, just to break the deadening stupor, I set my Corporations casebook on fire. Although I found this deeply satisfying, I would be irresponsible to recommend either smoking or torching your books.

To determine the best way to study, let's begin with your goal. Let's put aside your loftier goals, those you felt compelled to adopt for purposes of your law school application. Let's descend to the bottom of Maslow's pyramid: "My goal is to pass the test."

Fair enough.

Assume that in your torts class you discover that there are some things called "intentional torts" and that the courts generally look at three or four key factors to decide whether an intentional tort was committed. These factors are sometimes called the "elements" of the particular tort.

Now, many students, recalling their undergraduate days, sit down and try to memorize these elements. This would be a good approach *if* law school exams asked questions like, "What are the four elements in an intentional tort?"

They don't.

Law school essay exams are short little stories, some more compelling than others, all ending with one or more persons pretty angry. Your job is *to help the reader* (here, your professor) *understand how a court might approach and resolve the conflict.* Your first job is to "spot" the legal issues raised in the drama. Had you read the drama before law school, you probably wouldn't have spotted these issues; now you will be able to do so. "Here is an intentional tort issue!"

Next, to help your reader assess the situation, you must tell the reader something about intentional torts. Here is where the elements come in.

However, it is not enough to write: "This situation raises an intentional tort issue, and the court will look at the following four elements." That is somewhat helpful, but what the reader really needs to know is *how the elements will play out in the particular situation.*

That's why mere memorization will never work. What you need to do when you are studying is to *practice applying the elements.*

A sports analogy might help. Grant Gilmore, law professor extraordinaire, once argued that law is not something we *know* but rather something we *do*. He compared it to baseball. Knowing all the rules of the game won't get you to first base. How do you become good at something you *do*, whether it's playing ball, playing the piano, dancing ballet, or acting Shakespeare?

By practicing!

Learn law by *practicing* law. View your assignments, not as tasks to learn specific legal doctrines, but as opportunities to practice lawyering skills. You can no longer be a passive observer in your studies; you must become an active participant. When you are struggling to figure out a case, when you are struggling to see if two cases are consistent or inconsistent, when you are struggling to interpret a statute, you are doing what lawyers do, and you are in fact practicing law.

A huge fear of first-year students is that they aren't "getting it," that, even as hard as they work, they still aren't getting the legal rules just right. Relax. It is okay to be wrong as long as you are practicing. Assume you worked for several hours trying to understand a case, and during class, it becomes painfully obvious that you really didn't understand it at all. Don't despair. Don't run out and buy commercial study aids, such as "canned briefs" (briefs written by experts that will tell you the correct answers). By doing so, you have deprived yourself of the opportunity to practice.

No one ever learns to play Mozart the first time out, and no one ever learns to play Mozart by watching others play Mozart. The only way is to hang in there and develop your own skills. And it won't always be pretty.

If you study by practicing law, you will learn the legal doctrines almost as a by-product. On the exam the issues will *jump out at you*, and you will know what factors a court might consider in resolving them.

I have already illustrated this by giving you two practice questions after our discussions of *Globe* and *K v. Landlord* in Chapters One and Two. Recall that those discussions did not focus on the "law" of those two cases and I did not advise you to try to memorize the holdings of those cases. Our discussion was rather on how lawyers distinguish cases. My belief is that you would have learned the "law" as a by-product of struggling with the cases. If you had written answers to the two questions I gave you, you would have found the issues jumping out at you and that you were able to discuss them intelligently. You were able to do this without sitting down and trying to "learn" the law; your knowledge came as a by-product of your practicing law. (It is not too late to go back and answer those questions.)

Let me illustrate how to *practice* law. Consider the issue of the modification of on-going contracts (where a builder, say, comes to the homeowner and says, "I have run into difficulty with some of my suppliers and will need an extra $1000 to complete on time," and the homeowner says, "Fine, I'll split the cost with you."). When are these modifications enforceable? What follows is a slightly rewritten Restatement Section which governs the situation.

Section 89: Modification of Contract

*A promise modifying a duty under a contract
not fully performed on either side is binding if
the modification is fair and equitable in view of
circumstances not anticipated by the parties
when the contract was made.*

Let's parse this section for the elements needed
to make a contract modification enforceable.

　　1.　The contract must have not been fully performed at the time of modification; and

　　2.　The modification must be fair and equitable; and

　　3.　The circumstances causing the modification
must not have been "anticipated" by the parties when the contract was made.

It would be quite possible to sit down and memorize these three elements. But, if you were facing a
modification problem on the exam, you would need
to say more than simply, "The issue is whether the
promise modifying a duty is binding and, to determine it, the court will look to the following elements...." Again, to help the reader understand
how the particular case described in the question
would play out in court, you must discuss *how* these
elements would play out. You can do this if you
used this section, not as something to memorize,
but as an opportunity to practice law. How to
practice law with this section?

　　1.　*Try to figure out the justification of each of
the three elements*. Why did the drafters add this

business of circumstances "not anticipated"? Why did they require the contract not to have been fully performed?

2. *Run the section against real or hypothetical situations.* To get a feel for how the section works, make up cases that would clearly pass each issue and cases that would clearly fail each issue. Run the section against difficult cases. Did the builder in our example "anticipate" trouble with the suppliers? That will lead to the question of what the drafters meant when they used the term. In one sense, all problems can be anticipated. This is probably too broad an interpretation (indeed, it "eats Pittsburgh"). Did the drafters intend that the circumstances were "anticipated" only if the parties actually talked about them before the contract was signed?

Practice with these questions. And recall our discussion of statutory interpretation in Chapter Five.

The key to success is to engage the material and to view each assignment as an opportunity to practice your legal skills.

All of this is not to suggest that memorization has no place in law study. But make it your *last* move, not your first. At the end of the day, once you are done with practice, it is a good idea to write out the elements you have worked on for later review and perhaps memorization. But for now, when your mind later accesses these memories, more than sterile words will come. What will come is your deeper understanding born of long and difficult practice.

CHAPTER 8

READING CASES

"Who's on first?"

"No, Who's on second."

"What?"

"What's on third!"

"Who's on third?"

"No. I already told you. Who's on second!"

"But who's Pennoyer?"

"He's Neff."

I'm a basketball fan. A highly touted high school All–American comes to the University. After a few months, the coach is quoted as saying, "He's got great talent, but he has to learn to play with intensity."

"Play with intensity? I've been playing with intensity my whole life. I can't play harder and better than this."

But he can ... and he will.

In your first weeks of law school, you will work very hard and spend long hours struggling with the cases. You will read closely and with great care. You will think that you can't do more.

"I just can't read with greater concentration."

But you can ... and you will.

We all have levels of competence that we cannot even fathom. With hard work, we can amaze ourselves.

What follows is a rather famous case, known as *Walker-Thomas*. I want you to read my slightly edited version of it and then answer some questions about it. Part of the difficulty you will encounter in reading cases is that you will meet with a new vocabulary and come across procedures that you are unfamiliar with. To help you in this regard:

-For the District of Columbia, Congress acts as would a state legislature. That is why we will see it dealing with a contract law question, which is usually a matter left to the states.

-The **Uniform Commercial Code**, or **UCC**, is a code written by various experts covering, among other things, the sale of goods. That Code covers much (but not all) of the same ground as the common law (court-made law) of contracts. Most states, and as you will see, Congress for the District of Columbia, have adopted the UCC.

-**Statutes trump common law**: once you have a statute covering an area, it is the primary source of law.

With these things in mind, read *Walker-Thomas*.

WILLIAMS v. WALKER–THOMAS FURNITURE CO.

U.S. Court of Appeals.
District of Columbia Cir., 1965.

J. SKELLY WRIGHT, CIRCUIT JUDGE. *Walker-Thomas Furniture Company operates a retail furniture store in the District of Columbia. During the period of 1957 to 1962, Ms. Williams purchased a number of household items from Walker–Thomas, for which payment was to be made in installments. The terms of each purchase were contained in a printed form contract which provided that, in the event of a default in the payment of any monthly installment, Walker–Thomas could repossess the item.*

*The contract further provided that "the amount of each periodical installment payment ... **shall be credited pro rata on all outstanding bills** ...." The effect of this rather obscure provision, known as a cross-collateral clause, was to keep a balance due on every item purchased until the balance due on all items, whenever purchased, was paid. As a result, the debt incurred at the time of purchase of each item was secured by the right to repossess all the items previously purchased by the same purchaser.*

On April 17, 1962, Ms. Williams bought a stereo set of stated value of $514.95. At that time, she had an outstanding balance of previous purchases of $164. The total of all of the purchases she had made at the store over the years came to $1,800. Over the years she had paid $1,400. At the time of this purchase, Walker–Thomas was aware of Ms. Wil-

liam's financial position. The reverse side of the
stereo contract listed the name of her social worker
and her $218 monthly stipend from the government.
Nevertheless, with full knowledge that Ms. Williams
had to feed, clothe, and support both herself and
seven children on this amount, Walker–Thomas sold
her a $514 stereo set.

Shortly after purchasing the stereo, Ms. Williams
failed to make her payments, and Walker–Thomas
brought this action to repossess every item she had
purchased at its store over the years. The court below
found that, under the contract, Walker–Thomas had
the right to do so and granted judgment for it. Ms.
Williams appeals that decision to this court.

Ms. Williams' principal contention, rejected by the
trial court, is that cross-collateral clauses are unconscionable and, hence, not enforceable. The trial court
explained its rejection of this contention as follows:

"I cannot condemn too strongly appellee's conduct. It raises serious questions of sharp practice
and irresponsible business dealings. A review of
the legislation in the District of Columbia affecting retail sales and the pertinent decisions of the
highest court in this jurisdiction disclose, however, no ground upon which this court can declare
the contracts in question contrary to public policy. I think Congress should consider corrective
legislation to protect the public from such exploi-
tive contracts as were utilized in the case at bar."

We do not agree that the court lacked the power to
refuse enforcement to contracts found to be uncon-

*scionable. In other jurisdictions, it has been held as
a matter of common law that unconscionable contracts are not enforceable. While no decision of this
court so holding has been found, the notion that an
unconscionable bargain should not be given full
enforcement is by no means novel. In* **Scott v. United States** *(1870), the Supreme Court stated:*

*"If a contract be unreasonable and unconsciona-
ble, but not void for fraud, a court of law will give to
the party who sues for its breach damages, not
according to its letter, but only such as he is equita-
bly entitled to."*

*Since we have never adopted or rejected such a
rule, the question here presented is actually one of
first impression.*

*Congress has recently enacted the Uniform Com-
mercial Code, which specifically provides that the
court may refuse to enforce a contract which it finds
to be unconscionable at the time it was made. The
enactment of this section, which occurred subsequent
to the contracts here in suit, does not mean that the
common law of the District of Columbia was otherwise at the time of enactment nor does it preclude
the court from adopting a similar rule in the exercise of its powers to develop the common law for the
District of Columbia. In fact, in view of the absence
of prior authority on the point, we consider the
Congressional adoption of that section persuasive
authority for following the rationale of the cases
from which the section is explicitly derived. Accord-
ingly, we hold that where the element of unconscio-*

nability is present at the time a contract is made, the contract should not be enforced.

Unconscionability has generally been recognized to include an absence of meaningful choice on the part of one of the parties together with contract terms which are unreasonably favorable to the other party. Whether a meaningful choice is present in a particular case can only be determined by consideration of all the circumstances surrounding the transaction. In many cases, the meaningfulness of the choice is negated by a gross inequality of bargaining power. The manner in which the contract was entered is also relevant to this consideration. Did each party to the contract, considering his obvious education or lack of it, have a reasonable opportunity to understand the terms of the contract, or were the important terms hidden in a maze of fine print and minimized by deceptive sales practices? Ordinarily, one who signs an agreement without full knowledge of its terms might be held to assume the risk that he has entered a one-sided bargain. But when a party of little bargaining power, and hence little real choice, signs a commercially unreasonable contract with little or no knowledge of its terms, it is hardly likely that his consent, or even an objective manifestation of his consent, was ever given to all the terms. In such a case the usual rule that the terms of the agreement are not to be questioned should be abandoned, and the court should consider whether the terms of the contract are so unfair that enforcement should be withheld.

In determining reasonableness or fairness, the primary concern must be with the terms of the contract considered in light of the circumstances existing when the contract was made. The test is not simple, nor can it be mechanically applied. The terms are to be considered "in the light of the general commercial background and the commercial needs of the particular trade or case." Professor Corbin, a leading expert in the field, suggests the test as being whether the terms are "so extreme as to appear unconscionable according to the mores and business practices of the time and place." We think this formulation correctly states the test to be applied in those cases where no meaningful choice was exercised upon entering the contract.

Because the trial court did not feel that enforcement could be refused, no findings were made on the possible unconscionability of the contracts in these cases. Since the record is not sufficient for our deciding the issue as a matter of law, the cases must be remanded to the trial court for further proceedings.

So ordered.

Discussion

If you were reading the case with the intensity that is required (and the intensity that you are capable of), you would be able to answer the questions that follow with at most a quick glance back to the case for reference. I don't expect that you will be able to do so now; if you can, I told the basket-ball story to the wrong person!

1. What was the precise issue before this court?

2. Which side cited the case of *Scott v. United States*? What argument was made based upon that case?

3. Why didn't the court simply apply the UCC to this case? Congress had passed it and made it the law.

4. What argument did the store make based upon the fact that Congress passed the UCC?

5. Assume that a customer proves that he had "no meaningful choice" in agreeing to a certain term in a contract because every store in his area had the same contract term in their contracts. Under the doctrine of **unconscionability** as developed by the court, would that customer win?

Don't panic: "I'm supposed to learn all that from each case? Like who cited which case?"

No ... you're not!

I am talking about the care with which you must read cases. I am **not** talking about what you want to take away from a case; that is the subject of the next chapter on case briefing. A careful reader would know, as she read along or with a moment's reflection, which side cited *Scott* and for what purpose; a careful reader would not, however, try to "learn it." Who cited *Scott* in terms of legal doctrine doesn't matter.

Now reread the case and answer the questions. Write them, and then we can compare answers.

My answers:

1. The precise issue was whether the courts of D.C. have the **power** to refuse to enforce parts of contracts if they are **unconscionable**. The court below didn't think it had the power. This case **does not** decide whether the particular clause was unconscionable; the case is sent back to the lower court to make that determination.

2. The customers cited *Scott* in support of their argument that the courts have an inherent power to refuse to enforce contracts, at least not to their "letter," if they are "unconscionable."

A somewhat plausible "wrong answer" would be that the store cited *Scott* for the proposition that the courts enforce, even if not to their "letter," unconscionable contracts. The problem with this answer is that the store, given the tenor of trial court opinion, knows that the "letter" the court would refuse to enforce would be the cross-collateral clause.

3. The court couldn't just apply the UCC to the case, because the contracts in question were signed **before** the UCC was passed. Statutes, generally, cannot have **retroactive effect**.

This raises a fascinating jurisprudential issue: *Congress* can't retroactively change the rules on Walker–Thomas ("unconscionable contracts will not be enforced") because that would be unfair to Walker–Thomas. But apparently there is nothing wrong with the *courts* changing the rules ("unconscionable contracts will not be enforced"). Of course it can be argued that the court really wasn't changing the rules at all; that in some sense the common law in D.C. always had a doctrine of unconscionability; it's just that no one realized it before Judge Wright came along and told us.

But what happens when a court overrules prior decisions? Aren't they changing the rules, upsetting apple carts, **retroactively**? Ask your profs.

4. What argument the store made based on Congress's passage of the UCC is a difficult question, as you must **infer** what the argument was. It is that, prior to its passage (and when the contracts were signed), it must have been that the courts of D.C. **could not** refuse to enforce contracts on the basis of unconscionability: if they already had that power, why would Congress have to pass the UCC?

Note here the **reversibility** of many legal arguments. The court, adopting something of an "in your face" style, writes:

The enactment of the UCC does not mean that the common law of the District of Columbia was

otherwise at the time of enactment. **In fact** ...
we consider the congressional adoption persua-
sive authority for following the rationale of the
cases from which the section is explicitly de-
rived.

5.   To show a contract provision unconscionable,
the customer must show **both** lack of meaningful choice **and** terms unreasonably favorable to the other party.

Unconscionability has generally been recog-
nized to include an absence of meaningful
choice on the part of one of the parties **togeth-**
er with *contract terms which are unreason-*
ably favorable to the other party.

It is critical that you focus on the *relationship*
between elements. In our prior math notation,
here we find a 1 + 2 = VICTORY equation,
not a 1 **or** 2 = VICTORY one.

A Few Tricks to Reading Closely

1.   First, figure out what the **issue** is: what legal
point must the court decide in order to resolve the case?

2.   Be clear on the basics:

What happened in the court below?

Who is appealing?

On what theory?

Who wins and why?

What happens next?

3. As to each case cited, and as to each argument the judges make, ask, "Who did they steal that one from?" Remember that judges don't think for themselves at all. Who cited the case to the court and for what purpose? This question forces you to restage the ping-pong game that legal argument is.

4. Be clear about the **relationship between arguments and between elements**. If the court is making two points, the relationship can be:

$$1 + 2 = \text{VICTORY}$$

or

$$1 \text{ or } 2 = \text{VICTORY}$$

Again, to prevail on unconscionability, the customer must show "lack of meaningful choice" **and** "unreasonable terms": one is not enough.

5. **Play loser.** Pretend you are the lawyer representing the losing side in the case and that the court's opinion is simply your opponent's argument. How will you respond to it? Often, opinions seem so clearly right that we ask ourselves, "Why did the losing side even bother?" Always remember that the losing side thought that it would win! Judicial opinions are "winners' history."

Now that you have some idea of the intensity with which you should read cases, we turn to what you are supposed to learn from them.

CHAPTER 9

BRIEFING CASES

In law school, you "brief" cases. As we will see, it is a brilliant educational device. I will begin this chapter by asking you to brief a case.

"You can't do that. You haven't told us *how*!"

A better point: I haven't told you *why*.

You brief cases partly for the same reason you take notes—*to review* later on. You don't want to reread all those cases again. For review purposes, *brevity is a virtue*. However, the main reason you brief cases is to force yourself to grapple with them, to reduce them to their core. Here, too, brevity is a virtue.

At its core, a case is a **rule of law** announced in a specific **factual context** and justified by a particular **rationale.** The *traditional briefing format* uses these categories of analysis:

1. Statement of Facts

    The factual context of the case.

2. Issue and holding

    The *issue* is the legal question the court must answer to resolve the case. The *holding* is the court's answer. It is often stated as a *rule of law*.

3. Rationale

    The reasons the court gives for reaching the result it did.

If you are called on in class to recite a case, you will say something like, "The facts of the case are ... and the issue before the court was ... and the court held that ... for the following reasons...." (assuming that you don't just freeze up and sit there).

The case you will brief is a classic and is found in most Contracts casebooks. Decided in 1917 by the highest court in New York, the opinion was written by a famous judge, Justice Cardozo, whose prose helps a case. It involves a marvelous character, Lucy, Lady Duff–Gordon (who is seen, alas, not at her finest). Lucy was a very "high profile" designer and, leading the way for today's superstars, was one of the first celebrities to endorse products. Whether she was a role model is lost in the historical record. She did, however, survive the Titanic.

But we are not here to gossip.

To help you brief the case, you will need to know some background law. As you will learn in your Contracts course, there is a doctrine called "mutuality of obligation" which requires that both sides to a contract must be bound or **neither is**. In this case Lucy, who is the defendant, made a promise to Wood, who is the plaintiff. She broke her promise to

Wood and, when he sued, she defended on the basis of "mutuality of obligation." Said Lucy:

> *"Sure, I made a promise to Wood, but Wood never actually promised to do anything for me. He could walk away from the contract any time he wanted to. Because he didn't have any promises to live up to, under the doctrine of mutuality, I don't have to live up to mine."*

One word of warning. Before you can begin to brief a case, you must read it all, probably more than once. Never just start writing; you must think long and hard before you begin.

Your brief shouldn't be more than a page. Follow, for now, the traditional format: facts, issue, holding, and rationale. After you have done the brief, we'll critique it together.

WOOD v. LUCY, LADY DUFF–GORDON

New York Court of Appeals, 1917.
222 N.Y. 88, 118 N.E. 214.

CARDOZO J. *The defendant styles herself "a creator of fashions." Her favor helps a sale. Manufacturers of dresses, millinery, and like articles are glad to pay for a certificate of her approval. The things which she designs, fabrics, parasols, and what not, have a new value in the public mind when issued in her name. She employed the plaintiff to help her to turn this vogue into money. He was to have the exclusive rights, subject always to her approval, to place her indorsement on the designs of others. He was also to have the exclusive right to place her own designs on sale, or to license others to market them. In return she was to have one-half of "all profits and revenues" derived from any contracts he might make. The exclusive right was to last at least one year from April 1, 1915, and thereafter from year to year unless terminated by notice of 90 days. The plaintiff says that he kept the contract on his part, and that the defendant broke it. She placed her indorsement on fabrics, dresses, and millinery without his knowledge, and withheld the profits. He sues her for the damages, and the case comes here on demurrer.*

The agreement of employment is signed by both parties. It has a wealth of recitals. The defendant insists, however, that it lacks the elements of a contract. She says that the plaintiff does not bind himself to anything. It is true that he does not promise in so many words that he will use reasonable efforts to place the defendant's indorsement and market her designs. We think, however, that such a promise is fairly to be implied. The law has outgrown its primitive stage of formalism when the precise word was the sovereign talisman, and every slip was fatal. It takes a broader view today. A promise may be lacking, and yet the whole writing may be "instinct with an obligation," imperfectly expressed (Scott, J., in McCall Co. v. Wright, 133 App. Div. 62, 117 N.Y.S. 775). If that is so, there is a contract.

The implication of a promise here finds support in many circumstances. The defendant gave an exclusive privilege. She was to have no right for at least a

*year to place her own indorsement or market her
own designs except through the agency of the plaintiff. The acceptance of the exclusive agency was an
assumption of its duties. Many other terms of the
agreement point the same way. We are told at the
outset by way of recital that:*

*"The said Otis F. Wood possesses a business orga-
nization adapted to the placing of such indorsement
as the said Lucy, Lady Duff–Gordon, has approved."*

*The implication is that the plaintiff's business
organization will be used for the purpose for which
it is adapted. But the terms of the defendant's compensation are even more significant. Her sole compensation for the grant of an exclusive agency is to
be one-half of all the profits resulting from the
plaintiff's efforts. Unless he gave his efforts, she
could never get anything. Without an implied promise, the transaction cannot have such business "effi-
cacy, as both parties must have intended that at all
events it should have." Bowen, L.J., in the Moor-
cock, 14 P.D. 64, 68. But the contract does not stop
there. The plaintiff goes on to promise that he will
account monthly for all moneys received by him, and
that he will take out all such patents and copyrights
and trademarks as may in his judgment be necessary to protect the rights and articles affected by the
agreement. It is true, of course, as the Appellate
Division has said, that if he was under no duty to
try to market designs or to place certificates of
indorsement, his promise to account for profits or
take out copyrights would be valueless. But in determining the intention of the parties the promise has a*

value. It helps to enforce the conclusion that the plaintiff had some duties. His promise to pay the defendant one-half of the profits and revenues resulting from the exclusive agency and to render accounts monthly was a promise to use reasonable efforts to bring profits and revenues into existence. For this conclusion the authorities are ample.

The judgment of the Appellate Division should be reversed . . . .

After you brief this case, we'll discuss it.

Discussion of Briefing

First I will discuss the essentials of briefing: the need to focus on the issue and holding of the case, the need to include the critical facts and the need to understand the court's reasoning by expressing it in your own words. Then I will discuss things you might or might not want to include, such as the procedural history of the case, the name of the judge, the court that issued the opinion and its date. I will close with my recommended brief format. Unlike the traditional format, it puts the issue, not the facts, first. Why? Because, without knowing what the issue is, there is no way of knowing what facts are important.

Issue/Holding/Rule

The *issue* in a case is the legal question the court must resolve in order to determine who wins. The *holding* of a case is how the court answered that legal question, and it can be thought of as the *rule* of the case.

Unfortunately, often courts don't come right out and tell you what the issue is or what its holding is. Sometimes they do: "The issue we have to resolve is...." or "We therefore hold that...." When they do, hog heaven. But generally they don't; you have to root around some. (Sorry for the imagery.)

In *Lucy,* you had to root around. The *issue* was whether the court would imply a promise on the part of Wood to use "reasonable efforts" in marketing Lucy's endorsements. If that promise was not implied, Lucy would not be held to her promise under the "mutuality of obligation" doctrine. The court *held* that the promise would be implied, and thus Lucy could not get out of her promise on the basis of mutuality.

There is no magic way of stating the issue/holding. Good lawyers can differ as to their statements of it. For your purposes, what you want to come away with is the notion that sometimes courts can imply promises to save ("create"?) contracts and that *Lucy* is one such instance.

> **Issue**: Should the court imply a promise to use reasonable efforts to make the contract enforceable? **Holding**: Yep.

While conceptually *issue* and *holding* are quite distinct, in the workaday world of briefs, they often merge:

Issue: Will Lucy be able to get out of her promise under the doctrine of mutuality?

Holding: Nope, because the court will imply a promise to use reasonable effort to make the contract enforceable.

Take a look at the issue that you stated. Does it come close to stating the main fight? Coming close, in this business, *is* a cigar.

Operative Facts

Knowing the issue the court has to decide, now you can tackle the *Facts*. The key facts that led the court to decide the issue as it did are known as the *operative facts*.

While operative facts have their own dignified label, their counterparts don't. Let's call them "tidbits." Tidbits are easier to recognize than are operative facts. In *Lucy,* some of the tidbits were that Lucy designed parasols, that the contract was dated a certain date, and, alas, that her favor helps a sale.

Reread your statement of facts: have you included tidbits, facts that played no part in the court's decision? Including tidbits is a "no-no." They make your brief longer, and hence less helpful when it comes time to review. More importantly, including tidbits may indicate that you are "looking busy" rather than concentrating on the case as much as you should.

As to what were the operative facts, some are clear, such as the fact that Wood did not, in so many words, promise to undertake any work for

Lucy. Reasonable minds can differ on some of the facts at the margin. Is Wood's promise to "account monthly" an operative fact, or is it a tidbit? Another way of asking that question is, "If he hadn't made that promise, would the court refuse to imply the promise of *reasonable efforts*?" I don't think so. As I don't think the court's decision would have been different, I don't think "monthly accounting" was an operative fact.

But who am I to say? Perhaps, down the road, a court might distinguish *Lucy* on that very basis:

> *"In the case before us, we are asked to imply a promise on the part of an agent to use reasonable efforts to market his principal's endorsement. Admittedly this was done in the case of* Wood v. Lucy. *However, in that case the agent had made some express promises, including to account monthly to his principal. Given the fact the agent made some express promises, it is easy to imply others. In the case before us, the agent made no express promises at all, and hence we refuse to follow* Wood v. Lucy *and will not imply a promise to use reasonable efforts."*

This illustrates a central point: what is, and what isn't, an operative fact is very much at issue in applying and distinguishing cases. Recall our discussion in Chapter 2 of whether *Globe* controlled *K v. Landlord* or whether the cases were distinguishable based on the differences in the facts of the cases.

Given uncertainty as to centrality, there may be a tendency to err on the side of inclusion. "Well I'm not sure if that fact matters, so I'll put it in." Bad idea. Best to do your work *now*: "Is this fact important or isn't it?" If you can't decide now, you won't be able to decide when you review.

Warning. Often you will work hard on a brief and go to class, only to discover that others (alas, perhaps the Prof) saw things differently, saw your omitted tidbits as pivotal, and your operative facts as not being worthy of mention. Don't get depressed. You brief cases, *not* primarily to get them right, but as a way of getting into the thick of things. By forcing yourself to work hard on figuring out which facts are operative and which are tidbits, you are lawyering even though others might disagree with your results.

Court's Reasoning

In addition to a statement of the issue before the court and its resolution, and in addition to a retelling of the operative facts, your brief should recount the court's reasoning. Why did it rule as it did? This is known as the court's *rationale*. Remember, at its core, a case is a *rule* announced in a specific *factual context* and justified by a particular *rationale*.

Put the court's reasoning in your *own* words. Don't just copy what the judge wrote. If you copy, you really won't be sure you understand it.

> *The law has outgrown its primitive stage of formalism when the precise word was the sovereign talisman, and every slip was fatal. It takes a broader view today. A promise may be lacking,*

> *and yet the whole writing may be "instinct with*
> *an obligation," imperfectly expressed.*

I don't care how many times you copy that over. To understand it, you simply must try to express it in your own words. What does it mean? Talk about "imperfectly expressed"!

What did you have for the rationale in *Lucy*? I would have put something to the effect that the court seems to justify its decision on the common-sense notion that, "Come on, the parties obviously intended that Wood would sing for his supper. Even though he didn't come out and say so, we will imply a promise to use reasonable efforts."

Viewing cases as opportunities to practice law, don't overlook the intellectual dividends that can flow if you *challenge* the court's reasoning. Can you think of any reasons why Wood would not want to promise Lucy that he would use "reasonable efforts?" Can you think of any reasons why Lucy might have agreed to give him an exclusive contract even though he didn't promise "reasonable efforts"? Try to answer those questions before I do.

Of course Wood planned to work hard for Lucy, or he wouldn't make any money. But if he *promised* to use "reasonable efforts," then no matter how much work he did for Lucy, she could still sue him claiming that he had been "dogging it." Sure, he might win down the road, but he would still be facing a lawsuit and all the heartache that entails.

Would Lucy ever agree to give him exclusive rights even if he promised her nothing in terms of the effort he would put in on her behalf? Sure, and if you ever tried to get a book published, you know why. You'll promise a literary agent *anything* as long as he takes your book and tries to sell it. But I digress into unseemly personal chitchat. As to Lucy, if Wood was good at what he did, it would be rational for her to rely upon his self-interest, rather than the threat of a lawsuit, to motivate him.

A Way to Check Your Brief

A good way check your brief is to put it in the following form:

> *We decided X (holding) because*
>
>   1. *Of these operative facts and*
>
>   2. *For these good reasons (rationale).*

If you do put your briefs in this format, you may find some strange constructions:

> *We decided to imply a promise of "reasonable efforts" on Wood's part **because** Lucy designed parasols.*

I recommend that you put the issue/holding *first*. The traditional format, which puts facts first, has always struck me as strange. How do we know what facts are important unless we know what the issue is? Let's say the issue is, "Was Lucy a woman of many talents?" Now what had been just an interesting tidbit becomes the smoking gun:

> We decided that Lucy was a woman of many
> talents **because**, among other things, she de-
> signed parasols.

We have covered the big three of briefs: issue/holding, facts, and rationale. Now let's turn to collateral matters and whether you should include them. Bottom line: include them *only if* you have a good reason, a reason you can articulate, to do so; otherwise you're just looking busy and filling up paper.

Holding/Dicta

Is it important to flag in your brief which legal rules are *holding* and which are *dicta*? First I had better tell you what these terms mean.

Holdings are statements of law necessary for the decision in the case; *dicta* are statements of law which aren't necessary for that decision. Take the case of *Brown v. Finney*, which involved two men meeting in a bar and, after a few drinks, making a supposed contract for the sale of coal. The evidence disclosed that the seller may have been joking. The appellate court reversed the judgment for the buyer on the basis that the jury should have been instructed that, if the seller was joking, he should not be held to the contract. Suppose, in the course of that opinion, the court stated:

> "We reverse the lower court decision on the
> basis that the jury should have been instructed

> *as to the issue of seriousness. We also note that*
> *intoxicated persons do not have contractual ca-*
> *pacity."*

Was the statement about intoxication *necessary* for
the court's decision to reverse the lower court?
Think.

———————

No, it wasn't. The court reversed on the seriousness issue. It didn't even have to mention the
intoxication point. Compare the situation where the
court reverses on the intoxication issue:

> *"We reverse this case on the basis that the jury*
> *should have been instructed that, if one of the*
> *parties was intoxicated at the time the contract*
> *was made, that party cannot be held to it. We*
> *also note that persons who are not serious at the*
> *time of the contract can defend on those*
> *grounds."*

Here the *holding* is the intoxication point, the *dicta*,
the seriousness point.

Why do we split these hairs?

It goes to the heart of *stare decisis*. When something is really at issue, when the case turns on it,
the court will think long and hard about it before
reaching a decision. The reason we follow prior
decisions is that we respect that effort. Compare
that to a statement of law that has the quality of,
"Oh, by the way, did you know that. . . ."

Dictum is not ("are" not, for you real hair splitters) worthy of the same respect because it is not the product of long, serious thought; this is because nothing in the case turned on it.

Thus, in a case after *Brown*, a drunk, wobbly on his feet, slurs:

> *"Your Honor,* Brown *is a controlling decision here. It says, 'Intoxicated folks don't have the capacity to contract.' So there! I win! Let's celebrate! Drinks on me!"*

Here, "Learned Opponent" stands and with great sobriety, sneers:

> *"This court is not obligated to follow the statement in* Brown *that 'Intoxicated persons do not have contractual capacity.' It is merely dicta. It was not necessary for the decision in that case.* Brown *involved pranksters, not drunks. It held that pranksters should be able to get out of their contracts. Its comments about drunks are totally beside the point. Hence this court is not obligated to follow the statement in* Brown.*"*

Such stark realities drove our friend to drink in the first place.

For a law student, the distinction between holding and dicta is a useful analytic ploy. Which statements of law are absolutely necessary for the result reached? Which are not? Once you determine something is dicta, however, don't ignore it. Much of the law you will learn will come from judicial asides. Both drunks and pranksters have defenses.

Citation and Dates

A typical caption might be:

Brown v. Finney

Penn. Supreme Court 1866

Opinion by Judge Thompson

Is this information necessary?

No, hardly ever. It won't help you review, nor does it further your understanding of the case.

If you were citing *Brown* to a judge in an actual case, the information *might* be important. Some courts are more equal than others. In the development of common law principles, some courts led the way, such as the New York Court of Appeals (the highest state court in New York) with Justice Cardozo and the California Supreme Court under Justice Traynor. Opinions of those courts carry particular weight.

In Constitutional Law courses, it's interesting to see how a particular Justice's philosophy plays out in several areas. However, in most courses, who wrote the opinion is of little interest.

Dates are important *if* you are studying the historical development of a particular legal doctrine. Sometimes you are. *Usually* you aren't. Most cases are included in casebooks not to show you what the law *was* but to show you what the law *is*. The rule of *Brown v. Finney* is as good today as it was in 1866.

Legal education generally ignores history. The sense the student gets from reading old cases as current law is that the problems facing the law have always been the same and that the law itself is above history, that it is the product of neutral rational principles rather than the clash of competing philosophical, economic, and political positions. It isn't.

Oliver Wendell Holmes, in his great essay, "The Path of the Law" (10 Harv. L. Rev. 457, 1897), said it best:

> *I cannot but believe that if the training of lawyers led them habitually to consider more definitely and explicitly the social advantage on which the rule they lay down must be justified, they sometimes would hesitate where now they are confident, and see that really they were taking sides upon debatable and often burning questions.*

Law cannot and should not escape its historical context. Yet we tend to teach law as a set of timeless principles.

I lament this with great fanfare. But, bottom line, I am part of the problem. Don't include dates. Include them only if you think them important. And be explicit as to why the date is important. Do you feel the case would not be followed today because it reflects different times?

Procedural History of the Case

Some profs *insist* on it and, well, it's their nickel.

For my money, don't *routinely* include the procedural history of the case.

Jury found for plaintiff. Defendant appeals on basis of improper jury instruction.

Appellate court reversed and plaintiff appeals. Affirmed.

This tells you nothing about the law and simply takes up space. Your interest is in what the error was in the jury instruction.

This is not to say, however, that procedural history is irrelevant. I return to the notion that I developed in the last chapter. There are things that you should understand about a case (such as which party cited which case) that you need not "take away" from the opinion. The procedural history of a case is one such thing. Forcing yourself to sort it out will help you to understand how courts operate and will help you understand which party is arguing what.

The procedural history of a case can also tell you some very interesting things. *Lucy won at the lower court*. Reading the flowing prose of Justice Cardozo, we are swept along, "But of course a promise should be implied." But not according to the New York courts of the time. Cardozo was working a major shift in the law, but he doesn't seem to be making a ripple. Courts of the time were reluctant, in the name of party autonomy, to "imply terms" to contracts. And note that even the great Cardozo was not above name-calling: "The law has outgrown its primitive stage of formalism...." etc.

In addition to the procedural history of a case, be sure you are clear as to *what happens next*. Often the decision will put an end to the matter, once and for all. But what about the case of *Wood v. Lucy*? Has Wood won his case? Think.

Wood has won the battle but not the war. Cardozo simply held that Lucy cannot get out of her promise simply because of the apparent defect in Wood's promise. Now the matter must go back for trial. At trial, Wood still must prove that Lucy broke her promise and, indeed, she might be able to defend her own breach on the basis that Wood breached first, by "dogging" it.

After an appellate case is decided, the lawyers always plan their next move. By putting yourself in their shoes, by asking "What next?" you will reread the case with greater care and will begin thinking like a lawyer.

Bottom line, put in your brief the case's procedural history and consider what happens next *if* you think it will help you. Never do anything simply as a matter of routine.

Some Final Pointers on Briefing

1. Leave wide margins so that you can add points from class discussion and make further notes when you review.

2. Don't expect to write your brief the first time you read the case.

3. Some advise *not* to brief a case until you have read all of the cases in the same assignment. This helps you see how the particular tree fits.

4. Include a "puzzling points" section at the end. What don't you understand about the case? Do you agree with it?

Here is a format you might try out. If you find that it doesn't always work (and it won't), this discovery doesn't make me an idiot; it makes you a genius. It shows that you are not mechanically filling in the blanks; it shows you are struggling with the material.

1. Issue/holding (What legal issue did the court have to resolve and how did it resolve it? Note: in some cases you will find more that one issue.)

2. Operative facts (don't include the kitchen sink ... unless the case is about a plumber)

3. Rationale (in your own words)

4. Procedural history and future (when of interest)

5. Puzzling points

The End

"That's it? That's the end of the chapter? I'm puzzled. Why would anyone end a chapter here?"

CHAPTER 10

GENERAL STUDY TIPS

I'll begin and end this chapter with the importance of writing out your own thoughts. In between, I'll cover how to maximize your time in class, how to prepare course outlines, how to use old exams to review, how to use (and abuse) study aids, and why to consider a study group. I'll give you some figures on how many hours law students traditionally study and warn against letting law school consume the rest of your life. I'll close with an idea on how to solve the forest/tree problem and then return to the topic of writing and recommend that you consider keeping a journal during what is an intense period of your life—your first year in law school.

Before we begin, a cautionary tale. After finals, some students come to discuss their grades.

"I thought I would do better. I really *know* Contracts."

That might be the problem. Your study goal should not be to know the subject. It should be to deepen your understanding of it. If you are approaching law study correctly, then the last time you go through your notes before the final, you will not come away convinced you know the subject. There will still be areas that are fuzzy to you. There are areas of the law that are fuzzy. If knowledge is your goal, once you have learned a rule or doctrine, likely you will feel compelled to protect that knowledge by closing your eyes to ambiguities and the nagging questions which threaten your understanding. If your goal is to deepen your understanding of a subject, you will relish the ambiguities and the difficult questions. By pursuing these ambiguities and difficult questions you will be learning the subject at an even deeper level.

If you push yourself, if you refuse to be satisfied with easy understandings and insist on asking yourself difficult questions, you never walk away from a subject smug. You simply run out of time.

Learning by Writing

Write in the margins; when you run out of room, draw arrows to the top and write upside down ... a well-used casebook is a mess.

Reading, you skim along and all is right with the world. Put pen to paper, or fingers to key board, and your mind slows. "Wait, that point really doesn't make sense. And how did the court get from point A to point C? I thought I understood that."

Underlining and decorating your book with various color markers gives you a sense of accomplishment, but leaves the real work of understanding to a later day. There will likely not be time to go back.

In order to *write,* you need room. Leave *sufficient margins* on your briefs, class notes and outlines to allow you to write questions and comments.

Maximizing Your Class Time

Law school classes are usually an intense intellectual experience. In order to hit the floor running, take five or ten minutes *before* class to review your briefs on the cases you will discuss. That way you won't waste valuable time trying to remember who the plaintiff was or what the dispute was about.

Note-taking presents a problem. If you take too-detailed notes, you will quickly lose the thread of the discussion and get further and further behind. Best to jot down key words during the class and then, as soon as possible after class, go over your notes and fill in the details. Some students wait a week or even longer before reviewing class notes; this is a mistake as then the notes are lifeless. If you spend 10 minutes or so each day reviewing the notes you took in each class, not only will you be able to fill in the blanks, but in a very real sense you will be repeating that class, seeing new relationships between the topics, and perhaps, just perhaps, seeing what the professor was getting at.

Volunteering in class presents a problem as well. I think it is very important to jump into the fray every now and then to test your ideas and your ability to think on your feet. On the other hand, while your arm waves, you are blocking out what is happening in class in order to hold on to your comment. Given this, volunteer, but not all the time.

And don't wait until you have "something really good to say." That idea can freeze you for semesters, for years. You won't know if what you have to say is really good until you say it. Jump in with some obvious point. It may develop that you are the only person who thought of it.

Outlines and Old Exams

"Outlining" is a law school tradition. It is the stuff of dreams:

> *"Hello. My name is Tom Berriman, and I am the head of the Law Book Division of West Publishing. A copy of your Contracts Outline came into my possession and, if you haven't sold it to Foundation or Little Brown, we are prepared to offer you big bucks."*

Outlining can also be the stuff of nightmares. Freud once noted what he called the "Graduate School Nightmare," where you dream that you are about to take an exam in a course you forget to attend.

> *"Have your started your Contracts outline yet?"*

> *"Contracts!!?? Oh no ... I forgot to go to Contracts this semester."*

Outlines combine case briefs, class notes, and any outside reading you have done. For the major categories, consider using the Table of Contents of the casebook.

There is nothing magical about outlining except doing it. Its value is not the product but the production. It is yet another way to be actively involved with the material. ("Where does this interesting tidbit fit? Should it go under Topic A or Topic B?")

Most students start outlining about halfway though the semester. Outline each course and review it several times. Some students, in order to run through the class yet again, outline their outlines.

Some students find it very helpful, toward the end of the semester, to review old finals, either by themselves or in a study group. Many schools maintain files of them. There are also books giving typical exam questions. As a student I didn't get much value out of them. I would look at an old exam and simply freeze—there was simply no way I could answer it. In the real test situation, of course, I had to overcome this panic and go ahead and answer the question.

Like other study devices, going over old test questions is helpful to many students but not all.

Study Aids, Canned Briefs, and Commercial Outlines

Most professors advise not to rely on canned briefs or commercial outlines. I will join this chorus—knowing full well that you will believe the second-year student sitting across the table in the library who assures you that someone in his class used nothing but canned briefs ("Didn't even buy the book!") and did great. Probably the most important advice in this entire book: *Believe second-year students at your own risk.*

One problem with study aids is that they may teach you more than you need to know, may teach you more than it is possible to know, and, indeed, may drive you crazy. I recall a short story:

> *A man commits murder in the victim's living room. "I must wipe my fingerprints off the glass I was drinking from!" Fair enough, he does. "What about the table? Did I touch it? Why take a chance?" He wipes the table.*
>
> *"Maybe I went into the kitchen! I don't think I did, but I can't be too sure; it will take just a few minutes!"*
>
> *The next morning, the murderer is found in the attic ... slavishly wiping off old trunks.*

First-year courses do *not* cover "everything" about Torts, Civil Procedure, or whatever. There are scores and scores of tort doctrines, of Contract doctrines, that you just don't cover in your classes. Treatises and hornbooks cover them. The risk of using collateral resources is that you might fall into the abyss. You may get further and further afield from the topics covered in class; eventually you may end up in the attic.

If you don't use outside materials to do *your* work and are aware of their dangers, they can be valuable. Make them your last, not your first, choice. If you are having a particularly difficult time with an area, a treatise might help. Once you have finished a topic, it is helpful to read a Nutshell or commercial treatise *as a method of coming at the material from a different perspective*. It is helpful to see how others have organized the material, to read how others have described the rules, and to think about examples others have used to illustrate the doctrines.

Treatises can also help overcome the discreteness of the case method by showing where a particular topic is in the forest.

Study Groups

You should be talking law with other students. It is simply a great way to try out your ideas, get additional insights, and have some fun. One of the real joys of law practice is discussing difficult cases and problems with your colleagues. After law school I practiced with a Legal Services Program. Every Friday afternoon, we sat around the table in our small law library and talked "cases."

"How is your feed-lot case going?"

"I am moving for an injunction next week."

"But won't you have a problem with the Knowles case?"

"Well, I think I can get around it by arguing X."

"Yeah, but what if they come back with Y?"

"Then I'll argue Z."

"I dunno. Do that and they'll come back with W."

These were intellectually exciting times, hard-headed legal analysis on the run. Lay folks may not, however, recognize our elegance. A reporter, who once sat in, summed up our fine legal discourse:

"Oh, no! They've overrun the Nitpicks! Retreat to the Quibbles!"

Many students find formal study groups productive. Working with others is a tricky business. Some may dominate; others seek free rides. Study groups will require you to negotiate, often implicitly, the critical dynamics of working with others, including, perhaps, some explicit breaks:

> *"Let's stop for a few moments. This group doesn't seem to be working out. We never get as far as we plan. There are too many distractions. What can we do to improve this?"*

Or, more to the point:

> "Lee, shut up!"

A few tips:

1. Everyone should feel comfortable enough to ask "dumb questions" and to admit confusion. Learn, don't maintain image.

2. Structure the sessions. Will you go over more than one subject? Will you review by discussing the cases or by working on problems, possibly old exam questions? How much time will be spent?

3. Consider having discussion leaders. Rotate them. "Next week, you do Property, I'll do Contracts." One effective way to learn is to teach: planning and conducting a review session can be quite educational.

4. It is *not* a good idea to divide the first-year curriculum among the group to prepare outlines. "Kingsfield, you take Contracts." The true value of outlines comes in putting them

together. Each person should outline each course.

Don't feel bad if you're not in a study group. You can do brilliantly without one, and they are not for everyone. Some people work better alone. So be it! But, outside the formal structure of study groups, be sure to "talk law" with other students every chance you get.

How Much Time?

About half way through the first semester one of my students came to me.

"I'm doing all the reading and briefing and have even started on my outlines. But I still have time for my family and going to an occasional movie. What am I doing wrong?"

Don't get all caught up in the law school hype. Sure, it is demanding, and, sure, it will probably take more time and intense preparation than you are used to. But you don't have to become a mole. Several years ago there was a national study that indicated that law students average about 2½ hours of study for each hour in class. Assuming you are carrying 15 units, this works out to about 53 hours per week. This is surely a full-time load, but don't think that all your classmates are studying all the time and that you must do so to keep up.

You may be setting a pattern that you will follow your entire career. If you put your studies before your family or health now, it is likely your job will come first when you graduate. Actually, this might not be such a bad thing: some of the happiest people I know are "workaholics." It is, however, lousy for your family. No one ever dies thinking, "I should have spent more time at the office."

If you, like me, planned your entire undergraduate life around a single guiding principle, "No classes before 11," you will be shocked to learn that studying in the early morning hours is the most productive. After you wake up, you are as alert as you will be; thereafter, it is all downhill. I find that if I start working around 6 a.m., I can get as much done in one hour as I can in two or three in the late afternoon or evening.

The Forest/Tree Problem

You'll face a real forest/tree problem. Usually your focus will be quite narrow, on a particular case or, indeed, a particular paragraph. Every now and then, step back and try to get an orientation as to where you are and how a particular case fits with the others you have read.

A good table of contents helps. Assume that you're using Dobbs, *Torts and Compensation*, and have just read a case by the name of *Cullison v. Medley*. Where it fits in the big picture? Turn to the table of contents and see where the case is.

Chapter 2: Establishing a Claim of Intentional Tort to Person or Property

Section 1: Battery

. . . .

Section 2: Assault

  McCraney v. Flanagan

  Dickens v. Puryear

  Holcombe v. Whitaker

  Cullison v. Medley

Section 3: False Imprisonment

To put a case in context, begin with it and expand outward along the book's outline.

a. What does *Cullison v. Medley* add to your understanding of "Assault" that the other cases did not? Was it added to the casebook to show the same rule of law in a different factual context? To show a variation on the rule of law?

b. How does the subsection "Assault" relate to the one of equal rank: "Battery"? How are the cases in those two sections the same? How are they different?

You can use this technique to go where no one has gone before: the future.

"Wow, look here. Next we'll read about 'False Imprisonment.' I wonder what that is. How might it be different from the assault cases? How might it be the same? How will it fit into the general topic of Chapter 2?"

The periodic journeys into the vast unknown shouldn't take very long, only a few minutes. I don't even suggest you write anything: just sit, look at the table of contents, and ask yourself questions.

At first it will be difficult even to begin to answer the questions I have suggested, and indeed, some may be without rational answer. (Some cases seem to be in casebooks simply "Because they're there.") Still, the questions take you beyond the narrow focus of the particular case and, ever so slowly, the overall picture clears. The trick is knowing both the particular and the general, in seeing both the tree and the forest.

Treatises, hornbooks, nutshells and law review articles can also help put the tree into the forest.

As you wander the halls of your first year, you are something of a tree yourself. How can you keep your orientation?

Keep a Journal

Law study is turbulent and overwhelming. Expect moments of exhilaration and expect moments of deep self-doubt. Every now and then, quit the hurly-burly and step back to reflect on what is happening to you.

Consider keeping a journal. Take 20 to 30 minutes a few times a week to be with yourself and your thoughts.

When I require my students to do this, afterwards many tell me they got a great deal out of it. Graduates tell me that they reread what they had to say as first-year students and rejoice.

Write your thoughts, because, until you write them, you really don't know what they are. In your head they are just vague impressions and fragments of ideas; on paper they take shape and content. Write *now* while you are experiencing what will be an intense and highly significant period in your life. Next year it will be too late:

"First year? I liked it, at least some of it, I think."

Many journal entries will be first year gossip. But occasionally force yourself to attempt something in the nature of an essay.

- *Reflections on a particular case or legal doctrine.* Did you find it just? Were there certain aspects of the case that you found of special interest that your classmates and professor did not?

  Once an anthropology graduate student was sitting in a Torts class. It was a 1935 case. The plaintiff went to the circus in Ames, Iowa, and, as fate would have it, an elephant backed up and, there is no nice way of saying this, defecated on him.

  "I wasn't interested in assumption of risk," the student told me. "But why would someone in a rural state be so upset to sue?"

- *Reflections on law school.* How is it affecting you? Is it what you thought it would be? How does law school compare with undergraduate education? What about competition? What of male/female reactions in the classroom? Do you participate in class? Why or why not?

- *Reflections on lawyering.* Based on what you see, do you think you will like being a lawyer?

What do you think the lawyers who handled a particular case were feeling? Were thinking? Could they have done something to avoid litigation?

Consider writing yourself a letter. Address it to yourself as a third year student. What will you want to tell that person about you? "Why I came to law school" might be a good topic. In the years to come, maybe even next year, when you are considering what kind of job to take, it will be good to recall why you came to law school.

Finally, what if you think keeping a journal is a waste of time? Write an essay: "Why keeping a journal is a waste of time."

You can't win. It's my book.

CHAPTER 11

WRITING LAW SCHOOL EXAMS: THE ONLY SKILL WORTH HAVING!

The first thing you'll notice is that law school exams are written in Greek. You will confront an indistinguishable mass of words, all blurred, all running together. Let me give you an example from an exam I gave last year.

Question 1

Acme Construction Inc. *allkdfj pqwiur nbvmznx kdk ieur pire jdjo ghjhgfiyr oiyu re otjhg lkpqyr pqlxh plvhgfd qwert yuiop asdf fgh zxcvb mjuik opk kiuy juyhgr dqwsxcgy plmbht fdghj qmpzwno hyde nhyu cdew mkoiy asdfqwer.* Discuss. Be concise but don't overlook anything. Pay particular attention to *kuzt op mdzopor yuiopt.*

You look around the room. Everyone else has already started writing. Sweat runs into your eyes and drops onto the page, smudging the only words you understood.

Take a deep breath. Remember this: All law school exam questions relate to the material you covered in the course. Eventually you will be able to understand the question, and you will be able to

141

answer it. The folks who have started writing are writing home.

Don't worry that you didn't get "enough" sleep the night before. While advisable, sometimes sleep just doesn't come. No one has ever, not ever, gone to sleep during a law school exam.

What should be your *goal*? It is not to fill up a lot of space, nor is it to use a lot of legal terms. More surprisingly, it is *not* to show how much law you learned during the semester, nor is it even to appear brilliant.

All good legal writing is alike. Your goal is always to help the reader (here, the professor) understand how the law would impact a specific factual situation. Law school exams generally give you a fact pattern which ends with folks being disappointed, mad or injured. (There are no happy endings.) How can you help the reader understand how the law would resolve the conflict?

First, you must identify the *legal issues* buried in the problem. Most law exams have several issues. You must discuss each *separately*. To convey this information to the reader, you might begin:

> *"The first issue is ...."* or
>
> *"The plaintiff's first theory of recovery will be...."* or
>
> *"The defendant will argue that...."*

There are no magic formulations; what you must do is flag the legal issue you are about to discuss.

Second, you have to tell what *legal rule* or *legal doctrine* a court would look to in order to resolve the issue presented. There is no need to have memorized the exact wording of the legal rule you are to apply; it is enough to give the reader a fairly accurate statement of it. As to form, again there are no magic words:

"The law is that . . . ." or

"The courts have held that . . . ." or

"The U.C.C. requires that . . . ."

Third, you must give the reader your best thinking as to the factors the court would consider in applying the legal rule to the case before it. You must consider *both sides*. An error many first year students make is *taking sides*. They conclude that the plaintiff or defendant should win and then go about writing their exam. Naturally, as partisans, they now overlook all of the good arguments the other side might have. *To help the reader understand how the law might resolve the issue,* both sides must be presented with equal vigor. As I indicated in earlier chapters, you must adopt *"yes . . .but"* reasoning: *"Yes,* the plaintiff has this good point, *but* the defendant can answer it with . . . . "

Another typical error occurs when the student states the legal rule and then discusses the facts of the case without showing how those facts relate to the legal rule. You must be *explicit* as to the relationship between the facts you discuss and the law you have stated. As I indicated in earlier chapters, in order to assure explicitness when you are discussing a fact, always ask, *"So what?"*

Thus far I have given you the famous *IRAC* approach to exam-taking, without the *C*.

*I*ssue

*R*ule

*A*nalysis

*C*onclusion

The reason I leave off the "C" is that it tends to suggest that you must resolve the case—*"Plaintiff will win."* Such conclusions generally don't help the reader understand how a court might resolve the conflict. Write as if the reader is the decision-maker. That reader wants your best thinking on the issues presented and is not particularly interested in your conclusions unless they further your analysis: *"Having looked at the plaintiff's and defendant's arguments as to this point, it strikes me that the plaintiff has the better arguments in that...."*

That said, *IRAC* works well as an approach to individual issues. However, it totally fails to draw your attention to the critical need to account for the relationship *between* the various issues. Let's say there are three issues, A, B, and C. To prevail, must the plaintiff win on all three issues (A *and* B *and* C) or is it enough if the plaintiff prevails on only one (A *or* B *or* C)? Or are we dealing with some form of new math: ([A *or* B] *and* C)?

After you have identified the issues a problem presents, be clear on the relationship between them before you start to write. Then, when you move from one issue to the next, tell the reader the relationship between the issue you just discussed and the one you are about to discuss. I'll show you a neat way of doing this later in the chapter.

Practice Test

What follows is a typical (at least for me) law school exam question. I follow it with two possible answers which I then analyze. If you wish, you can try your hand at writing an answer before you see my answers, or you might wish to wait until after you read them.

Isn't the latter cheating? No. It is one thing to read something and say, "That's good." It is something more to articulate why it is good. However, you must learn not only to recognize good writing and how to describe what constitutes it. You must *write* it.

In art museums, you will see aspiring artists copying the pictures of the masters; aspiring poets copy the work of masters as well, calling this "playing the sedulous ape." Play the ape: find a good piece of legal prose and *copy it* just to get a hands-on sense of how it is put together.

Rules of Law to Apply

These legal rules will come into play in answering the practice test. Reread them a couple of times before you begin writing your answer, and it is OK to refer back to them while you are writing.

1. If one is sued for breach of contract, it is a good defense to say, "I wasn't making a serious offer, and the person who is now suing me should have known it!" The law is that, after looking at the surrounding circumstances, if a reasonable third party would conclude that the person making the promise was not serious, then that promise is not enforceable.

2. The Statute of Frauds requires that some, not all, agreements be in writing. It generally goes something like this:

   The following contracts are invalid, unless the same, or note or memorandum thereof, is in writing and signed by the party to be charged:

   1. An agreement for the sale of real property.

   2.   * * *

   Cases interpreting the Statute of Frauds have indicated that it fulfills two purposes. The first purpose is to protect against false claims. A writing is good evidence that the parties actually agreed and that no one is making things up. The second purpose of the Statute is cautionary. People shouldn't enter into important legal transactions, such as the sale of realty, orally. Written contracts ensure greater reflection on the part of the contracting parties.

3. Contracts for an illegal purpose are void and unenforceable. For example, a "contract," as in "there is a contract out on the Godfather,"

is unenforceable. Even if the assassin does his part, he can't sue to recover his promised fee. Such contracts are illegal on their "face" in that the illegality appears in the agreement itself: "I'll shoot Jones for $5,000."

The Question

Sleazy Sam and Billy Bigmouth ran into each other at the Lazy J Bar. After several drinks, Billy said, "You know, I think I'll blow this town and get into pictures."

"Oh yeah? How are you going to support yourself in Hollywood until they discover your major talent?" asked Sam.

"Why, I'll sell my house. You can have it for $60,000. Last week it was appraised at $120,000."

"You must be joking; that deal is too good to be true," replied Sam, having another drink.

"Man, it's just that you don't have the money."

"Look, I can have $60,000 cash at the end of the week."

"Bring it by."

"Are you serious?"

"Sure," laughed Bigmouth.

"Well, I need a new place for my bookmaking activities."

"That's illegal, but what you do with the place is your business," said Bigmouth. "Let's shake." The men shook and left the bar.

Three days later Sam received the following letter from Bigmouth:

> *Dear Sam,*
>
> *Of course I was joking when I promised to sell you my house for $60,000 cash at the end of the week. In any event I don't want to do it. So there.*
>
> > *Yours truly,*
> > Billy Bigmouth

Discuss.

To help you think through the problem, fill in the following blanks.

Issue One:

Controlling law:

What P will argue:

What D will argue:

Issue Two and its relationship to Issue One:

Statement of issue and its relationship to first issue:

Controlling law:

What P will argue:

What D will argue:

Issue Three and its relationship to Issue Two:
  Statement of issue and its relationship to second issue:

  Controlling law:

  What P will argue:

  What D will argue:

If you wish, you can write an answer now or wait until after my discussion of the model answers.

Model Answers

As you work your way through these two examples, jot down what you like and don't like about them.

Answer Number One

This case is about Sam and Bill, who met in a bar and began to talk about the selling of Bill's house to

Sam for $60,000. The issue is whether the alleged contract is enforceable or not.

First, Bill was clearly drunk.

Second, Bill was joking. He said as much in his letter to Sam. Who on earth would sell a $120,000 house for $60,000 in order to get into pictures? Sam was going to use the house for bookmaking activities, and that's illegal. And remember that Sam didn't think Bill was serious because he asked him "Are you serious?" Sam knew Bill was joking.

Because this deals with the sale of real property, the Statute of Frauds applies. The first English Statute of Frauds was enacted nearly 300 years ago to prevent fraud. In California the Statute is Civil Code § 1624. Many commentators in law reviews have argued that the statute, which has been adopted with modifications in many states, causes more fraud than it prevents. That is, it allows people who have made promises to get out of them simply because they are not in writing. Courts often try to get around the Statute of Frauds.

Bill will clearly win.

Answer Number Two

[Ed. Note: I put words of contrast in bold
to illustrate their importance.]

There are several issues to be considered in this question:

1. *Did Bill make a serious offer to sell his house to Sam?*

2. Assuming that the Statute of Frauds applies, does the letter from Bill to Sam satisfy it?

3. Is the contract void because Sam intended to use the house for an illegal activity?

The first issue is whether Bill was making a serious offer to sell his house. If he wasn't, then he has a good defense to any suit Sam files. The test will be, considering all of the circumstances, would a reasonable person conclude Bill was making a serious offer? Bill will claim he was joking and that Sam should have known it. He will point out that both men accidentally met in a bar. There is no indication that they met to discuss the sale of the house. He will also point out that both men were drinking. (If Bill had been drunk, that would be another defense.) He will argue that no reasonable person would believe he wanted to sell a $120,000 house for $60,000 in order to go into pictures. Note that there was nothing put in writing—it is reasonable to assume that if Bill were seriously thinking about selling a house, it would be in writing.

On the other hand, Sam will argue that Bill appeared seriously to want to sell his home. First, Bill initiated the discussion. Second, he mentioned that the house had been recently appraised—one does that when one is planning to sell. Third, Bill told Sam he was serious, and both men shook hands, a traditional way to conclude a deal. If Bill had been joking, he would have told Sam just that rather than shake hands. Finally, Bill himself thought the deal serious because he wrote the letter to Sam—had the joke been clear, he wouldn't have thought to write claiming it was a joke.

Even if it is found that Bill was making a serious offer, the agreement might still be unenforceable under the Statute of Frauds. The Statute applies because the deal concerns the sale of real property. It requires that some writing be signed by the party to be charged (here Bill). The original agreement was oral. However, Bill wrote Sam saying he wanted out of the deal. He signed that letter. **The question becomes**, then, can a letter denying the seriousness of a prior oral promise be used to satisfy the Statute of Frauds? **On the one hand**, it appears as though it might. One of the purposes of the Statute is to prevent fraud—by signing the letter, Bill admits he made the promise to sell the house. Sam didn't make up the agreement. **On the other hand**, another purpose of the Statute is cautionary—to ensure that people reflect before committing themselves to important deals. Obviously a letter trying to get out of a deal cannot be said to fulfill any cautionary function: it comes too late.

Assuming Bill was serious in making the offer and **even if** his letter satisfies the Statute of Frauds, there **is another** possible defense, that of illegality. The law states that contracts illegal on their face are unenforceable. **However**, this contract isn't illegal on its face—it is not for bookmaking, it is for the sale of a house. Assuming a seller knows that the buyer is to use what is purchased for an illegal activity, can he, must he, refuse to go ahead with the deal? I assume that contracts for illegal acts are not *enforced in order to deter illegal activity. That policy would apply here and make the contract unenforceable.*

———

Before continuing, I would advise you to go back and reread both answers, noting in the margins what you liked and disliked about each. The more you put into this exercise, the more you will get out of it. Again I hope you will take the opportunity to write an answer yourself.

Given the length of this chapter, and your growing weariness, I'm going to stop right here and pick up my analysis of the two answers in the next chapter. Get some rest.

CHAPTER 12

THE TALE OF TWO ANSWERS

A cartoon shows Dickens in the office of a New York literary agent. The agent is looking up from a manuscript and is clearly irritated, "Come on Charles, which was it? Was it the best of times or the worst of times?"

In this chapter, we'll look closely at the two answers given to the practice exam in the last chapter. Most would agree that Answer Two is far better. I wrote both answers. The first illustrates common first-year errors:

1. Taking sides,

2. Failing to state the controlling law and making implicit statements,

3. Failing to note the relationship between issues,

4. Mixing legal categories, and

5. Discussing law "because it's there."

The second answer I wrote to give you a feel for a really good answer. Don't be depressed by it; it took me a long time to write it, and I *wrote* the question.

Reading and analyzing it will, however, give you a feel for good legal writing.

Before you look at my analysis of the answers, I think you will find it helpful if you reread Answer One, looking for the common errors I just mentioned. Then reread Answer Two to see how it avoided those errors. If you do this, you will get more from the analysis that follows.

Answer One

Answer One begins:

This case is about Sam and Bill, who met in a bar and began to talk about the selling of Bill's house to Sam for $60,000. The issue is whether the alleged contract is enforceable or not.

This is a rather weak opening. It tells the reader nothing that is not already known and does not focus the issues at all. The issue "is the contract enforceable" is so broad as to be meaningless.

The major fault, however, is that one senses that the student just started writing without first *analyzing* the problem. While student approaches vary, you must spend some portion of your allotted time thinking about and organizing your answer.

Look at the opening paragraph in the second answer:

There are several issues to be considered in this question:

1. Did Bill make a serious offer to sell his house to Sam?

2. *Assuming that the Statute of Frauds applies, does the letter from Bill to Sam satisfy it?*

3. *Is the contract void because Sam intended to use the house for an illegal activity?*

Why is this such an improvement?

Here the student *planned* before writing. The student has a good sense of the issues to be discussed and probably a sense of how they all fit together.

In terms of exam style, it is *not* necessary to list all of the issues you are to discuss up front. You can start:

The first issue is whether Bill made a serious offer.

However, even if you don't list all the issues you are going to discuss, be sure you have a fairly good idea of them before you start writing. It is a mistake to suddenly take off on the first issue you see.

Stating all of the issues up front does have some advantages. It forces you to organize your thoughts and gives you instant credibility (as long as you have listed most of the issues the prof is looking for).

Answer One continues:

First, Bill was clearly drunk.

There are two problems with this. First the student has *manufactured* facts—the question did not say Bill was drunk, simply that he was drinking. Be *very* careful to get the facts straight. Two important lawyer skills are careful reading and an acute awareness of the critical distinction between *observed data* and *inference*. Exams often test for this awareness. Don't jump to conclusions.

The second problem is that the statement is *implicit*: *So what* if Bill was drunk? If Bill was drunk, it would make a legal *difference*—but it is the student's job to tell us what that difference would be.

Observe how the second answer avoids both of these problems:

"If Bill had been drunk, that would be another defense." This doesn't assume Bill was drunk and tells us the legal significance of being drunk.

The first answer continues:

Second, Bill was joking. He said as much in his letter to Sam. Who would sell a $120,000 house for $60,000 in order to get into pictures? Sam was going to use the house for bookmaking activities, and that's illegal. And remember that Sam didn't think Bill was serious because he asked him "Are you serious?" Sam knew Bill was joking.

There are multiple problems here.

First, there is no attempt to state the controlling law. Without some knowledge of the legal principles to be applied, the reader will not be able to understand how they would apply in the specific case. Compare Answer Two:

The first issue is whether Bill was making a serious offer to sell his house. If he wasn't, then he has a good defense to any suit Sam files. The test will be, considering all of the circumstances, would a reasonable person conclude Bill was making a serious offer?

In stating the controlling law, you *don't* have to cite case names, Restatements, or statutes. All you have to do is alert the reader to the governing law. And note that you can use your own words in describing it.

Second, our first writer is *taking sides*, looking only at Bill's position. Had the student asked the right question—"What would the other side say when Bill's lawyer argued Bill was joking?"—all the counter facts would have jumped out. The problem with "taking sides" is that you fail to see the other side's point of view: without rubbing contention against counter-contention, your analysis is doomed to remain superficial.

Always ask, "How will the other side respond?" Or, more simply, keep in mind, *"Yes, that's true, but...."*

Third, our first writer is making an *implicit* argument. *So what* if Bill were joking? The *so what* of it is, the *explicitness* of it is, if a reasonable person would have known Bill was joking, then Bill has a defense to Sam's suit.

Fourth, the writer mixes legal categories—the business of illegality is thrown into a discussion of seriousness. Not good.

Legal analysis is *analysis by category*. "Illegality" and "seriousness" are *separate* legal categories; each, on their own, could make the contract unenforceable. Always keep categories separate. (We will see, however, that the same fact can be used in more than one category, *viz*, the lack of writing going to the seriousness issue and triggering the Statute of Frauds issue.)

Finally, there is no basis in the facts recounted to conclude, "Sam knew Bill was joking." When one takes sides, when one becomes contentious, one is more likely to manufacture facts.

Because this deals with the sale of real property, the Statute of Frauds applies. The first English Statute of Frauds was enacted nearly 300 years ago to prevent fraud. In California the Statute is Civil Code § 1624. Many commentators in law reviews have argued that the statute, which has been adopted with modifications in many states, causes more fraud than it prevents. That is, it allows people who have made promises to get out of them simply because they are not in writing. Courts often try to get around the Statute of Frauds.

This paragraph reads like a good undergraduate essay, and that's its fatal flaw.

Why is writing like an undergraduate a flaw? Writing law always *involves the interplay of law and fact*. Recounting the history of the Statute of Frauds does not help the reader understand how the law would impact the controversy between Bill and Sam. Note that *"So what?"* applies to long discussions of law as well as long discussions of fact. You must explicitly tie the law you are discussing to the facts of the case, and you must explicitly tie the facts you are discussing to the law.

Fortunately, there is usually little need, in law exams, to cite specific code sections ("Civil Code § 1624") or, for that matter, specific case names. Case names may be important in some courses, such as Constitutional Law. In most first year courses, however, case names are not significant. Ask your professor.

Finally:

Bill will clearly win.

If it were that clear, the question would not have been asked.

On the Need to Show the Relationship Between Issues and Their Legal Significance

A final criticism of Answer One is that it fails to show the relationship between the issues and, when it introduces a new issue, fails to indicate its legal significance. Consider the first sentences of the first two paragraphs.

First, Bill was clearly drunk.

Second, Bill was joking.

What is the legal significance of Bill being drunk? He would have a defense to the contract action, and it would be helpful to the reader to know this. Let's rewrite:

First, Bill was clearly drunk, and this would constitute a defense to any suit filed by Sam.

We should rewrite the second topic sentence as well:

Second, Bill was joking, and the law says that individuals are not to be held to their jokes.

But what is the relationship *between* the *intoxication* issue and the *prankster* issue? It could be either an *and* relation or an *or* relation. To successfully defend the action, must Bill show both that he was drunk *and* that he was joking, or is it enough if he shows one or the other?

To show an *or* relationship:

Second, assuming Bill could not show he was drunk, if he could show he was joking this would constitute a defense.

To show an *and* relationship:

Not only must Bill show he was drunk, in addition he must show he was joking.

Compare the two major transitions in Answer Two:

1. *Even if* it is found that Bill was making a serious offer, the agreement might still be unenforceable under the Statute of Frauds.

2. *Assuming* Bill was serious in making the offer and *even if* his letter satisfies the Statute of

Frauds, *there is another* possible defense, that of illegality.

I call these *RILS* transitions. Not only do they introduce the next topic, but also relate it to the last topic or topics discussed *and* tell the reader the legal significance of the topic.

*R*elate

*I*ntroduce

*L*egal *S*ignificance

Forcing yourself to think and write in terms of RILS transitions not only will help the reader understand your writing, but also will help you to think through the relationships. I return to this topic in my chapter on legal writing.

Now let's turn to the good cop, Answer Two.

Answer Two

There are several issues to be considered in this question:

1. *Did Bill make a serious offer to sell his house to Sam?*

2. *Assuming that the Statute of Frauds applies, does the letter from Bill to Sam satisfy it?*

3. *Is the contract void because Sam intended to use the house for an illegal activity?*

The first issue is whether Bill was making a serious offer to sell his house. If he wasn't, then he has a good defense to any suit Sam files. The test will be, considering all of the circumstances, would *a reasonable person conclude Bill was making a serious offer? Bill will claim he was joking and that Sam should have known it. He will point out that both men accidentally met in a bar. There is no indication that they met to discuss the sale of the house. He will also point out that both men were drinking. (If Bill had been drunk, that would be another defense.) He will argue that no reasonable person would believe he wanted to sell a $120,000 house for $60,000 in order to go into pictures. Note that there was nothing put in writing—it is reasonable to assume that if Bill were seriously thinking about selling a house, it would be in writing.*

This is really good. It starts off discussing the law. Again *precise statements of law* are not required, nor need you memorize the language of statutes or Restatements or the key language from opinions.

The seriousness issue requires the student to apply a relatively clear legal standard to an ambiguous fact pattern. The paragraph shows good factual analysis. For example, note the use of the fact that the deal was not in writing. There is a *separate* issue concerning the Statute of Frauds, but here the fact of no writing is skillfully used as evidence of lack of serious intent. Well done!

On the other hand, Sam will argue that Bill appeared seriously to want to sell his home. First, Bill initiated the discussion. Second, he mentioned that the house had been recently appraised—one does that when one is planning to sell. Third, Bill told Sam he was serious and both men shook hands, a traditional way to conclude a deal. If Bill had been joking, he would have told Sam just that, rather than shake hands. Finally, Bill himself thought the deal serious because he wrote the letter to Sam—had the joke been clear, he wouldn't have thought to write claiming it was a joke.

This paragraph answers the essential question, "What will the other side say?" (or, to state the matter differently, employs *"Yes, but"* analysis). Is it necessary to reach a conclusion as to which side has the better arguments? Not necessarily.

This is a tricky point. Physicians often don't make good law students as they have been trained in a system where coming to the right answer is crucial: "Does the patient have TB?" In law, it is our analyses, not our conclusions, that matter. Take the issue of whether Bill's letter satisfies the Statute of Frauds. The competing contentions would be:

> *Bill: My letter could not satisfy the Statute of Frauds because the goal of the Statute is to force people to reflect before they enter into important deals. My letter was written after I made my hasty promise. To allow it to satisfy the Statute would defeat its purpose.*

> *Sam: Not so. The main purpose of the Statute of Frauds is to prevent false claims from being made. It requires that before one person can sue another for the breach of certain kinds of promises, that person must produce writ-*

> *ten evidence that the promise was made.*
> *And there is that evidence, Bill's letter.*

Developing the competing contentions is your main work. It helps the reader see how a court would approach the issue, and it shows that you know how to analyze problems as a lawyer would. To further that analysis, it may be proper to reach a conclusion—not because it is necessary to reach the "right" conclusion, but rather to round off the analysis, to show the reader that you have a legal sense that some arguments are better than others. Two important lessons come from this discussion:

1. *Don't freeze up in fear that you won't reach the proper conclusion.*

2. *Don't simply assert your conclusion; always justify it.*

Take the following conclusion:

> *I think that Sam will win the Statute of Frauds issue.*

Well and good. Perhaps, in a real court, he would. Yet, as written, the conclusion tells us nothing about the only thing we are really interested in: the student's ability to analyze problems. Perhaps the student simply made a lucky guess—after all, the odds aren't all that bad. Compare:

> *I think Sam will win the Statute of Frauds issue. Although Bill's letter was written after the promise, and hence could not fulfill any cautionary function, it seems that the main thrust of the Statute is to prevent false claims. Here we know*

Bill made the promise because we have his signed letter to prove it.

In sum, while analysis may stand without conclusion, conclusion can seldom stand without analysis.

Continuing with Answer Two:

Even if *it is found that Bill was making a serious offer, the agreement might still be unenforceable under the Statute of Frauds. The Statute applies because the deal concerns the sale of real property. It requires that some writing be signed by the party to be charged (here Bill). The original agreement was oral.* ***However****, Bill wrote Sam saying he wanted out of the deal. He signed that letter.* ***The question becomes****, then, can a letter denying the seriousness of a prior oral promise be used to satisfy the Statute of Frauds?* ***On the one hand****, it appears as though it might. One of the purposes of the Statute is to prevent fraud—by signing the letter, Bill admits he made the promise to sell the house. Sam didn't make up the agreement.* ***On the other hand****, another purpose of the Statute is cautionary—to ensure that people reflect before committing themselves to important deals. Obviously a letter trying to get out of a deal cannot be said to fulfill any cautionary function: it comes too late.*

Another job well done. Nice transition. It shows we are dealing with an **"or"** relationship between seriousness and the Statute. Good statement of the law and of the issue.

Note that this analysis is essentially different from the "seriousness" analysis. There we had a clear legal standard and had to apply it to an ambiguous fact pattern. Here the facts are clear and the law is ambiguous: Should the letter satisfy the Statute? The model answer uses the proper mode of analysis. Because the Statute does not tell us what it means by "note" or "memorandum," we must define those terms in light of the **purposes and goals** of the Statute. Would they be furthered or defeated by allowing the letter to count? This is something a court would have to decide.

Continuing with Answer Two

Even if *Bill were serious in making the offer and* ***even if*** *his letter satisfies the Statute of Frauds,* ***there is another*** *possible defense, that of illegality. The law is that contracts illegal on their face are unenforceable.* ***However****, this contract isn't illegal on its face—it is not for bookmaking, it is for the sale of a house. Assuming a seller knows that the buyer is to use what is purchased for an illegal activity, can he, must he, refuse to go ahead with the deal? I assume that contracts for illegal acts are not enforced in order to deter illegal activity. That policy would apply here and make the contract unenforceable.*

This starts well. There is a good transition. We know that even if Sam wins on the serious issue and on the Statute of Frauds point, he still may be a loser if he blows the illegality point. The discussion of illegality would be much improved had the student asked, "What will the other side argue?" There are powerful arguments against Bill's position here, so powerful, in fact, that courts will likely reject the defense—although that is an issue I will leave to your Contracts course.

Finally, one last point. You are to discuss *all* issues that are *fairly raised* in the problem *even though* you may think one would be determinative. For example, even if you were convinced Bill would win his case on the Statute of Frauds point, you must still discuss seriousness and illegality because they are fairly raised in the problem.

Assignment

23 minutes

I cannot overemphasize the importance of transitions that not only introduce a new topic but also show its legal significance and how it relates to prior topics. I call these RILS transitions. They will prove invaluable in helping you and your reader sort through difficult material. I want you to practice writing them.

1. Reread pages 161 to 162.

2. Even though you understand the concept perfectly, do me a favor. Write out the following:

* *Even if* it is found that Bill was making a serious offer, the agreement might still be unenforceable under the Statute of Frauds.

* *Assuming* Bill was serious in making the offer and *even if* his letter satisfies the Statute of

Frauds, *there is another* possible defense, that of illegality.

3.   By copying, you have a sense of how these are constructed. Now write five or six RILS transitions of your own. Vary the words of contrast you use, not always "even if" but perhaps:

Despite the fact that Bill may have made a serious offer, the agreement. . . .

One defense to the contract would be lack of seriousness; *another would be.* . . .

Play around with these constructions until you are comfortable with them. Introduce the seriousness issue assuming that your prior discussion concerned the Statute of Frauds. Introduce illegality issue after a discussion of seriousness. Be sure to tell the reader the legal significance of the topic: what turns on resolution of the issue?

Okay. *27 minutes.*

CHAPTER 13

EXAM TIPS

In the last chapter, I walked you through how to write law exams. In this, I will suggest some things that might help you spot the issues, organize your answers and deepen your analysis. There may be some repetition. While repetition on an *exam* is a vice, generally, repetition is a virtue. This stuff is difficult; hearing it more than once, described differently, helps.

The basic points I'll cover are:

-Your goal

-Not letting extraneous matters come between you and the exam

-Spotting issues (the law exam as art)

-Outlining your answers (briefly)

-Asking "So what?" and "Yes ... but ..."

-And writing down the middle.

Your Goal

Your goal in writing an exam is *not* to discuss as much law as you can, it is *not* to use as much legal jargon as you can, and it is *not* to resolve the question in this sense: "The plaintiff will win this one." The goal of all legal writing is the same. It is to *help* the reader understand how the law will apply to a specific factual situation. This is true whether your reader is a law professor, a senior partner, a judge, or, indeed, a client.

Write as if the reader *is* the decision-maker; he or she wants your best thinking on the factors that should be considered in making the decision. Faced with a tough decision, the reader is not helped by long discussions of the law, nor by being bamboozled with a lot of legal jargon, or even by being told what to decide. What this person *needs* is your help in sorting out the problem.

What do you know about your reader? If the reader is a lawyer, he or she has a background knowledge of the law *but* is *not* 100% on top of the specific law that applies to the case at hand. I stress this because often students fail to mention the controlling legal rule or standard on their exams.

"I didn't bother telling the law, I mean, like, you know, you're the professor."

This is error; you must always state the controlling law. First, you must show you know it. Second, once you have stated it, it will structure your analysis.

What does this reader need to know?

1. What legal issues the problem presents;

2. What legal rules will apply;

3. Your analysis of how these rules will apply to the given facts; and

4. The relationship between the issues you discuss.

This is basically the traditional exam writing format, IRAC (Issue, Rule, Analysis, Conclusion), without the C, but with an added emphasis on the relationship between issues. As I explained in the last chapter, conclusions which further analysis are fine but free-standing conclusions ("The plaintiff will win") are not needed and do nothing to help the reader figure out why the plaintiff should win. I stress the need to tell the reader the relationship between issues because it helps both the reader and *you* sort out the problem.

So, forget IRAC and embrace IRARI (Issue, Rule, Analysis, and Relationship between Issues).

The Dreaded Day

After all that study, after all that struggle, one morning you will enter the room, and it's just you and your bluebook. It all comes to this. You will be given a copy of the exam about the size of a telephone book. You sit, waiting further instructions. Sweat pours into your eyes. Then, a smiling face:

"You may begin." The smiling face, of course, gets to go get coffee.

Expect to be nervous and expect to have a hard time getting started. After the panic, however, likely you will *enjoy* the exam. It will be a fascinating intellectual puzzle. It will push you, confound you, and ultimately delight you.

Exams are not awful. The prospect of exams is awful. Grades may be awful. Exams themselves are adrenaline, discovery, and adventure. The hard part about exams is generally not having too little to say, but having too much to say.

If you bring too much baggage into the exam with you, you may interfere with this creative process. Here, a Zen-like insight:

Be with the exam. Ooommm. Thinking of things outside the exam while taking the exam, such as "Do's and Don't of Taking Exams," will deflect your concentration on the problem. Some students swear by "checklists" which reduce all the learning of a course into one mnemonic device, perhaps "Tippecanoe and Tyler too." Running through a checklist during the exam, however, gets in your way of focusing on the actual question. Often, while there may be a "Tippecanoe" on the exam, there won't be a "Tyler too." But, because you are looking for it, you may falsely see a "Tyler too." And there will be issues on the exam that you didn't put in your mnemonic, perhaps an "I like Ike." By focusing on the checklist, you may overlook them.

Advice of second year students gets in your way as well. "Professor Rehnquist is a liberal, so always take the bleeding-heart position," or "Professor Cro–Magnon isn't that sophisticated; you really have to draw pictures for him."

Second year students don't know what worked for them. Perhaps Rehnquist, deep down, loves hard-headed, heartless analysis, and the very thing that prevented the student from doing much better on the exam was his wishy-washy, bleeding-heart position.

And maybe Professor Cro–Magnon is just sick and tired of that bison.

Frankly, no one is smart enough to psych out the professor. Don't try a special writing or analytical style based on what you think the professor wants. You're going to be busy enough just sorting out the problem.

Of course, there are no controlled studies as to what is effective exam writing. However, some hunches are better than others. To reassure yourself as to this matter of "no controlled studies," look at the lower-right hand corner of the title page of this book: make sure it doesn't say, in teeny-tiny print.

Placebo Edition.

Learn from your experiences. After your first exam, before studying for the next, ask:

> *What did the exam teach me about the way I studied? Did I spend enough time analyzing the questions? Did I carefully consider the facts and address the important facts in the discussion? Did I develop both sides of the arguments? What did I do well? What should I do differently next Tuesday? Is it on Tuesday? Oh, no, it was yesterday!*

Spotting Issues

After your Torts exam, the person you had thought was your best friend will ask, "Did you see the assumption of risk issue?"

Don't discuss exams with others. Nothing will make you more miserable. But take heart. Few students, no students, get all of the issues. Usually in my classes the top exams have missed maybe two, three, or more of the key issues: they developed the others with such depth and flare that these omissions are overwhelmed.

It is, of course, better to spot as many issues as you can.

-Read the question a couple of times, underlining or making notes in the margins.

-Read *aggressively*. Assume that *every fact in the problem is there for a reason*. Why is it that the defendant kicked the plaintiff's *ugly* dog? "Why is that fact there? Why not a cute dog? Why not a rabid dog who always wanted to be a good dog?" Remember, there is very little filler in law school exams.

Once you have spotted several issues, discuss them *all*, even if you believe that one would resolve the case.

Although the defendant has a very good chance of winning on the Statute of Frauds issue, there are two other defenses that should be considered.

Don't put all your eggs in one basket.

Sometimes students make up false issues, either because they expected them to be on the exam (they were, after all, on the checklist) or because they want to show the professor they learned something during the semester.

> *Had the plaintiff assumed the risk, then that would be a defense. The doctrine was first developed in the case of Jones v. Smith, and today the elements of "assumption of risk" are blah, blah, blah. Of course, because the plaintiff was at home, in bed, asleep, when the defendant's car smashed through the wall, it doesn't seem he assumed the risk.*

Discuss only issues that were *fairly raised* by the problem. If you are not *sure* whether an issue was fairly raised, err on the side of inclusion but don't spend much time developing your answer. Recall how Answer 2 in the last chapter dealt with the possible issue of intoxication:

> *If Bill had been drunk, that would be another defense.*

This gives you some protection against overlooking an issue but doesn't get you sidetracked on to long discussions that may lead nowhere.

Capturing and Organizing Your Thoughts

Questions will trigger a tidal wave of ideas: a towering mixture of issues, good points, and counter-arguments that rushes towards you and threatens to overcome you. You can't run because the sand is too soft.

Make a rough outline. In the problem I discussed in the last chapter, there were three issues: Were the parties serious in making the contract? Did a letter withdrawing from an oral agreement satisfy the Statute of Frauds? Was the contract void for illegality? Your rough outline:

Serious?

Letter/Statute of Frauds

Illegal?

Then you will use the outline to jot down ideas that come to you, such as

Serious?

   met in bar

   discussed details

You will find, when you are writing on one issue, that thoughts jump into your mind concerning other issues. How can you remember them without breaking the flow of your answer? Jot a word or two on your outline:

Illegal

   not illegal on face

Once you have your rough outline, which issue should you discuss first? There is no set order. Probably it is best to start with the most difficult or challenging issues, as those will win the most points for good analysis. *Time is always a factor,* and you must keep track of it. If you run out, far better to miss the minor issues.

Don't spend time *not* making points. Long recitals of the facts and long conclusions where you essentially repeat what you have said just kill the clock. Introductions and conclusions are great in most legal writing, since previews and repetitions help recall. However, the prof will be focused and hence these devices are not needed.

Before you start writing, be sure you are clear on the relationship between the issues. For example, must the defendant win *both* the seriousness issue *and* that of the Statute of Frauds or is one enough (1 + 2 or 1 or 2)? As I discussed previously, RILS transitions show these relationships. They introduce the next issue, relate it to the prior issue, and indicate its legal significance.

Thinking in terms of RILS transition will help you think through the problem. If you do so, good transitions will come naturally. Although I do not grade on style, looking back at the best papers, it strikes me how well they read. *Style follows understanding*.

Analyzing the Issues

The two most common errors are the failure to be *explicit* and the failure to consider *both sides*.

By failure to be explicit, I mean the failure to show how the facts you are discussing relate to the legal standard you are discussing. For example, out of the blue, a student may write:

"The two men met in a bar."

Without more, the reader is forced to ask, "What should I make of this interesting tidbit?" I like to think of these free-floating tidbits as *"free radicals."* Their cure: ask yourself, as you merrily go along, *"So what?"*

"The two guys met at a bar."

So what?

"Well, that might mean that they weren't serious in their negotiations."

So what?

"If they weren't serious, that means, under a doctrine of contract law, that the contract is not enforceable."

Long discussions of law, not grounded in the specific facts of the case, are also *free radicals*.

In addition to the failure to be explicit, the other common failure is to consider both sides of the issue. Sometimes this is because the student has *taken sides* by concluding, early on, that the plaintiff or defendant should win. Being an advocate is not conducive to seeing both sides.

While there may not be two sides to every issue, unless there are, the issue isn't worth discussing. Here the mantra is, *"Yes ... but ..."* For every point, there is generally an answer.

Some students, while considering both sides, make a bad error by first considering all of the points for one side and then all of the points for the other side.

   Plaintiff will argue:

   As to the seriousness issue, blah, blah, blah.

   As to the Statute of Frauds issue, blah, blah, blah.

   As to the illegality issue, blah, blah, blah.

Defendant will argue:

As to the seriousness issue, blah, blah, blah.

As to the Statute of Frauds, blah.

The format is confusing and wordy. More significantly, it doesn't produce sparks. The proper format is:

As to the seriousness issue, Plaintiff will argue . . . and defendant will respond.

Only by running contention against contention will your analysis deepen.

However, when it comes to writing your answer, consider dropping the "sing-song" of "plaintiff argues, defendant responds." You can do this by *writing down the middle.*

Instead of:

As to the seriousness issue, Plaintiff will argue . . . and defendant will respond.

Try:

As to the seriousness issue, on the one hand. . . . on the other hand . . . . .

Or:

As to the seriousness issue, even though. . . . it is true that. . . .

Finally, to sharpen your analysis, do a pre-exam warm-up. Opera singers bellow a few notes before going out; ball players practice their mean stares (for opponents) and their innocent "What, me?" expressions (for refs). During your warm-up, repeat, and repeat, "So what?" and "Yes. . . . but. . . ."

CHAPTER 14

FEAR AND LOATHING IN THE FIRST YEAR

Visualize yourself, once again, a cute, lovable baby. You are lying in your crib, playing with a teddy. Next to you is another crib, with another baby. You look over and life's first rock smacks you!

"That baby's standing! I can't do that. I can't even pull myself up; I always fall down. I'll never make it. I'll never stand, or walk! My life is ruined. You're not so cute and that's not a smile. That's a smirk! Talk about stuck-up! . . . . I hate that baby . . . I really hate that baby!"

If you don't get this story, you haven't started law school yet.

Not so long ago, a creative-writing professor from Stanford decided to go to law school. It would be a piece of cake, what with his academic record, what with his history of intellectual achievement. Not so.

Why was I afraid?

Imagine, is all that I can answer.

You have a stake. You have given up a job, a career, to do this. Or you have wanted to be a lawyer all your life.

181

You've studied hours on a case that is a half page long. You couldn't understand most of what you read at first, but you have turned the passage inside out, drawn diagrams, written briefs. You could not be more prepared.

And when you get to class that demigod who knows all the answers finds another student to say things you never could have. Clearer statements, more precise. And worse—far worse—notions, concepts, whole constellations of ideas that never turned inside your head.

Yes, there are achievements in the past. They're nice to bandage up your wounded self-esteem. But "I graduated college magna cum laude*" is not the proper answer when the professor has just posed a question and awaits your response with the 140 other persons in the class.*

The feeling aroused by all of that was something near to panic, a ferocious, grasping sense of uncertainty.... On many occasions I discovered that I didn't even understand what I didn't know until I was halfway through a class. Nor could I ever see how anyone else seemed to arrive at the right answer. Maybe they were all geniuses. Maybe I was the dumbest guy around.

The writer was Scott Turow. He went on to great things as a lawyer/novelist. Isn't it nice to know that someone whose books routinely appear on the *New York Times Best Sellers List* once sat where you sit, terrified?

Why is the first semester so scary?

Partly, it's the hype. Professor Kingsfield, dreaded Contracts Professor of *Paperchase*, bellows at his first-year class:

Your minds are filled with mush. You will teach yourself the law. I will teach you how to think!

Whatever that means, it doesn't seem to bode well to entering students.

Partly, it's that law school is a brand new game. Had you gone into other graduate programs—schools of education, philosophy, social work—you would have a fairly good idea what to expect, how to study, and how you would do.

And there is very little feedback. There are no term papers or midterms. You will sit in a large class (classes over 100 are not uncommon), awaiting the *one and only* test.

Why the lack of feedback? Economics. Legal education is graduate education on the cheap—one demigod handling a class of 140! Things are getting better. Some schools offer at least one small section in the first semester, and, in the second and third years, there will be seminars and clinical courses that have a lower student/faculty ratio and hence more feedback. With these exceptions, the general model holds: large classes followed by a single final.

In this chapter, I will look at the psychological tensions of the first year. In your darker moments, you will come to believe that "I'm the dumbest one here" and "Everyone here is viciously competitive, except me and my friends." And you will, most likely, assign a wildly inappropriate meaning to first year's grades. I will also cover the almost universal fear of being called on in class. I will explain why we teach the way we do, the so-called Socratic Method, and I will urge you to help us out, by raising your hand and volunteering.

"I'm the Dumbest One Here!"

Take heart! *Every* first year student believes this, even the smug guy from Princeton sitting next to you.

Flunking out is no longer much of an issue. In the old days, deans would welcome incoming students with,

"Look to the person to your right, look to the person at your left. Only one of you will be here second semester."

We now pre-flunk most of the class with high admission standards. Flunking out usually isn't a real threat. Nonetheless, the "ferocious, grasping sense of uncertainty" remains. Why?

The psychologist Carl Rogers wrote of our basic insecurity, that we know, deep down, that we really aren't all that "hot." We know that our prior successes have been, at bottom, luck. Sure, we've been able to fool the others, but this is law school, and that "demigod" up front might prove too much. She'll expose us, once and for all, as the incompetents we are.

The brilliant things your classmates will say feed this basic insecurity. Realize this. There are so many interesting and profound things to say. Student A and student B will both have interesting, insightful comments to make, comments which are, however, quite different. Student A recites; student B is dumbstruck—"I would never have thought of that; there are notions, concepts, whole constellations of ideas that never turn inside my head!"

If only B had talked first!

Insecurity, although understandable, can lead us to what will not be our finer moments. One is the pathetic posturing that occurs:

> *"I don't study more than an hour a day and understand everything."*

> *"Why did everyone in class have such a problem with Pennoyer v. Neff? I understood it immediately."*

One of my favorite stories involves an ex-professional football player who was, wittingly or not, something of a Zen Master. His friends would often tease him with the fact that others who played his position, defensive lineman, often sacked the quarterback while he seldom did. Would he bite? No.

> *"Did you ever consider that those guys were better players?"*

Concession often entails victory. To admit that you didn't understand *Pennoyer* will convince the braggart that you are, not only more secure and honest, but probably smarter and better-looking.

"Law Students Are Viciously Competitive"

Law students are aggressive, competitive, humorless and, worst of all, they study all the time. Now, of course, *I* wasn't that way as a law student, nor were my close friends. I am sure you and your friends aren't that way either. But we can agree that everyone else is.

One of my students wrote of her first day at law school. She met another woman and thought, "She's smarter than I am, better educated, better looking and, obviously, more stable." Instant hatred.

Don't reject people simply because they had the effrontery to come to law school.

Note a curious fact. Although you may feel a little like jelly, in fact *you* are that smart, educated, good looking and stable person everyone is afraid of. That sentence is worth rereading and pondering.

Competitiveness and aggressiveness are not just psychological projections. They are real. Your classmates are competitive, and so are you. It is important to confront and contain your aggressiveness and competitiveness. It will not do simply to deny these feelings, "Oh, I don't care what grades I get or how I do; I just want to get by!" Some students take denial to the extreme of not trying; they do a minimum amount of studying and miss class frequently. (If you refuse to try, then failure will be less painful. On the other hand, there is always the possibility of the ultimate seventh-grade fantasy— an "A" in Contracts and an "F" for Effort.)

You are competitive, or you wouldn't be in law school. You have achieved recognition and pleasure in competing successfully in the past. This is not shameful. Accept this part of yourself; however, do not let it consume you.

Scott Turow describes how he was almost consumed as a first year student. He found himself telling a friend, *"I don't give a damn about anybody else. I want to do better than them."*

My tone was ugly.... What had been suppressed all year was in the open now. All along there had been a tension between looking out for ourselves and helping each other; in the end, I did not expect anybody—not myself, either—to renounce a wish to prosper, to succeed. But I could not believe how extreme I had let things become, the kind of grasping creature I had been reduced to. I had not been talking about gentlemanly competition. There had been murder in my voice.

That night I sat in my study and counseled myself. It's a tough place, I told myself. Bad things are happening. Work hard. Do your best. Learn the law. But don't suffer, I thought. Don't fear. And for God's sake, don't give up your decency. (Another sentence worth rereading and pondering.)

The Socratic Method

Where there is understanding,
  Let me sow confusion.
Where there is light,
  Darkness.

No, although sometimes it may seem like it, law professors are not committed to a terrible misreading of the Prayer of Saint Francis.

The "Socratic Method" involves a professor randomly calling upon students to "state the case," and then to answer a series of follow-up questions, either directed at the coherence of the case itself or its future application. Critics argue that this method keeps students in terror and is designed to humiliate; that it teaches future lawyers that is it proper to abuse people. Other critics argue that the process of demanding justifications and meeting argument with counter-argument leads to extreme relativism. This is not a new fear.

Suppose the student is confronted by the question, "What does 'honorable' mean?" He gives the answer he has been taught, but he is argued out of his position. He is refuted again and again from many different points of view and at last is reduced to thinking that what he called honorable might just as well be called disgraceful. He comes to the same conclusion about justice, goodness, and all the things most revered. We shall see him renounce all morality and become a lawless rebel.

Plato, *The Republic*

Admittedly, when I was a student, these criticisms of the Socratic Method rang more true than they do now, now that I am a professor. Let me say a few nice things about it.

When it comes to legal doctrine, you are not learning it in the classroom. In the classroom, you are learning how to "do law." By tearing apart the cases, testing their coherence and rejoicing in their ambiguities, your professors are showing you how to do it.

The goal of the method is *not* to inculcate relativism; the goal is *not* to expose student ignorance; the goal is *not* to ridicule. The goal of the method is *to force students to justify their positions, to consider other points of view, and to realize that even the best of arguments suffer from "inconvenient facts."*

To illustrate, take a familiar case: a tenant is suing the landlord for negligently maintaining a common stairway. The landlord sets up as a defense a clause in the lease in which the tenant agreed not to sue the landlord for negligence. Is the clause valid?

> *Student: I don't think the tenant should be held to her promise not to sue if that promise was buried in the small print in the lease.*
>
> *Professor: Why not?*
>
> *Student: It just isn't fair.*
>
> *Professor: Why not?*

Here the student may feel that she is being attacked. Still worse, the student may feel that she is being argued out of her sense of fairness. This is not the professor's goal; rather it is to force the student to bedrock why she feels the way she does.

> *Student: Well, it seems to me that one reason we enforce promises is to protect free choices. If the tenant didn't know what she was signing, then the whole justification for enforcing promises collapses.*

Behind our sense of justice often lie good sound reasons. For the professor to insist upon their verbalization is not to attack them.

> *Professor: Good. But what if the evidence showed she read the contract? Would you still think the agreement unfair?*

> *Student: Yes. The facts show that she was poor and probably not that well educated. She really didn't know that she was giving up valuable rights.*

> *Professor: Good. But isn't that a little paternalistic? If the law doesn't enforce her promise because she is poor and not well educated, aren't we saying that she is legally incompetent? That she doesn't have that most basic of rights, the right to mean what she says?*

The professor is not attacking the student, not trying to trip her up and humiliate her. Nor is the professor trying to argue her out of her position and turn her into a mouthpiece for landlords. The professor is attempting to force her to consider other points of view, to adopt the "yes.... but" form of reasoning. "*Yes*, my initial reaction is valid, *but* there are counter-considerations."

Max Weber, the great sociologist, wrote that the "primary task of a useful teacher is to teach his students to recognize *inconvenient facts.*" The teacher should force students to understand what their opinions and arguments entail. Weber continues:

> *If you take such and such a stand, then you have to use such and such means in order to carry out your conviction. Now, these means are perhaps such that you believe you must reject them. Does the end "justify" the means? Or does it not? The teacher can confront you with the necessity of this choice.*
>
> *The teacher can force the individual, or at least we can help him, to give himself an account of the ultimate meaning of his own conduct. This appears to me as not so trifling a thing to do, even for one's own personal life. Again, I am tempted to say of a teacher who succeeds in this: he stands in the service of "moral" forces; he fulfills the duty of bringing about self-clarification and a sense of responsibility.*

Having made a very compelling argument why the tenant should be excused from her promise to pay, it is discomforting to have the professor point out that the argument entails paternalism and denies tenants the very basic right to "mean what they say." Again, in Weber's analysis, the professor is not suggesting that the promise should be enforced; the professor is forcing the student to realize the important values which would be sacrificed if the promise were not enforced. *"The teacher can confront you with the necessity of choice."*

Our goal is not to hurt feelings. Of course we screw up. Teaching law is not easy. We don't lecture from well-worn notes. All is movement, and you never know exactly what will happen next. No doubt in the hurly-burly of class we reject what the student believes is a valid point; undoubtedly, we are too abrupt with students who seem to be meandering; and, undoubtedly, the shock and dismay we occasionally experience shows. These are but inadvertent and unfortunate slights and insults caused by the intellectually challenging and unplanned nature of Socratic discourse.

When the Socratic Method Happens to You

You'll be in class one day, just sitting there, minding your own business, actually rather enjoying the discussion, when, without warning, you hear someone calling your name. The Professor! All eyes turn to you. There is total silence.

Relax! Take a deep breath, loosen your jaw. Shift your attention from "Oh, no, it's happening to me!" Focus on the question. If necessary, ask that it be repeated. While answering the question, remember that you are probably doing a whole lot better than you think you are. Just because *you* thought of something, just because *you* understood a point, that doesn't mean that it is so obvious it doesn't justify discussion. What you have to say might be terrific. Realize that you appear less nervous than you feel. When your classmates recite, they do not *appear* nervous even though they surely are. The guy sitting next to you, from Princeton? Jelly. It's just that you don't hear the pounding of his heart nor feel the quiver in his lips.

Confront, finally, the dreaded fear: You make a total fool of yourself. Your classmates laugh. You bumble, meander, and eventually give up. The professor moves on and asks the person behind you what has to be, and I'm not making things up here, the easiest question you have ever heard.

Shattered, you walk from class. You overhear smatterings of conversations and are greatly relieved.

*"They're **not** talking about me and what a fool I was. They're talking about the cases and lunch. But wait! It's worse than I feared. They just don't care!"*

Play the fool and the world continues to turn. This is a valuable lesson even if a disappointing one. The willingness to take risks is absolutely essential to effective lawyering. Who was foolish enough to first assert that separate means unequal? To argue that, despite tradition and practice, police must warn defendants of their right to remain silent? To suggest that manufacturers of goods could be held "strictly liable" for injuries their products cause?

Law demands creativity; creativity demands we try new things; creativity demands we play the fool.

Volunteering in Class

For a law school class to succeed, students must participate and share their insights, questions, and experiences. You can't sit on your hands and then complain that the class is boring. A good class is as much the doing of the students as it is of the professor.

Give me a good class that is on my side and is willing to take risks, I am pretty good. Give me a silent, resentful class, I stink.

Recently, in Contracts I brought up the hard/soft metaphor and how it plays out in law study. Some courses are "soft"—family law, clinical courses, interviewing and negotiation; and some courses are "hard"—Antitrust, Federal Jurisdiction, Tax. And "hard" always trumps "soft." I thought the discussion was very important because I believe that the metaphor guides a lot of our choices. But I noticed a student in the back, looking bored and resentful. "That student thinks this is a waste of time. Probably he's right."

"Let's get back to offer and acceptance."

"Wait." My silent critic raised his hand. "Before we leave hard/soft, that is about masculine/feminine. When I was a boy, growing up, I liked books, and they are soft. My friends all liked sports, and it was very painful for me . . . ." His voice trailed off.

The discussion he facilitated, the discussion he almost shut down, was one of the best ever.

You have a stake in your classes. *You can make them better, and you can make them worse.* Take part. Raise your hand. Ask a question. Stab at an answer.

Volunteering pays off. Even if it isn't counted towards your grade, volunteering gives you experience in trying out your ideas and thinking on your feet—important lawyering skills.

Don't volunteer all the time, as there is a definite drawback. Volunteering requires blocking out remarks of other students while you wait until you are called on. It is difficult to listen and retain what you want to say or ask. (Try jotting down a few words and then turn attention to the class). And, if you volunteer too much, other students will resent you.

Realize that in the first few weeks of law school you are making important choices about yourself. William Blake had a marvelous phrase, "mind-forged manacles." Don't forge: "I'm just not the kind of student who raises his hand!" Volunteer at least occasionally; otherwise, you'll lock yourself in a closet.

Grades

Finally, you are not your first-semester grades.

"Of course not," you laugh nervously.

Just wait.

You work really hard all semester. Suddenly it all comes crashing down into a letter or a number. "So that's it, huh. I'm a C."

No, you are not a C. You are whoever you were before you came to law school, the same person who, as a small child, took such good care of the puppy. Only you're different: you have a lot more knowledge and a lot more skills. You are well on your way to becoming a competent professional.

Remember why you came to law school. You didn't come to be a successful law student; you came to be a successful lawyer. Some students, disappointed in their grades, forget this and drop out in place. Keep working hard on your studies; you will know more law and will have better lawyer skills when you really need to, when another individual puts important matters into your hands. From now on, it's about your clients.

If you do well on your exams, more power to you. Feel good; celebrate. But don't fall victim to your own success. A good friend of mine, a regular Joe, did remarkably well his first semester and he suddenly became a character of Shakespearian dimension, walking the law school halls

> *". . . . dressed in an opinion*
>
> *Of wisdom, gravity, profound conceit–*
>
> *As who should say, 'I am Sir Oracle,*
>
> *And when I ope my lips, let no dog bark!"*

Fast forward to a recent movie. An elderly man is asked advice by a younger person.

> *"Get to be my age, everyone thinks you know what you are talking about. But I'm the same old [expletive deleted] I have always been."*

On your way to the Law Review office, just remember that you're the same kid who was always picked last.

———

This chapter has been kind of a downer. It focused on the negatives. It started with Professor Kingsfield, who, I admit, is one of my heroes:

> *Your minds are filled with mush. I will teach you how to think.*

He's right and you will come to know it. When you aren't complaining, you'll be talking law and loving it.

You are going to meet many wonderful people and make life-long friends. Expect bumps and moments of despair. You are mastering a new and difficult discipline. At first you will be doing it wrong; you will garble facts, misstate issues, and confuse holdings. After much hard work, you will do it right.

"Hey, look at me! I'm not only standing. I'm walking!"

*

PART THREE
LITIGATION

*Perhaps nine-tenths of legal uncertainty is caused
by uncertainty as to what courts will find, on
conflicting evidence, to be the facts of the case.*

Jerome Frank, *Zell v. America Seating,*
138 F.2d 641 (1943)

In your first year of law school *legal* uncertainty
will be your daily bread.

> "In the case of *Globe*, involving a business
> contract and financial loss, the court held that
> a clause in a contract agreeing not to sue for
> negligence is valid. Would that holding apply in
> the next case, one involving a landlord/tenant
> relationship and personal injuries? Well,
> maybe."

But as Judge Frank points out, you ain't heard the
half of it. Even if we figure out what legal rule to
apply, the outcome is not certain, because of *factual*
uncertainty. Assuming the injured tenant gets
around *Globe* and the court throws out the agreement not to sue, to win her case she now must
prove that the landlord was negligent. On the basis
of conflicting evidence, will the jury find that the
landlord was negligent?

Well, maybe.

In this part, we take a detailed look at the factual side of things, the litigation process. Now, you won't be trying lawsuits for years, so why four chapters devoted to this topic? As a first year student, your job is to master legal doctrine, not the art of cross-examination nor that of closing argument. The reason I walk you through the litigation process is that it will deepen your understanding of the legal doctrines you will study.

"How will this rule play out in the courtroom? If it were my case, how would I prove it?"

On a less grand and more immediate level, these chapters will be a great help in understanding the cases you read as judges throw around unfamiliar terms. What's a "motion to dismiss"? An "affirmative defense"? "Impermissible hearsay"? I will introduce you to these terms and show you how they fit into the bigger picture of a lawsuit.

This part will also put your Civil Procedure class in context.

There are no exams, and, again, you won't be going to court for a long time to come. (I hope.) Therefore, don't try to sit back and memorize the points I will make. Simply read along in order to get a sense of how lawyers try lawsuits.

Chapter 15 begins, naturally enough, with late-night lawyer advertising and then describes something of the lawyer/client relationship, including the important matter of fees. It then describes how lawyers plan and investigate cases, backwards, from potential jury instructions. Chapter 16 shows you how lawyers reduce the factual chaos of the world into Complaints and Answers and then describes how the law tests for the legal adequacy of those factual stories, in motions to dismiss. It will also cover the discovery process. The last two chapters show you how all of this comes together in trial.

Sit back, get a good light, and enjoy!

CHAPTER 15

CASE PLANNING: THE INTERPLAY OF LAW AND FACT—BACKWARDS

The Return of Ms. K

You remember Ms. K. She had tripped on a defective step in her apartment house. Recuperating, she watched a lot of T.V. Late one night, during the reruns, after the ad giving the 1–900 number for an authentic psychic, the lawyer C. Darrow appeared on the screen. Solemnly, indeed reluctantly, she broke the bad news:

"Insurance companies are sleaze! Physicians are murderers! Even, I hate to tell you, authentic psychics are frauds. I am your only friend." A warm, inviting smile:

"If you've been injured, been worrying you might get injured, or if the person who saved your life bruised your arm, hurry on down and we will see just how much money you get."

The next day, Ms. K hurried on down.

"Don't tell me what happened," instructed Darrow. "Just tell me how badly you were hurt."

Ms. K did. Her injuries were substantial.

"That bad, huh? You have a *great* case. Now tell me what happened."

Lawyer Fees and Retainers

Eventually, after much talk of sugar plums, it gets to the unpleasant part of the interview, fees. Rather than an *hourly fee* (used most often in business representation) or a *flat fee* (used often in criminal defense), they agree that Darrow will work on a *contingency fee* basis. If settled prior to trial, Darrow will receive 25% of the recovery, if litigated, 35%. If there is no recovery, Darrow gets nothing.

The idea behind the contingent fee is to assure access to the courts for folks who have been injured. If they don't win their case, they don't have to pay their attorney. Without a contingent fee arrangement, many people could not afford to hire a lawyer because of high hourly fees and hence could not get compensation for their injuries. Some argue that contingent fees are a bad idea because, first, they encourage lawyers to bring unmerited law suits and, second, with meritorious cases, they put too much of a successful plaintiff's recovery in the lawyer's pocket.

Contingent fees are permissible only for personal injury cases and not, for example, in criminal, divorce, or child-custody cases.

However, even personal injury plaintiffs do have to pay *costs*: filing fees, reporter's fees for depositions, juror fees, and expert witness fees. Depending on the complexity of the case and the extent of discovery, these costs can run into quite a bit. If Ms. K wins her case, however, most likely the defendant will be ordered to pay these costs. If not, she's stuck.

Two quick points about attorney fees and court costs. Usually a large amount of money can be saved by both parties if they settle prior to trial: litigation costs and attorney fees. In addition to uncertainty of outcome, the saving of pretrial costs is a major incentive for settlement.

Second, the tradition in this country is that each side pays its own lawyer, even if it wins. In many European countries, loser pays for both lawyers. The rule concerning attorney fees has tremendous impact. "Each side pays its own" prevents people with small claims from getting legal representation—"Sure, I can get you the $400 you spent on the refrigerator back, but my fee would be $2000." On the other hand, "loser pays" tends to discourage novel law suits, people thinking, "If I sue Big Tobacco and lose, I will be out the money I paid my lawyer plus the zillions they paid theirs."

After they settle the matter of fees, Darrow and Ms. K sign a *retainer agreement*. It spells out the fee arrangement and states what Darrow is to do. Does the fee include representation of any possible appeals? A major source of lawyer/client fights is misunderstanding the lawyer's commitment. (Another is the failure of the lawyer to keep the client informed as to what is happening with the case.)

Hands are shaken. Ms. K leaves. Darrow, left alone with her books, will start preparing for trial even though she knows the chances are high the case will be settled; without some trial preparation, she won't know how strong the case is and won't know what a fair settlement would be. Where does she start? At the very end of the trial. What will the jury be told?

Jury Instructions and Their Politics

After all the witnesses and all of the objections, the judge will instruct the jury as to the law. Lawyers prepare cases backwards. They begin with finding out what must be proven, by whom and by what standard. This is the stuff of jury instructions.

Visualize a warm courtroom, with jurors nodding off. The judge clears her throat and instructs:

*Ladies and Gentlemen of the Jury. I will now tell you the rules of law which you must follow to decide this case. (1) If you find that the defendant was **not** negligent **or** that the defendant's negligence did **not** cause plaintiff's injuries, your verdict must be for the defendant. (2) If you find that the defendant **was** negligent, **and** that his negligence caused the plaintiff's injuries, then your verdict must be for the plaintiff.*

Plaintiff claims that defendant was negligent.

Negligence is the failure to use reasonable care. Negligence may consist of action or inaction. A person is negligent if he fails to act as an ordinarily careful person would act under the circumstances.

Before you can find the defendant liable, you must find that the defendant's negligence caused the plaintiff's injury. Negligence causes an injury if it helps produce the injury, and if the injury would not have happened without the negligence.

If you decide for the plaintiff on the question of liability, you must then fix the amount of money which will reasonably and fairly compensate for any of the following damages proved by the evidence to have resulted from the defendant's negligence:

(1) The nature, extent and duration of the injury;

(2) The pain, discomfort, suffering, and anxiety experienced and to be experienced in the future as a result of the injury;

(3) Reasonable expenses of necessary medical care, treatment, and services rendered and reasonably probable to be incurred in the future; and

(4) Earnings which were lost by the plaintiff to date, and any decrease in earning power or capacity by the plaintiff in the future.

The plaintiff has the burden of proving by a preponderance of the evidence:

(1) That the defendant was negligent;

(2) That the plaintiff was injured;

(3) That the defendant's negligence was a cause of the injury to the plaintiff; and

(4) The amount of money that will compensate the plaintiff for her injury.

I will now tell you the standard of proof in this case.
Preponderance of the evidence means such evidence
as, when weighed with that opposed to it, has more
convincing force and the greater probability of truth.
In the event that the evidence is evenly balanced, so
that you are unable to say that the evidence on either
side of an issue preponderates, then your finding
upon that issue must be against the party who had
the burden of proving it.

Now that's a mouth full, and there is even more.
The judge will also instruct as to witness credibility
and the role of jurors.

"Where do jury instructions come from?" asks
the precocious child. Appellate cases and relevant
statutes. In most jurisdictions, you can find them in
form jury instruction books. While these instructions seem quite dull, they mask vibrant political
and legal battles.

Here the jury is instructed that Ms. K must prove
both neglect and injury ("*burden of proof*") and she
must prove it by a "preponderance of the evidence"
("*quantum of proof*"). These are not neutral or self-
evident decisions; they turn on political assessments. Do we want to encourage or discourage
personal injury suits? Do we want to shift losses, or
do we wish to let them stay where they have fallen?

If we wanted to help people in Ms. K's position
(to shift losses to folks who might be better able to
absorb them or prevent them), we could put the
burden of proof on the defendant to prove he wasn't

negligent. As the judge has told us, if the evidence is balanced, he who has the burden *loses*.

On the other hand, if we wanted to further discourage people like Ms. K from bringing suit, we could increase the quantum of proof required of her from "preponderance of the evidence" to "clear and convincing evidence" or even, as in criminal cases, to "beyond a reasonable doubt."

"Pain and suffering" awards are a hotly debated element of recovery. The huge jury awards one reads about are mostly for "pain and suffering." Insurance companies argue that they threaten Western Civilization. Others argue that huge jury awards do not harm American business but rather assures that it will be conducted in a safe manner. Both sides can keep you awake with compelling war stories and can put you to sleep with statistics.

Consider the following instruction:

> *Ladies and Gentlemen of the Jury, you are to decide the facts of this case. I will tell you the law. It is your* **duty** *to follow the law as I give it to you even if you disagree with it.*

Again, this seems to be an unremarkable statement but, like so much of law, it masks great debates. Why not tell juries, "If you think the law is unjust, don't follow it"? This is known as *jury nullification* and, in the early days of our country, was a proud tradition: local juries protecting neighbors from the unjust edicts of the King.

We don't tell juries that they have the power to disregard the law, and in fact we tell them that they have to duty to apply it as the judge instructs. Woe to the lawyer who tries to argue to the jury, "The law in this case would be unjust. Don't follow it." She will find herself in contempt of court. I hope you have the opportunity to consider the issue of jury nullification sometime in your law school career. It turns on assessments of how much we trust legislatures to do the right thing, how much we fear juries will do the wrong thing, and how much we believe that general rules can capture the nuisances of justice, "If you think the law would be unjust in *this* case, don't follow it."

Investigating and Proving a Negligence Suit

From the jury instructions, Darrow knows she must prove:

(1) That the defendant was negligent;

(2) That the plaintiff was injured;

(3) That the defendant's negligence was a cause of the injury to the plaintiff; and

(4) That the amount of money suggested is needed to compensate the plaintiff for her injury.

Two and three look fairly easy and may be established by Ms. K's testimony, "Before my fall, my leg and back were fine but not afterwards." But how can Darrow convert physical injury into dollars?

Ms. K broke her leg, hurt her back, and incurred hospital and doctor's bills. She also missed 10 days of work. Darrow knows that it will be relatively easy to prove the amount of the "reasonable expenses of necessary medical care" by simply introducing the bills at trial. She can easily prove "lost earnings" by having Ms. K testify as to their amount. It will be more difficult to prove that the injuries will cause her lost income in the future, and it may be hard to convince the jury to put a high monetary value on the "pain, discomfort, suffering and anxiety experienced" by Ms. K.

The real problem for Darrow, however, is proving that "the defendant was negligent." Ms. K says she fell because the step at the top of the stairs was loose. Darrow and her photographer visit the scene and inspect the staircase. They will find that the top step, made of wood, is cracked so that, when one steps on its outside edge, it gives. But neither Darrow nor her photographer can tell how long the step has been cracked.

Does the mere existence of a cracked step prove, by a "preponderance of the evidence," that Landlord was neglectful? Without more, it seems pretty weak. If this is all she has, maybe Darrow won't even be able to get to the jury. If the judge thinks the evidence is so weak that no reasonable juror could find for the plaintiff, she can take it away from the jury after the plaintiff has presented her case, by granting a motion for a *directed verdict*, or even after the jury comes back with a judgment in favor of the plaintiff, by entering a *judgment notwithstanding the verdict—"a judgment n.o.v."*

Darrow needs more evidence of Larry's negligence. She would like to argue that Larry knew of the defective stair for months prior to Ms. K's accident, that he knew that many people used the stairs and that he was seen, beer in hand, laughing the villain's laugh, "Let them tumble!"

The odds are that Larry will deny knowing anything about the step's defective condition and will claim that he inspects them often (on his way to Temperance meetings), and that he has nothing but love for all his tenants, and that his heart goes out to Ms. K, but that, hey, it wasn't his fault.

In hopes of proving that Larry knew of the defect before the accident, Darrow will send an investigator to talk to other tenants. Did they ever report the condition to Larry? Were there other accidents on the stairs? Does Larry himself use the stairway, thus possibly having firsthand knowledge?

If Darrow can't prove Larry actually knew of the condition, what about arguing that, as a reasonable landlord, he should have inspected the stairs periodically? Darrow will do legal research in hopes of finding a statute or case imposing a duty of reasonable inspection on landlords. If she finds one, she can ask the judge to instruct the jury:

> *Ladies and Gentlemen, a landlord has a duty to make periodic inspections of common areas.*

If Darrow can get this instruction, she has saved herself a lot of work: now she must prove only that Larry didn't make the inspections, not that he should have.

Assuming Darrow can't get the instruction as a matter of *law* (because she can't find any statutes or cases), she can argue to the jury that, as a matter of *fact*, failure to inspect is negligence. It would strengthen that argument if she could call other landlords to testify that they always make inspections and think it would be unreasonable not to do so.

Now she has something else to research: would testimony of other landlords as to what they do be admissible evidence? As many trial lawyers have learned, everything you want to get before jury might not be allowed into evidence. She will likely write a *trial memorandum* to use at trial if the issue comes up. (Note that this research can help in negotiation: "Look, I will call three landlords who will testify your client should have made inspections, and that testimony is admissible.")

Darrow realizes, however, that even if she can establish a duty to inspect (either legally or factually), she still must show that the inspection would have disclosed the defect. She needs testimony that the stair was defective for a long time. She needs an *expert*. An expert need not have academic degrees nor even "book learnin'". An expert is simply someone who has special knowledge that will help the jury understand the facts of the case. Darrow will ask a carpenter to inspect the stairs and tell her, if he can, how long the step was broken.

Enter, stage left, *Quibble Weaver*.

While these investigations are going on, Larry has retained his own lawyer, Mr. Quibble Weaver. Of course, *Quibble Weaver* is a fictional name, but it isn't mine. It was the name given the lawyer in the first modern Italian novel, *The Betrothed,* written by Alessandro Manzoni. It was written in 1827. Even then and even there, "Quibble Weaver."

In any event, Darrow contacted Quibble looking for a possible settlement. Her initial overtures met sullen rejection:

"Larry Landlord wasn't negligent. Ms. K wasn't injured. Besides, there is a clause in the lease releasing the landlord from all liability."

"If that's the way it is going to be, see you in court."

Time to start drafting.

CHAPTER 16

COMPLAINTS, ANSWERS, PRETRIAL MOTIONS, AND DISCOVERY

Sometimes a case will settle before a lawsuit is filed. If one doesn't, it becomes time to rachet things up.

The Initial Court Papers

IN THE SUPERIOR COURT

IN AND FOR THE COUNTY OF KERN

STATE OF CONTENTION

Ms. K	.	**COMPLAINT FOR NEGLIGENCE**
Plaintiff	.	**AND STRICT LIABILITY**
vs.	.	
Larry Landlord	.	**Civil Action Number 1066**
Defendant	.	

. . . .

Comes now plaintiff and complains of the defendant as follows:

Count I

1. The court has jurisdiction of this matter as all events complained of occurred in this county, and both Ms. K and Larry Landlord are residents thereof.

2. At the times herein mentioned, defendant owned the Owl Apartment Building.

3. At the times herein mentioned, defendant retained control in the Owl Apartment Building of the halls, lobbies, and stairways used in common by all tenants of the building and others lawfully coming onto the premises.

4. Plaintiff was a tenant of defendant on or about November 17 last year.

5. On that date, while plaintiff was proceeding down the common stairway provided by defendant for the use of all tenants, plaintiff was tripped by a defective stair on the stairway, thrown violently down the stairway, and in falling broke her leg and sustained injuries to her back.

6. As a result of such injuries, plaintiff sustained damages in the amount of $300,000.

7. Defendant knew, or with the exercise of reasonable care should have known, of the defective condition of the stairway, but negligently failed to correct, remove, or repair such defective condition, and such negligence by defendant was a proximate cause of plaintiff's injuries and the damages incidental thereto.

Count II

1. *Plaintiff realleges 1–6 of her first cause of action.*

2. *Defendant is strictly liable for defective conditions in the stairway, and said defective conditions were a direct cause of plaintiff's injuries.*

THEREFORE, plaintiff prays judgment against the defendant for $300,000, for costs of suit, and for such other and further relief as the court deems proper.

C. Darrow
Attorney for Plaintiff

––––––––––

Reread Count II. What is Darrow up to? Why a Count II at all? Isn't it the same as Count I? Compare #7 in Count I with #2 in Count II. Read carefully.

––––––––––

The first thing a plaintiff must allege in his complaint is that the court has jurisdiction to decide the matter. As you will learn in your Civil Procedure class, whether a court has jurisdiction over a defendant can be hopelessly complicated. In the workaday world of lawyers, however, most defendants do not live out of state, and most do not commit obscure torts offshore that, as luck would have it, do harm in our town. Most defendants live next door and do their nasty deeds in place; usually jurisdiction is not at issue.

After the jurisdiction issue come the factual allegations that are needed to constitute a legal wrong. Note that *notice pleading* is all that is required. All you have to do is alert the defendant to your general factual contentions. It is, for example, enough to allege that the stair was "defective" and it is not necessary to say just how.

Returning now to the allegations in Count II, Darrow is asserting an alternative theory of liability. Unsure she can prove neglect, she is trying to avoid the problem by alleging that the landlord should be liable under the doctrine of strict liability. You will learn in Torts that, in cases involving very dangerous substances or activities, people can be liable for injuries they cause even if they were not negligent. This is true, for example, of people who store explosives. If the explosive goes off and injures someone, that person can recover without showing that the defendant was negligent: if you store explosives, and they go off, you are *strictly liable* for any injury caused. There is no need to show that you stored them in a negligent manner.

The law is always in a state of flux; Darrow hopes to convince a judge that the doctrine should apply to landlords and dangerous stairs. She does this by alleging that basis of liability. If Larry's lawyer is on his toes, he will file a motion saying that landlords are not strictly liable and then, as we are apt to say, the issue will be joined.

We'll see.

Proud of her work, Darrow takes it down to the County Courthouse, pays the County Clerk the filing fee, and files the complaint. The clerk gives it a case number, and we're off to the races. Darrow gives a copy of the complaint and a summons to a process server, who thereupon serves it on Larry Landlord.

Dismayed and no doubt quite fearful, Larry will take the compliant to his lawyer, Quibble Weaver, who now scurries to the law library. He has but twenty days to "answer."

IN THE SUPERIOR COURT

Ms. K	.	
Plaintiff	.	**ANSWER**
vs.	.	
Larry Landlord	.	**Civil Action Number 1066**
Defendant	.	

. . . .

Comes now defendant to answer plaintiff's complaint as follows:

1. *Admits allegations 1–4 inclusive.*

2. *Denies allegations 5, 6 and 7.*

3. *As to count two, denies all matters not admitted to in number 1 hereof.*

AFFIRMATIVE DEFENSE

As an affirmative defense to both counts, defendant alleges:

1. *That the lease between Ms. K and Larry Landlord, which Ms. K signed, provides: "The Landlord shall in no event be liable for any loss or damage which may occur to the Tenant."*

2. *Said clause bars plaintiff's suit.*

THEREFORE, defendant prays

1. *That plaintiff take nothing on her complaint.*

2. *That the court order plaintiff to pay defendant's costs of suit and order such other further relief as the court deems proper.*

> *Q. Weaver*
> *Lawyer for Defendant*

Weaver admits that the court has jurisdiction, that the defendant owned the apartment house and controlled common areas, and that the incident occurred on November 17. He denies the things he will contest at trial: the fall, the injuries, and the landlord's neglect. Ms. K, as plaintiff, will have the burden of proving them.

He also raises an *affirmative defense* concerning the lease provision protecting Larry from suits like this one.

Usually a plaintiff must prove all the elements of her case; sometimes, however, the law requires the defendant to bring up certain matters and then prove them. For example, the plaintiff must prove that the defendant was negligent; if the defendant claims that the plaintiff was *also* negligent (she was drunk) and this contributed to her injuries, the defendant must allege and prove it. Note, again, that these are political/legal decisions. One could, for example, require plaintiffs to prove not only that the defendant was negligent, but that they, the plaintiffs, were not.

You will spend time in your Civil Procedure class on how and why courts allocate issues between things the plaintiffs must prove and things the defense must prove (affirmative defenses).

As a matter of pretrial strategy, it is always best to try to avoid getting into a situation where you must prove something. It is far better to have the burden of persuasion placed on the other side. This is because if the evidence is evenly balanced, the party with the burden of persuasion loses. The general rule is that, if you allege something, you must prove it, so the general advice is try not to allege it. Assume that you represent a defendant in a negligence action and the law is unclear whether the plaintiff's contributory negligence is an affirmative defense or whether "due care" on the part of the plaintiff is part of her case. Don't just allege, in your answer, that the plaintiff was negligent. Rather file a motion which challenges the sufficiency of the complaint, arguing that it must allege that the plaintiff was acting with "due care." That way, if you can convince the judge of your position, you put the burden of persuasion on your opponent.

Discovery

Trials used to be a whole lot more dramatic. Weaver could call surprise witnesses. "The defense calls Mrs. Ortelere."

At counsel table, Darrow would turn to Ms. K and anxiously whisper, "Mrs. Ortelere? Who is Mrs. Ortelere, and what does she know?"

"I dunno. She was my third grade teacher. My God, they're not going to bring *that* up?"

In 1938, the Federal Rules of Civil Procedure were adopted with the goal of taking the surprise out of litigation. The basic idea was that, if both sides of a lawsuit knew all of the evidence that would be introduced at trial, more cases would be settled, and, as to those that weren't, they would be decided on their merits rather than on lawyer gamesmanship.

To illustrate something of discovery, by way of *written interrogatories*, parties can ask each other questions:

1. *List all of the witnesses you intend to call at the trial and summarize what testimony you will elicit from each.*

If Weaver didn't list Mrs. Ortelere, she would not be allowed to testify, except in very rare circumstances.

In your Civil Procedure class you will learn all about the various *discovery* methods available to lawyers. They are quite extensive. One, for example, allows for opposing lawyers to inspect premises and another can compel a personal injury plaintiff to undergo physical examinations by doctors hired by the defense.

The most popular discovery device is the *deposition*. In a deposition, a lawyer is allowed to question opposing witnesses, under oath, in order to see what they will testify in court and to get a sense of whether they will make good witnesses. Just how much sympathy will Ms. K elicit in describing her injuries?

Weaver will *depose* Ms. K in his office. Darrow will be there, and, before things start, she and Weaver will engage in that easy banter that lawyers love and clients hate ("What's my lawyer doing being nice to that sleaze?"). Once things start, Darrow probably won't do much except sit and listen. There is generally not much to object to in a deposition; Weaver can ask any question that can *lead* to admissible evidence, and that gives him a lot of room to question Ms. K about a whole manner of things. For example, he can ask her, "Tell me everything you were told by the neighbors about the stairs." As this calls for hearsay, such a question would not be permissible at trial; however, as it might *lead* to admissible evidence (calling one of the neighbors to testify), it is a fine question during discovery.

A court reporter will transcribe the questions and answers. Ms. K will be sworn in, and Weaver will try to pin her down, both as to the cause of her accident and as to the extent of her injuries. If Ms.

K changes her story at trial, she can be *impeached* by these prior statements. Suppose, for example, she testifies *at trial* that she hurt her left arm during the fall. Weaver has her deposition and is ready to *cross-examine*.

Cross Examination by Quibble Weaver

Q: *Ms. K, you testified on direct that you injured your arm during the fall, is that correct?*

A: *Yes.*

Q: *Do you remember coming to my office for your deposition?*

A: *Yes.*

Q: *Wasn't your attorney with you?*

A: *Yes.*

Q: *And you were sworn to tell the truth on that occasion?*

A: *Yes.*

Q: *And I told you before we began not to answer any question you didn't understand, isn't that a fact?*

A: *Yes, I remember. You seemed like such a nice man at the time.*

Q: *During the deposition I asked you to describe your injuries. You told me of your back pains and your broken leg, isn't that right?*

A: *Yes, my back was quite painful. And my leg was really smashed up. It was terrible.*

Q: *I appreciate your injuries. Please just answer my questions. Now, after you indicated your problems with your back and leg, didn't I ask you whether you were injured in any other way?*

A: *Yes, you asked me that.*

Q: *And didn't you tell me, "No, I had no other injuries." Weren't those your precise words?*

A: *Yes, but . . . . .*

Q: *(Cutting her off) Thank you, nothing further.*

If Ms. K has a good explanation for her inconsistency, Darrow can bring it out during redirect. In the jargon of the trial bar, this is known as *rehabilitation.*

Redirect by C. Darrow

Q: *Before you were cut off, I believe you were about to explain your inconsistency.*

A: *Yes. During the deposition, I was in pain. My back and leg hurt so much that I simply forgot about the injuries to my arm.*

Trial lawyers will tell you that some rehabilitation is better than others.

Despite the spirit of the discovery rules, lawyers, like kids, still love surprises. Unlike kids, however, they don't like to be surprised, they like to surprise. Lawyers resist full disclosure. For example, before a deposition, a party will be told by her lawyer:

"Just answer the questions. Don't volunteer anything. You will want to tell your side of the story. But remember that the lawyer asking you questions will never be convinced by you, and it is his job to turn anything you say against you. But, don't be nervous!"

Before trial, Darrow will undoubtedly depose Larry Landlord, hoping to find that he either knew of the condition or failed to make ordinary inspections of the stairs. Discovery is going per usual when suddenly Weaver makes a move designed *to end it all.*

Pretrial Motions Designed to Avoid Trial

IN THE SUPERIOR COURT

Ms. K   .

  Plaintiff   .

  vs.   .   **Civil Action Number 1066**

Larry Landlord   .

  Defendant   .

. . . .

DEFENDANT'S MOTION TO DISMISS COUNT 2 OF PLAINTIFF'S COMPLAINT

DEFENDANT'S MOTION FOR SUMMARY JUDGMENT

TAKE NOTICE THAT at 8:30 a.m. or as soon thereafter as the matter can be heard, on April 6 in

Courtroom 4 of the Superior Court of the County of Kern, defendant will move the court to dismiss Count 2 in plaintiff's complaint as it fails to state a claim upon which relief can be granted. DEFENDANT WILL FURTHER MOVE that summary judgment be granted it as to Count One, dealing with allegations of negligence, on the basis that there is no triable issue of fact in this case. As attested to in the attached affidavit of Larry Landlord, Ms. K signed a lease that provided she could not sue for negligence.

Respectfully submitted,
Quibble Weaver

If Weaver wins this motion, there will be no trial.

Why have a lengthy and expensive trial if it is clear that Ms. K will lose? Procedural law allows for various moves to abort cases without trial if there really isn't a true factual dispute.

A quick aside. *"Procedural law"* refers to the rules which govern the *method* by which disputes are resolved, such as rules governing which court should decide the controversy (jurisdiction), what issues may be joined in the same lawsuit, and how long one has to answer a complaint. *"Substantive law"* refers to rules which determine the *outcome* of the dispute, the rules of contract, property, and dog bite. Substantive law governs our daily lives and those of our dogs.

The two most common procedural devices to test the legal effect and sufficiency of fact are *motions to dismiss* and *motions for summary judgment.*

Motions to dismiss a pleading as insufficient as a matter of law

The plaintiff files a complaint making certain allegations. A motion to dismiss basically says "no soap"—what is alleged doesn't make it as a matter of substantive law.

In this case, defendant is moving to dismiss plaintiff's second count. Plaintiff alleged that the defendant landlord should be liable on a theory of strict liability, that he should be liable even though the plaintiff cannot prove that he was negligent in relation to the stairs. Darrow wanted a fallback position in the event she could not prove negligence. Clever idea. Defendant's motion to dismiss is saying, "Without showing negligence, there is no cause of action as a matter of law and hence the count should be dismissed. No need to have a trial on it."

Similar to a motion to dismiss, a motion to strike can be used to test the legal sufficiency of answers. Darrow could move to dismiss the affirmative defense, the one raising the exculpatory clause, by arguing that such clauses are void. If that motion was granted, then the defendant could not even introduce evidence of the clause at trial: *You can introduce evidence only in support of what you have alleged (or evidence which contradicts what your opponent has alleged).*

In olden days, days of grace and style, motions to dismiss were called "demurrers." You will find that term in some opinions you read. It is still used in our more romantic states, such as California.

Motions for Summary Judgment

A motion to dismiss is solely defensive in that it can only attack the sufficiency of the facts alleged by the opposition. But what if there is an important fact not alleged by the opposition that would abort the case? How can you get it before the court? By a Motion for Summary Judgment. Along with the Motion you file an affidavit by someone who swears that the fact is true. If the opposing party files an affidavit saying the fact is not true, then the matter will be set for trial. However, if the opposing party doesn't file an affidavit denying the fact, the court deems the fact admitted. Then the question becomes, with that fact admitted, should judgment be granted to one of the parties? The test, as you will learn, is whether there remains "a triable issue of fact". If there is, judgment will not be entered; if there is not, then it will be.

Now, in our case, Ms. K did not mention the exculpatory clause in her complaint. To get it before the court, Quibble files an affidavit attesting to it. K can't deny it. The issue is joined: does the clause, as a matter of law, bar her suit? Yes, if the clause is legally enforceable; no, if it is not. Thus we are thrown back to the first chapter of this book. Seamless web and all of that!

Come 8:30, April 6, Darrow and Weaver arrive in Courtroom 4. Most likely they have each previously submitted a *Memorandum of Points and Authorities,* which are legal briefs arguing their respective positions. Does the case law suggest it would be appropriate to impose strict liability on landlords? Do any cases or statutes address the issue of exculpatory clauses in apartment leases? At the hearing, both Darrow and Weaver will have the opportunity to quote precedent, argue policy, distinguish cases, wave their arms and predict doom. No doubt the judge will "take the matter under advisement." After a short interval the judge will enter judgment, in all likelihood striking the plaintiff's second count (nice try Darrow) and denying Weaver's motion for summary judgment, holding exculpatory clauses unenforceable.

The matter is set for trial of plaintiff's remaining count, the one alleging negligence. Can Darrow make it out *factually?*

Trial's set for tomorrow. Get some rest.

CHAPTER 17

TRIALS

A tree falls in the forest. No one is there to hear. Does it make a noise? Despite the mush you learned as an undergraduate, the correct answer depends on the jurisdiction in which it fell. We'll see.

Jury trials go something like this:

1. Jury selection.

2. Opening statements.

3. Plaintiff's (or State's/People's) case-in-chief.

4. Motions, such as a *directed verdict* motion, designed to test whether, at this point in the trial, a reasonable jury *could* (but not necessarily *would)* find for the plaintiff. If such a motion is granted, that's that.

5. Defendant's case-in-chief.

6. Plaintiff's rebuttal (witnesses called to contradict new testimony given in the defendant's case).

7. Defendant's rebuttal (witnesses called to rebut plaintiff's rebuttal witnesses).

8. Closing arguments.

9. Jury instructions. In some jurisdictions, jury instructions are given before closing arguments.

10. Jury deliberation.

11. The joy of victory, the agony of defeat.

Let's take a closer look at some of these phrases.

Jury Selection (Voir Dire)

The goal is to get an impartial jury. In the old days, whenever *they* were, jurors were neighbors; who better to know who is lying? Who is malingering? In today's enlightened society, we seek an ignorant jury. We get it by asking prospective jurors questions. This is known as "voir dire."

"Do you know any of the parties to this action?"

"This case involves a suit for personal injuries growing out of an automobile accident. Have you been in such an accident yourself?"

"The plaintiff is asking for money damages to compensate her for the pain and suffering she suffered as a result of the accident. The law allows for such damages. If you believed the evidence warranted damages for pain and suffering, would you award them?" (Some people simply don't believe that these damages should be available.)

"This is a criminal case involving burglary. Have you been the victim of a crime? Do you have any relatives in law enforcement?"

"If you are instructed not to put any more weight on a police officer's testimony than that of

any other witness, would you follow that instruc-
tion? If you were instructed not to consider what
will happen to the defendant if she is convicted,
will you follow that instruction?"

In some jurisdictions, the lawyers conduct the voir dire; in others, judges do. The reason that judges are replacing lawyers is that lawyers used the opportunity to "try their cases" by converting what will become their closing argument into a series of questions:

"Now, if the evidence showed Ms. K suffered
permanent leg damage, you wouldn't hesitate to
compensate her fully for that injury, say in the
neighborhood of $300,000, would you?"

After juror questioning comes juror selection. It is really juror *rejection*—those still standing after the rejections become the jury.

First come challenges *for cause,* and each side has an unlimited number. Say a potential juror is married to one of the police officers who investigated the crime. Defense counsel, no doubt insensitive to the dynamics of married life, would challenge this juror for cause. Of course the prosecutor, equally blind to life's subtleties, would attempt to keep this juror:

"Now the fact that you're married to the investi-
gating officer would not mean that you would
believe your spouse more than any other witnesses,
would it?"

It will be the judge's call. What about pretrial publicity? Even if a juror has read about the case in the newspaper, she will be kept if the judge feels that she can put all that aside and render a verdict upon the evidence presented at trial. In cases involving major media coverage, however, the case may have to be moved for trial in another city.

In addition to challenges for cause, each side will have a limited number of *peremptory* challenges. Exercised when the lawyer feels, for whatever reason, that it would be best not to have the person on the jury, peremptory challenges are the stuff of war stories and crude stereotypes (the prosecution wants Germans, preferably Lutheran, and ideally retired high school vice principals, while the defense wants drunken fraternity boys of all faiths and denominations). Peremptory challenges have created the cottage industry of "juror consultants" who, in high-profile cases, sit in the back of the courtroom and watch ever so closely for telltale body twitches.

As you will learn in your Constitutional Law class, peremptory challenges cannot be used to systematically exclude individuals based on race or sex.

Opening Statements

Opening statements are often referred to as "road maps" that help the jury fit the various pieces of evidence into an overall story. "We will call Dr. Dread to prove that Ms. K sustained serious injuries. He is not a real doctor but plays one on TV. He examined the plaintiff shortly after the accident. He will testify as to her injuries and as to the great pain she was in."

During their opening statements, lawyers are not supposed to "argue" their cases. Argument is the drawing of factual inferences and legal conclusions from the raw facts presented at trial. However, the line between "road map" (stating the facts that will be proven, e.g., the stairs were in disrepair) and "argument" (drawing inferences from those facts, e.g., "This means the landlord was negligent") is often a fine one, and lawyers often cross over. However, grand pleas for justice, or for the need to send landlords "messages," are clearly argument and must be saved for closing, where the only limit, frequently ignored, is good taste.

Case-in-Chief: Hearsay and Examining Witnesses

In the plaintiff's case-in-chief, evidence must be presented to establish all of the elements of the plaintiff's case. In a typical personal injury case, they are:

a.   That the defendant was negligent

b.   That the negligence caused plaintiff's injuries

c.   The extent of those injuries

The evidence can consist of *exhibits* (X-rays showing plaintiff's broken bones, photographs of the victim's injuries), *documents* (doctor bills) and, of course, *witnesses*, including *expert witnesses*.

Live witnesses are the most fun. A major limitation on what they can testify to is the *hearsay rule*. It basically prohibits a witness from testifying as to what others told him. Of course, in the real world, we love hearsay; our ears go on high alert when we hear the rich and promising phrase, "Guess what I just heard?"

The hearsay rule prohibits the introduction of "an out-of-court statement introduced to prove the truth of the matter asserted."

"Sam told me that he had tripped on the stair two weeks before Ms. K did."

As this would be introduced to prove the matter asserted, that Sam did indeed trip on the stair, it would be inadmissible hearsay. To admit it would be unfair to the other side. Sam isn't testifying, and hence there is no way for Landlord's attorney to cross-examine him as to his ability to recall and as to his possible motivation for lying.

Hearsay comes in many variations. Irving Younger, a professor of trial advocacy, would tell the following story:

From a distance, bystanders saw a man crawl out of a bedroom window. They were too far away to identify the man but watched as a dog began to chase him. Bystanders followed but were unable to keep the dog and man in vision at all times. A few minutes later they came upon the dog at the foot of a tree; in the tree was a man. Can the bystanders testify to this?

The hearsay problem doesn't jump out at you but, in essence, it is really as if the dog is testifying, "The guy in the tree is the same guy I chased from the house."

Younger would conclude, "It would seem that the testimony would be admissible because there really is no need to cross-examine the dog. We all know dogs never lie."

Younger would pause. "But, they have a great sense of humor!"

Like most legal rules, there are scores of exceptions to the hearsay rule, exceptions which will become the bane of your Evidence course. The two most common exceptions are *party admissions* and *prior inconsistent statements*.

Anything a party to a lawsuit said is admissible *against* that party. (A party is either the plaintiff or the defendant.)

"Now, you are a friend of Ms. K. Did she tell you what she was doing before she tripped on the stairs?"

"Yes. She said she was drinking beer and listening to Merle Haggart songs."

"How much beer?"

"She couldn't remember."

This testimony is being introduced to prove the matter asserted, that Ms. K was drinking (a lot) before she fell. But, because she's in the courtroom, she can take the stand and deny, or explain, her out-of-court statement.

A related rationale justifies the introduction of *prior inconsistent statements*. If a witness (any witness, not just a party) testifies one way at trial, the opposing lawyer can always bring up that witness's prior inconsistent out-of-court statement. This is why lawyers are fond of deposing opposing witnesses: if they change their story at trial, they can be *impeached* with their prior sworn deposition. This was illustrated in the last chapter.

In addition to the hearsay rule, the prohibition against *leading* witnesses on direct also helps ensure that the jury hears only what the witness has to say. When the lawyer calls his witnesses, he takes the witness on *direct* examination. Generally a lawyer cannot *lead* his own witness; that is, he cannot suggest the answer to him, as does the following:

> *Mr. Plaintiff, isn't it a fact that you received severe back injuries in the accident?*

> Only a dumb (or honest) witness would answer, "No."

On direct, you must ask non-leading questions:

> *Mr. Plaintiff, please describe the injuries you received as a result of the accident.*

Leading questions are prohibited on direct because we want the witness to testify, not the lawyer. Leading on direct is permissible as to non-contested matters (where the witness lives) or in the case where the witness is having a hard time remembering.

After each witness, the opposing lawyer has the opportunity to *cross-examine.*

> *"Mr. Plaintiff, you testified on direct that you injured your back in the accident. Now, isn't it a fact that you had injured your back several weeks prior to the accident?"*

On cross-examination the lawyer can, and usually does, ask leading questions. They are a great way to control the witness and force answers on unpleasant matters.

My colleague Paul Bergman points out the ultimate irony. Inexperienced lawyers tend to ask leading questions on direct (because they know the answers) and non-leading questions on cross (because they don't).

Let's examine one piece of lawyer lore: "Never ask a question on cross you don't know the answer to." War stories are offered in support:

> *The defendant was charged with biting off the victim's nose. An eye-witness, called by the prosecution, had testified on direct that indeed the defendant had done this heinous deed. On cross, the defendant's lawyer established that this witness was not looking in the direction of the defendant and his victim until after he heard a scream, thus throwing grave doubt on the testimony that he saw the crime. Then came the dreaded question: "If you weren't looking at the time, how can you know the defendant bit off the victim's nose?"*

> *"Because I saw him spit it out."*

Great story. Troubling story. It suggests that lawyers should use their craft to hide the truth. That is a highly debatable proposition. Further, the story assume that the prosecuting lawyer is incompetent. After cross-examination, there is always *redirect.*

> *"Now, on cross-examination, it was shown that you didn't see the fight. So how can you testify that the defendant bit off the victim's nose?"*

Cross-examination is a needed response to the human tendency to take sides and, once a partisan, to fudge their testimony: to recall a better look than they had and to fail to recall good points for their opponent. Wellman, in his classic book *The Art of Cross-Examination,* gives a striking example of witness partisanship. This is not a recent phenomenon. Wellman was writing at a time when folks traveled by ship. He wrote that when two ships collide, "almost invariably all the crew on one ship will testify in unison against the opposing crew, and, what is more significant, such passengers as happen to be on either ship will almost invariably be found corroborating the stories of their respective crews."

Cross-examination has been touted as the best known device for ferreting out truth (from weaseling witnesses). It usually doesn't work as well as it does on TV, but it can be quite powerful. Volunteer to play the role of a witness at a trial practice court. Feel the rush of combativeness and fear when the judge says, "You may cross-examine." It's only you and the lawyer, and you must answer the questions.

Gone are your jokes, your charm, your easy evasions.

"I didn't ask you that. Please answer my question."

Another limitation on witness testimony is that, unless the witness is called as an expert, the witness cannot testify as to her *opinions* or *conclusions*. This is best illustrated by the cartoon showing a rather smug dog on the stand, and the frustrated lawyer shouting, "We're not interested in what you think. We are only interested in what you smelled."

I'll illustrate the opinion rule in the next chapter.

Rebuttal

Certain things may come out during the defendant's case that plaintiff feels he can prove wrong. Rebuttal is his opportunity. Suppose defendant calls a witness who testifies he saw the accident. Plaintiff, during rebuttal, can call witnesses who will put the defendant's witness, at the time of the accident, in Nova Scotia. A defendant's rebuttal is quite infrequent. Perhaps witnesses could testify that plaintiff's rebuttal witnesses don't even know where Nova Scotia is.

Closing Argument

Once the evidence is in, and after (or in some jurisdictions, before) the judge instructs the jurors as to the law and their role as fact-finders, lawyers are allowed to make closing arguments. Here they "marshal" the evidence, wax poetic, and strut. We'll see this in the next chapter.

One criminal defense lawyer of the Civil War era used to call, as his only defense witnesses, his own small children.

"What would happen if Daddy were to die?"

They would mourn, cry, and ultimately have to be helped off the stand.

The lawyer's closing was short, focused, and effective.

"Ladies and Gentlemen of the Jury. If you convict my client, I am going to kill myself."

This is no longer considered good form.

Who goes first? The party with the overall burden of proof (the plaintiff in a civil action, the prosecution in a criminal action). Then it is the defense's turn. Finally, the opening party gets to rebut the defendant's argument. In theory, this can only be for rebuttal, and a lawyer should not bring up new matter; to do so would be unfair because her opponent would not have the opportunity to respond.

The two most common mistakes lawyers make in closing arguments is putting *their own credibility in issue* and *arguing evidence that is not in the record.* You put your credibility in issue by arguing, *"I know my client is telling the truth."* It is fine to argue, *"The evidence shows my client is telling the truth."* Subtle but important distinction.

The reason lawyers begin planning their closing argument as an almost first step, before even investigating the case, is because they know that unless they get the evidence in the record, through a document, exhibit, or witness testimony, they cannot argue it even if it is true. Good lawyers will make a list of the evidence they want to argue and, as the trial goes on, check off items that have been covered.

Legal planning begins at the end and looks backwards.

Finally what about the tree falling in the forest?

It's a question of *habit* evidence. Can you introduce evidence that someone has a "habit" of doing a particular thing as evidence that he probably did it at a particular time? In some jurisdictions you can; in others, you can't. Thus, as trees habitually make a noise when they fall, if they fall in a jurisdiction that admits habit evidence, they will make a noise even if no one is there to hear.

Of course, it may be that falling trees habitually make noise *only* when there is someone there to hear. It would make for a great law school exam question:

> *A tree, standing in a jurisdiction that admits habit evidence, falls into one that does not. It is in that jurisdiction that the person who wasn't there to hear would have been.*
>
> *Discuss.*

CHAPTER 18

K v. LANDLORD, GREATEST HITS

In this chapter we take a more detailed look at trial dynamics. As you are years away from your first trial, now is not the time to take notes or to try to memorize things. Just sit back and observe what a trial looks like. There will be a few jokes *and* you will learn the secret identity of Ms. K. Whose sister is she, anyway?

We will use the case of *K v. Landlord*. As you will recall, Ms. K is bringing suit for injuries she sustained when she tripped and fell on common stairs in her apartment house. Her basic claim is that Landlord failed in his duty to provide a safe place to live by failing to repair a defective step. Ms. K is represented by Ms. C. Darrow and Landlord by Mr. Quibble Weaver. In the last chapters, we went through their pretrial haggling.

Darrow, for the plaintiff, has the burden of proof and, therefore, goes first. She plans to call Ms. K to testify to her fall and injuries. She plans to call Dr. Dread to establish the extent of those injuries. To establish Larry Landlord's negligence, she will call Joe Ham, a tenant of the apartment house, who will testify that he complained of the loose stairs to

Larry Landlord two weeks before the unfortunate accident. Darrow will also call a carpenter, with the unlikely name of Woody Nails, who inspected the stairs shortly after the accident and concluded that they had been in a dangerous condition for at least two months.

Quibble Weaver, for the defense, will call Larry Landlord and Chuck Pile, a tenant who will testify that he takes out the garbage by way of the back stairs every week and has not once tumbled. Weaver will also call, to rebut the seriousness of Ms. K's injuries, a doctor who usually testifies for insurance companies, Dr. Polly Anna. Pursuant to a discovery order, Dr. Anna, hired by Weaver, gave Ms. K a complete physical. She think Ms. K is a malingerer. Or worse!

Waiting in the wings, for the defense, is Billy Knowles. When Weaver deposed plaintiff's witness Joe Ham, he learned just how devastating his testimony would be. Weaver decided he needed an *impeachment witness*. His investigator found Billy Knowles, who will testify that Ham hates Larry Landlord; Landlord has threatened to evict him and has called the police on his parties. Joe told Billy that he would get even with Landlord. When Weaver gets to cross-examine Joe during the trial, he plans to ask him about these matters. If Joe denies them, then Weaver, with great fanfare, will call Billy Knowles as part of the defense case.

Darrow can call her witnesses in any order she pleases. Trial lawyers will tell you that you should

open and close with strong witnesses, putting the
weaker one in the middle. People tend to remember
best the first thing they hear and the last thing
they hear, tending to fuzz over points in the middle.
Knowing this, Darrow decides to put Dr. Dread on
first and to put on Ms. K last. She wants to begin
and end with a powerful presentation of her client's
suffering. The weak part of her case, that of Larry's
negligence, she plans to sandwich in between high
points.

One reason she puts Ms. K last, rather than first,
is that this will allow Ms. K to hear of the evidence
before she testifies. There is nothing worse than
having your client testify and then be contradicted
by her own witnesses who testify after her. Witnesses in a case are usually prohibited from listening to other witnesses testify before they testify.
This rule does not apply to *parties,* and, to allow
them to hear what others have to say before they
take the stand, they usually testify last.

As to each witness, Darrow knows she can develop the testimony in any order she selects. Chrono-
logical order is often the easiest to follow but,
frankly, it lacks flair. Take the testimony of Ms. K.
The chronology of it is:

1. She trips.

2. She goes to the hospital.

3. She misses some work and loses some wages.

4. The mail arrives, with the doctor bills.

To have Ms. K testify in this order would put even me to sleep, and I'm getting paid. Darrow first sits down and lists what points she wants to make with Ms. K.

First she plans to use Ms. K to prove up medical bills and loss of earnings. These matters are not controversial and lack emotional impact; they should go in the middle of the testimony. Second, Darrow wants Ms. K to testify as to the terror of the fall. She also wants to establish that Ms. K was being careful at the time of her fall. Darrow is concerned that during jury deliberations, a juror might remark, "If she had been looking where she was going, this never would have happened." Darrow wants to shut this down if she can. Third, Darrow wants to have Ms. K testify as to the pain and suffering she has experienced and continues to experience. Darrow decides on the following order:

1. Description of the accident and the fact that Ms. K was being careful.

2. The amount of her medical bills and the extent of her loss of earnings.

3. The pain and suffering; the fear she would never walk again.

There is no magical order, but a good trial lawyer should be able to answer the question, "Why did you present the testimony in the order you did?"

Of course, the first problem Darrow faces is getting Ms. K on the stand, making her comfortable, and, if possible, bringing in some interesting tidbits

which will make her more human and compelling.
Most judges will allow such tidbits although they
are technically irrelevant. You wouldn't be allowed
to go on and on about things: "OK, those are all the
good and kind things you did in the third grade;
now, turning your attention to the fourth...."

It would be nice if Ms. K coached Little League or
chaired the United Way Campaign at her job. Alas,
you play the hand you get.

Q: *State your name and address for the record.*

A: *Ms. K., 1601 E. Kleindale.*

Q: *Are you nervous?*

A: *Yes. After what the judiciary did to my brother, Mr. K, you'd be nervous too. He woke up
one morning and found himself accused of a
heinous crime. No one ever told him what the
crime was. He ended up, like, you know,
killing himself.*

Q: *That's horrible. Do you have any other siblings?*

A: *Yes, another brother. He woke up one day and
found himself turned into, like, you know, a
giant cockroach.*

Pausing to wipe a tear, Darrow now turns to
developing the notion that Ms. K did not contribute
to her fall.

Q: *(by C. Darrow). Now, Ms. K, you weren't at
fault in this, were you?*

Q: *(by Q. Weaver). Objection. Leading. You can't lead on direct. You know better!*

Q: *(by C. Darrow). Of course I do. This is an instructional book, and the author keeps making me do things that are wrong. Then he can come in and be a big hero. Sometimes I wish I were real!*

Cut and back to fiction:

Q: *(by C. Darrow) The afternoon of the accident, had you been drinking?*

A: *No.*

Q: *Were you tired or sick?*

A: *No, I was feeling fine.*

Q: *Now, prior to the accident, did you know the step was loose?*

A: *No, I seldom use the back stairs. I hadn't used them before my fall for at least two months.*

Q: *Now, as you approached the top of the stairs, were you distracted in any way?*

A: *No, I was looking where I was going.*

Q: *Then why did you step on a step that was loose?*

A: *Well, I did look down and nothing seemed out of the ordinary. I had no idea that the step was going to give way like it did.*

Note how Darrow develops the facts. It is far more effective to develop a conclusion than it is to simply come to it:

Q: Were you careful?

A: Yes.

Details convince.

Q: After the accident, did you have occasion to inspect the top step?

A: Yes.

Q: Is it your opinion that Larry Landlord was negligent?

Q: (by Q. Weaver) Objection! That question is clearly improper as it calls for an opinion of a lay witness. Darrow knows better than that.

Court: Sustained.

Yes, Darrow does know better than that. She knows that the question is improper. She also knows that it is *unethical* to ask an improper question in order to sneak impermissible material before the jury. You can't ask, *"When did you stop beating your spouse?"* unless you have a good faith belief that the witness did.

I forced Darrow to ask the impermissible question in order to be a hero (I'm not one at home) and to tell you about the *opinion evidence rule*. One statement of the rule is found in the Federal Rules of Evidence:

Opinion Testimony By Lay Witnesses

If the witness is not testifying as an expert, his testimony in the form of opinions or inferences is limited to those opinions or inferences which are

(a) rationally based on the perception of the witness and (b) helpful to a clear understanding of his testimony or the determination of a fact in issue.

The rule forces witnesses to testify about the raw data of experience: what they saw, heard, smelled, tasted, and felt, not what they concluded from those experiences. Drawing conclusions is the job of the jury. A witness cannot testify, "Landlord was negligent." That opinion is neither "rationally based on perception"—the witness didn't *see* the landlord being negligent—nor is it helpful to a "clear understanding of his testimony." A witness can testify:

"I stepped on the stair and felt it give. I looked at the stair and found a crack about 6 inches long and a quarter of an inch wide. I told Landlord about it and heard him say, "That sounds dangerous. I will fix it immediately." A week later I looked at the stair and saw nothing had been done.

From the facts witnesses testify to, the jury concludes whether the landlord was negligent.

Some witnesses can testify as to their opinions: experts. For example, the Federal Rules provide:

Testimony by Experts

If scientific, technical, or other specialized knowledge will assist the trier of fact to understand the evidence or to determine a fact in issue, a witness qualified as an expert by knowledge, skill, experience, training, or education may testify thereto in the form of an opinion or otherwise.

Darrow plans to call two experts. Dr. Dread, based on his training in medical school and his experiences as a physician, will testify as to the extent of Ms. K's injuries and as to her prognosis. Woody Nails, carpenter, will be the other expert. He will testify about the condition of the stairs. Let's pick up the trial with him.

Court: Call your next witness.

Darrow: Plaintiff calls Woody Nails.

Witness is sworn.

Q: *(by C. Darrow) State your name and address for the record.*

A: *Woody Nails.*

Q: *And you live at 5010 Randlett Drive?* (A leading question, but it is OK as it goes to preliminary matters.)

A: *Yes, that's right.*

Q: *What is your occupation?*

A: *Carpenter. I have been a carpenter for thirty years.*

Q: *Have you ever built staircases?*

A: *More than I can count.*

Q: *Do you ever have occasion to inspect staircases for safety?*

A: *Quite often. Several insurance agents ask me to inspect buildings before they insure them. I* pay particular attention to stairways, because, if they're not built proper, folks can get hurt real bad.

Q: What happens if you find a staircase that is dangerous?

Q: (by Q. Weaver) I object, Your Honor. This line of questioning isn't relevant to the issues of this case. What happens when this witness inspects other staircases is beside the point.

Q: (by C. Darrow) Your Honor, this line of questioning is relevant to show this man's expertise. That insurance agents rely on him is evidence that he knows what he is talking about.

Court: Objection overruled.

Q: Again, what happens when you find a staircase that you think is unsafe?

A: I'll tell the owner or the agent. They have me repair it.

Q: Do they ever go ahead and insure the building without insisting on having the stairs repaired?

A: Not that I know of. It would be real dumb.

Q: Did you have occasion to inspect the back staircase at the Owl Apartments?

A: Yes. I went over there about two days after Ms. K fell.

Q: What was the result of your inspection?

A: The top stair was unsafe. It was loose and gave when you stepped on it. The problem was that it had a big crack in it, about 6 inches long and a quarter of an inch wide.

Q: Could you determine how long the crack had been there?

Q: (by Quibble Weaver) Objection, Your Honor. There is nothing about this witness that would make him an expert in this matter. I let his testimony about "unsafe" pass but not this. Without some showing that this witness has some expertise in knowing how long conditions have existed, I object to the testimony.

Court: I'm going to allow the question. I think carpenters can make these decisions. You can cross-examine Mr. Nails about how he came to his conclusion. How much weight to give his testimony will be up to the jury, but I will admit it.

Note here the very important distinction between *admissibility* of evidence and its *weight*. The judge decides whether or not to *admit* the evidence; once it is admitted, the jury decides whether or not to *believe* it. The fact that Nails' conclusion will be admitted into evidence does not mean the jury will believe it. Weaver will still argue that carpenters really can't make that determination; this time he will argue to the jury rather than to the judge. On the other hand, if the judge refused to admit the testimony, the jury would never hear Nails' conclusion.

To exclude evidence on the basis that it is untrustworthy strikes me as problematic. For example, if Woody Nails really doesn't have the expertise to offer an opinion, why shouldn't the jury be allowed to hear his opinion and then, after cross-examination, reject it? A lot of rules of law you will study seem to come from a deep suspicion that jurors are, not to put too fine a point on it, dunces.

But I digress. Here the judge let the evidence in.

Q: *(Darrow, continuing) How long would you say the stair had been in that condition?*

A: *Well, from the dirt and grime embedded in the crack, I'd say a fairly long time.*

Q: *Could you be more specific?*

A: *At least a couple of months.*

Q: *Thank you, no further questions. You may cross-examine.*

Cross–Examination.

Q: *(by Q. Weaver) Now, isn't it a fact that life's a stage and we're but actors?*

A: *(nervously) Well ... er ...I guess you can say that.*

Q: *And isn't it true that your testimony has been sound and fury, signifying nothing?*

A: *(looking desperately at C. Darrow) I, I ... just don't know.*

Q: *Well, you know this, **Mister** Woody Nails. That isn't even your real name, is it!? And not even a very clever one, at that!?*

Note that leading questions are *not* questions. They are statements of fact disguised as questions. Note too that when you ask a question, your voice goes up at the end and this encourages an answer. When you make a statement of fact, your voice stays flat and does not invite long responses but, at most, an agreeing grunt. Try it! Cross-examining a witness, you don't want answers, you want agreeing grunts.

A: *(beginning to sob) I, I don't have a real name.*

Q: *Of course you don't. That's because you don't exist. You are not Prince Hamlet, nor were you meant to be. You're a bit player in an instructional manual. Your Honor, I move to strike his entire testimony! Your Honor? Where's the judge? What's happening in here?*

The rest is silence. Exeunt.

To illustrate something of cross-examination, let's take the testimony of Joe Ham who, on direct, stated that two weeks before the accident he had told Larry Landlord of the bad condition of the stair and that Larry had said, "That sounds dangerous. I will get it fixed immediately." What Larry said to Joe seems like inadmissible hearsay but it isn't. Note that, to be hearsay, the out-of-court statement must be introduced to prove the *truth* of the matter asserted, that the situation was "dangerous." Here it is being introduced to show Larry's "state of mind," that he knew of the condition. That he spoke those words, not whether they were "true," is the issue. Larry can, and probably will, get up and testify he never said those words.

If the statement was introduced to prove that the stair situation was dangerous, then it would be hearsay. While hearsay is generally not admitted, it is admitted if the statement was made by a party to the lawsuit. It would be admissible as a party admission. But of course you knew that from our discussion in the last chapter.

However, Larry has told his lawyer, Q. Weaver, that the conversation never happened. As this is not something Joe could merely be mistaken about (like an eyewitness identification), it must be that Joe is lying (or Larry is). The purpose of cross examination in such cases is to suggest possible motives for perjury. Note, however, that Weaver realizes that even hostile witnesses can be used to make needed points, here to throw doubt on the testimony of Woody Nails. Note too that the questions on cross are leading.

Cross-Examination of Joe Ham

Q: *(by Q. Weaver) It's true that you used those stairs on several occasions both before and after Ms. K's fall.* (Note: a period, not a question mark: you want an agreeing grunt.)"

A: (Grunting) *Yes.*

Q: *And you never noticed the defective condition before the time you reported it to Larry Landlord.*

A: That's right.

Q: So, as far as you know, the condition was of fairly recent origin; isn't that right.

A: Well, I didn't notice it before.

Q: So as far as you know, the stairway was not cracked before the time you reported it?

A: Yes.

Q: And that was two weeks before Ms. K's fall, and not a couple of months.

A: Yes.

Q: Thank you. Now you never fell on those stairs, did you?

A: No.

Q: And you never heard of anyone else tripping on those stairs, isn't that right.

Q: (by C. Darrow) Objection, Your Honor. The question is not relevant.

Q: (by Q. Weaver) Your Honor, the lack of other accidents is relevant to the issue of whether the stairs were safe.

Court: Objection overruled. You may answer the question.

Note: This might be an error on part of the judge. Maybe, under the law, the lack of other accidents cannot be used to show that the stairs were safe. If Ms. K loses, she can appeal and base her appeal on judicial error. But good luck if this is all she has, even if the judge was wrong. Appellate courts don't like to reverse cases and make the parties start all over again. Despite what you may have read in the local press, appellate judges are not vultures looking with sharp eyes for mere technicalities to reverse convictions and thus thwart justice. Appellate courts reverse only when the judge below really screws up. (One particularly flamboyant trial court judge used to brag, "I've overruled the Supreme Court many more times than it has overruled me.")

A: No, I never heard of anyone else falling.

Q: Thank you. Now, you are a very good friend of Ms. K's, isn't that right.

A: Yes.

Q: And you want her to win this lawsuit, don't you?

A: I think she should.

Q: Please answer the question. Do you want her to win this lawsuit or don't you?

A: I guess I do.

Q: Do you guess or do you?

A: I do.

Note how Weaver pursues the witness. Most witnesses will try to deflect the lawyer's questions; you must become something of a bulldog.

Q: And isn't it a fact that you don't like Larry Landlord?

A: Well, maybe not.

Q: *Maybe not? Isn't it a fact that he has called the police on your wild parties?*

A: *Well. They weren't wild, but yes.*

Q: *And hasn't he threatened to evict you?*

A: *Yes.*

Q: *And didn't you tell Billy Knowles that you would get even with Landlord?*

A: *No, I didn't say that.*

Bingo! Now, as part of his case, Weaver can call Billy Knowles to testify as to that conversation. It is admissible as a prior inconsistent statement.

During trial, lawyers make points to use in closing argument. Weaver's closing argument, as it relates to Joe, will run something like this:

Ladies and Gentlemen, there is one glaring contradiction in this case. You remember Joe, the tenant who had been evicted by Larry. He testified that he told Larry of the faulty condition of the stairs a good two weeks before the accident. Not only did he tell him, but he told you Larry said, "That sounds dangerous. I'll get it fixed immediately."

Now that's quite convenient Larry said that. Note how well it fits into the plaintiff's theory. It shows not only that Larry knew of the condition, but also, that Larry knew it was quite dangerous. What better evidence could you ask for?

Larry testified he never had that conversation with Joe. You must decide who to believe. Some-

one is lying to you. How can you decide who is telling the truth? His Honor will instruct you that you can consider the "character and quality of the testimony" and the existence of any bias or interest.

Does Joe's testimony make sense? To believe that that conversation actually took place, you must believe that Larry knew that there was a very dangerous condition on the stairway but simply failed to do anything about it. Joe would have you believe that Larry was content to wait until someone tripped and fell, to wait until someone sued. Joe's story doesn't make sense. Further, Joe continued to use the stairs. Does it make sense to go on using a staircase after you have reported its dangerous condition to the landlord?

Joe's story just doesn't hold together. Had he told Larry of the condition, it is reasonable to assume Larry would have acted, not only to prevent someone's injury but also to avoid a lawsuit. Does Joe have a motive to make up his testimony? A motive to lie to you? You bet. He is a good friend of the plaintiff. He admitted that he wants her to win this case and obviously he knows his testimony is essential for her victory. And he dislikes Larry. He threatened to get even with Larry. Sure, he denies that, but Billy Knowles, who has no interest in this case, came in here, raised his right hand, and swore that he did.

Now you have two witnesses, Larry and Billy, against one.

No, Joe is not to be believed. He was simply lying about his conversation with Larry. Larry told you it never happened because it never did.

Closing Argument: Weaving Law and Fact

Effective closing argument relies on the primary lawyering skill, the ability to bring law and fact together. That's what you do when you write your exams. Here you'll do it in public.

The witnesses and the documents and the exhibits have put before the jury bits of information: that Joe was threatened with eviction, that the carpenter believes that the stairs had been in a state of bad repair for a long time, that Ms. K fell. At closing, the lawyer *marshals these bits of information into factual conclusions that have legal relevance*. To illustrate this, let's pick up part of Darrow's closing argument.

Closing Argument: C. Darrow

From the fact that Joe told Larry of the condition of the stairs and from the fact that they had been in disrepair for a long time, we can conclude that Larry knew or should have known that the stair was dangerous.

Next Darrow shows the jury what these factual conclusions mean in terms of law.

That Larry Landlord knew of the dangerous condition and yet did nothing about it means that he was not acting as would an ordinarily careful person under the circumstances. An ordinarily

*careful person would have done something to pre-
vent the accident. As the judge will instruct, if you
find that Larry did not do as would an ordinarily
careful person, you are to find him negligent.*

This mode of analysis is quite familiar. In an exam
the bits of information in the question are turned
into factual conclusions which are then turned into
legal conclusions.

Closing arguments are, however, more, much
more, than logic. They are emotion and power. In
the hands of a good criminal defense lawyer, "reasonable doubt" becomes the finest and most deli-
cate flower of Western Civilization, a flower about
to be ground under the shiny black boot of the
State. Listening to a good personal injury lawyer
you experience the victim's anguish as he lies sleep-
less in a hospital bed thinking of what might have
been.

When it comes your time to make a closing argument, there are few experiences so intense and
immediate. When you start, there will be distrac-
tions. You will be nervous, you will be aware of the
spectators, of the judge, and of your trembling
hands.

Soon, however, you soar. Forgotten are your
notes and gone is the judge; for awhile it is just you,
your argument, and the jurors.

Just once makes three years of law school worthwhile.

Most law schools offer Trial Advocacy courses. I urge you to take one. As one of my students told me, "Now I know I don't want to be a trial lawyer."

There are several excellent books on trial advocacy. One of my favorites, by the way, is Hegland, *Trial and Practice Skills in a Nutshell*.

*

PART FOUR

LEGAL WRITING AND ORAL ADVOCACY: THE ESSENTIAL SKILLS

All writing is persuasive writing. You have to persuade the reader to keep going.

Kay Kavanagh

This Part deals with legal writing and oral argument. Both rest on your ability to do legal analysis. Expect old friends, "Yes, but ..." and "So what?" and a plethora of "on the other hands."

Good legal writing is writing that is easy to understand. When you read the prose of a legal giant, such as Professor Corbin, you will ask, "Why is this person famous? What he says is self-evident."

Right.

The basic requirement for good legal writing is good legal analysis; order will emerge from chaos. Chapter 19 offers a lot of tips for good writing and gives some examples for your consideration. Chapter 20 is on editing your work.

Moot Court, the subject of Chapter 21, is a grand first year tradition: your opportunity to dress up and dazzle the judges with the depth of your knowledge and the sparkle of your wit. You will learn how not to pass out (or what to do when you wake up);

you will learn the central importance of fact (and how to tell a compelling story); you will learn how to meet and defeat traditional arguments, and finally you will learn what your role as a appellate advocate should be. You will be surprised. Chapter 22 deals with the mechanics of legal argument.

These chapters need not be read early on. Read the chapters on legal writing when you must take pen to paper. Most law schools have legal writing programs as part of the first year; each of these programs will use one of the many excellent texts on legal writing. Read the chapters in this book as an additional take on the subject.

As to the chapters on Moot Court, Chapter 21 presents a theory of judicial decision-making. What concerns motivate judges in rendering their decisions? I would read that chapter early on, and definitely before I had to write an argumentative brief. The last chapter, on the mechanics of oral argument, can wait until that dreaded day:

"Is Counsel for the Appellant ready?"

That will be you.

CHAPTER 19

LEGAL WRITING

A lawyer's teen-age daughter threw the gauntlet, "Dad, you can't write and I'm taking one of your briefs to my creative writing teacher to prove it!"

A week later, the verdict. Smugly. "I was right, Dad. My teacher says you can't write! He says your sentences are too short, your paragraphs are too short, and besides, anyone can understand it."

Your Goal

All good legal writing is alike. The goal is always the same: to help the reader make a difficult legal decision. A senior partner must decide whether to file a lawsuit or settle; a judge must decide whether to affirm or reverse a lower court's decision. These are always tough calls and these folks need your help.

What do they need to know?

1. The legal issues they must decide;

2. The legal standard or rule under which the decision must be made;

267

3.   Your best thinking on the factors they should consider;

4.   Your conclusion as to how the issues should be decided; and

5.   When the case presents more than one issue, the relationship between these issues.

If you read the chapters on exam-writing, you recognize this as our old friend, IRAC format (Issue, Rule, Analysis, Conclusion), with the added reminder of the need to show the relationship between the issues. All good legal writing covers these points because the reader, faced with a difficult decision, needs to know them.

Your Audience

What do you know about your audience?

First your reader is not 100% on top of the law.

Although a lawyer, your reader will not know the law of your subject as well as you do. Likely you will never know that area of law as well as you do now. What you struggled to understand will not be self-evident to your reader. Because the precise issue you are addressing will be downstream, you must back up and put it in context.

Recall *Lucy, Lady Duff Gordon*. Lucy gave her agent the exclusive right to market her endorsement, and the issue was whether the court would imply a promise to use reasonable efforts on the agent's part. A memo which simply discussed that issue ("Will the court imply a promise on the agent's part?''), would confuse your reader. "Why are we talking about this?"

Your reader must be told that, unless a promise was implied, then the agent's performance would be totally discretionary on his part, and thus, under the doctrine of mutuality of obligation, Lucy could not be held to her promise.

A good teacher always quickly reviews the basics and puts today's lesson in context before moving on to more difficult material.

Second, your reader will be in a hurry.

Brevity is always a virtue. In our first drafts, we tend to be wordy. Cut two words out of ten, which is a very realistic goal, and a cumbersome ten-page memo becomes a spiffy one of only eight. In the next chapter I offer an editing checklist, suggesting that you look at such things as passive verbs and throat-clearing phrases such as "In my considered opinion...."

Third, your reader might be more interested in some points than others.

If your memo or brief is going to cover several issues, which should you discuss first? If you are going to make three points about a particular issue, again, which goes first? Realize you have a *choice*; be able to answer the questions, "Why did you discuss this issue first? Why did you put that point where you did?"

As a rule of thumb, on exams and in office memos, I would start with the most difficult issue;

in briefs, given the fact that the first and last positions are usually the strongest, I would lead with my best argument, close with my second best, and sandwich the others in between.

Good topic sentences and subheads can help the reader quickly find the points he or she is most interested in.

Finally, and again, your reader wants your best thinking on the decision that must be made.

You must write so that the reader can *test* your analysis as he or she goes along. Novelists often write towards the finish, which is revealed, with great fanfare, on the last page: *"The butler did it!"* Science writers begin with a long description of how an experiment was conducted, and only after many pages of tedious detail do you learn that forcing rats to smoke two packs a day is bad for them.

This format doesn't help your reader understand or test your conclusion. While it may rob a novel of dramatic moment to know, up front, that the butler did it, at least we would be able to see whether all the clues add up or, as we often suspect, the writer simply wrote himself into a corner and the butler had the bad luck to be just wandering by. "Hey, you!"

While your conclusions are not terribly important in writing an exam, for the reasons I discussed previously, they are important in office memos and are critical in briefs as they are the conclusions you want the court to reach. By putting them up front, you allow the reader to test your reasoning.

Comparing Kinds of Legal Writing

The goal is always the same: to help your reader decide. What are the differences in format?

1. One difference between writing an *exam* for a professor and writing an *office memo* to a senior partner is that, writing a memo, you have the time to find and actually quote the controlling legal rule or standard. Another difference between the formats, of course, is that you have time for more than one draft (which, alas, few students take advantage of).

A more subtle difference between the two forms is the importance of your conclusion. On an exam, you are primarily spotting and developing the issues. Your conclusion *can* play a role in this process *if* it furthers analysis. A bare statement, "Plaintiff will win this one," does nothing to further analysis. A statement, "Plaintiff will win this one *because....*" may.

Writing an office memo, you have to reach a conclusion and then put it up front, so that the reader can test it as you go along. As you will see, your conclusion acts as an introduction to your analysis by flagging your key points. Note too that it is OK to conclude, "A court could go either way on this," if your opinion is that the question is too close to call.

2. The basic difference between *exams* and *office memos*, on the one hand, and *argumentative briefs* on the other, is your stance. When writing exams and office memos, you are to remain neutral be-

tween the parties to develop both sides with equal vigor. When writing a brief, you are trying to persuade the judge to come to a particular conclusion.

In a brief, your *conclusions* become *assertions*. They tell the judge what you believe should be the proper resolution of the case. I'll illustrate this in our discussion of argumentative briefs. For now, simply note that "A court could go either way on this," isn't your best foot forward.

In the chapter on exams, I walked you through an exam answer. To help you with matters of form, I will give you examples of the two other main forms of legal writing: the office memo and the argumentative brief. As to style, I will stress the importance of putting your reader in contact with the law, of using strong transitions, of being explicit as to the relationship of fact and law, and, finally, of putting your legal arguments in an overall context.

An Office Memo

This office memorandum is modeled on the case of *Mills v. Wyman*, a case found in many contracts casebooks. The memo follows one of many acceptable formats:

1. Caption
2. Facts
3. Issue
4. Conclusion
5. Statement of controlling law (when in statutory or Restatement form)
6. Analysis

OFFICE MEMORANDUM

To: *Senior Partner*

From: *Humble Associate*

Re: *Contract Claim of Charles Mills*

Facts

Levi Wyman, 25–year-old son of the defendant, fell sick upon his return from a sea voyage. The plaintiff, Charles Mills, cared for the young man for several weeks. Unfortunately, the young man died.

Upon hearing of the kindness plaintiff bestowed on his son, the defendant wrote plaintiff, promising to pay the expenses the plaintiff incurred in boarding and nursing his son. The defendant now refuses to pay on his promise.

Issue

Is Mr. Wyman's promise, made in recognition of services rendered to Wyman's son, enforceable under Section 89a of the Restatement (Second) of Contracts?

Conclusion

The Restatement enforces promises made "in recognition of a benefit" previously received. If the benefit must be a direct material one, then the father's promise is not enforceable because the services were rendered to the son. However, if the court interprets "benefit" to include the benefit of knowing

*one's child died in peace, then the promise is en-
forceable as the other requirements of the Restatement seem to be satisfied.*

Statement of Law

Section 89a of the Restatement of Contracts provides

(1) A promise made in recognition of a benefit
   previously received by the promisor is binding. . . .

(2) A promise is not binding under Subsection (1)

   (a) if the benefit was conferred as a gift . . . or

   (b) to the extent that its value is disproportionate to the benefit.

Analysis

[In skeleton format showing only the transitions]

*The first requirement under the Restatement is
that a promise must have been made. Was a promise
made? A promise is defined as* [definition omitted].
*Applying that definition to the facts of this case, it
seems a promise has been made.* [Analysis omitted].

Next, *was the promise "made in recognition of a
benefit previously received"? That depends upon
how the court would interpret "benefit."* [Analysis
continues].

But was the benefit conferred as a gift? *Mills
was acting voluntarily but that may not make his
act a gift. How should the court interpret "gift"?*
[Analysis continues].

The next question is whether the value of the promise is "disproportionate to the benefit"?
[Analysis continues].

Analysis of Memo

Good legal writing puts the reader in contact with the law, uses strong transitions and is as explicit as possible. No one has ever accused a lawyer of being too clear.

Put Your Reader in Contact with the Law

It is always a good idea to tell the reader what the controlling law is. Note that the model *Statement of Law* copies out, verbatim, the Restatement section. This puts the reader securely in contact with the source material. If you state the section in your own words, then the reader is unsure: is your interpretation correct? Compare:

> *"The Restatement would enforce a promise if it was made after the person making it receives some benefit and provided that the other person wasn't making a gift."*

This would be a great statement of law for an *exam*. You are not required to memorize definitions. However, this is *not* good enough for a legal memorandum. Your reader is forced to take your word that this is what the Restatement provides. If you quote the controlling language, there can be no doubt, and now your reader can confidently test your conclusions.

The same point goes to citing and discussing cases. Simply saying, *"Case Y held crude individuals cannot be denied free speech,"* forces the reader to take your word for it. It is far more effective if you cite language from the opinion that proves your point. *(In the case of Leto v. Cooper, the Court said "Even crude individuals have a right to free speech.")*

Copying forces concentration. When you read a statute, even when you read it carefully, you may read it incorrectly. Writing slows the mind, and little words like "not" tend to jump out.

Some provisions may not apply when you are copying controlling language. Edit them out, showing their omission with *". . . ."* Don't edit out inconvenient words, such as "not" and "except" as in *"Even crude individuals have a right to free speech but Cooper is way beyond crude."* For longer quotes, indent and single space.

Once you have copied the controlling law, in the body of your memo, you can refer back to it by simply highlighting specific words.

Compare

> *Was the promise made in recognition of a benefit previously received?*

With

> *Was the promise "made in recognition of a benefit previously received"?*

In the first example, the reader may think that this "benefit" matter is just an interesting twist you came up with. In the second, because of the high-lighting, the reader is reminded that this is indeed a legal requirement.

The only problem with the Statement of Law is its failure to *begin with the basics*. Your reader is not 100% on top of the legal doctrine in the area. You must begin by bringing this reader up to speed. Why isn't the promise simply enforceable? Indeed, why do we need a special Restatement section?

Statement of Law

Under common law, promises need consideration be to enforceable. A promise made in recognition of some prior benefit is not enforceable because there is no current consideration: the benefit came before the promise. The Restatement allows some such prom-ises to be enforced today. Section 89a provides.... [continuing as previously written].

Law is complicated stuff. Begin with basic propo-sitions of law before moving to the more complicat-ed.

Use Strong Transitions

Next, transitions. First, "Next, transitions" isn't much of one. Transitions can, and generally should do more than introduce the new topic. They can *tie that topic* to the previous material and can *explicitly state the legal significance* of that topic. To see how this works:

After a discussion of whether a promise was made:

Compare:

Next, was the promise "made in recognition of a benefit previously received"?

With:

***Even if** there was a promise, **it will not be** enforced unless it was made in "recognition of a benefit previously received." Was there a benefit here?*

After an analysis of whether a "benefit" was given:

Compare:

But did the promise confer the benefit as a gift?

With:

***If the court interprets** "benefit" to include the kind of benefit the father received, the next issue is whether the benefit was conferred by the Good Samaritan as a gift. If it was, then the father's **promise is not enforceable**.*

After a discussion of whether the benefit was conferred as a "gift":

Compare:

The next question is whether the value of the promise is "disproportionate to the benefit."

With:

***Assuming the court finds** the requisite benefit and that it was not conferred by the Good Samaritan as a gift, the father's **promise appears to be enforceable** as the value of the*

> *promise (to pay expenses) does not seem "dispro-portionate to the benefit."*

A transition can accomplish three goals: it can *relate* the new issue to the one discussed previously; it can *introduce* the issue; and it can show the *legal significance* of the issue: does resolution of the issue resolve the entire case or is it simply a building block? A mnemonic device might help you check your own work: RILS transitions.

*R*elate

*I*ntroduce

*L*egal *S*ignificance

It is one thing to understand something ("Oh, I see that!"), and it is quite another to do it. Practice writing RILS transitions. Take the following three elements:

-Promise

-Benefit

-Gift

Write out a transition introducing the "benefit" issue, showing its legal significance, and relating it to a prior discussion of the "promise" issue. Now introduce "gift," transitioning from a discussion of "benefit."

My writing students, when I explain RILS transitions, always tell me, "We understand." However, my experience is that unless they actually practice writing them, they seldom can.

Be Explicit (Ask, "So What?")

A common yet glaring failure in legal writing is the failure to make explicit the relationship between law and fact. Compare the following:

1. *The Good Samaritan cared for the son voluntarily.*

2. *The Good Samaritan cared for the son voluntarily, and thus it may be said that his action was a gift.*

3. *The Good Samaritan cared for the son voluntarily, and thus it may be said that his action was a gift. If so, then under the Restatement of Contracts, the father's promise to pay for the services would not be enforceable.*

The first statement simply identifies a fact. It fails to tell the reader why that fact is legally important. Maybe the author knows, maybe not. I have previously labeled such free-standing statements "free radicals." I think it's rather catchy.

The second statement is more explicit. It tells the reader that from the identified fact it may be concluded that the action was a gift. The third statement is even more explicit. It tells the reader the legal significance of that conclusion, that the promise would not be enforceable.

Explicitness helps both you and your reader understand how the law impacts the facts of the case. By simply stating that the Good Samaritan acted voluntarily and then going on to other matters, you will not consider the key legal issue. By tying your factual conclusions to principles of law, you come to the essential legal question: how should the word "gift" be interpreted?

When you are writing, your little voice should be chanting, "*So what? So what?*" When you are discussing facts, "*So what?*" will force you to be explicit as to how those facts relate to the law, and, when you are discussing propositions of law, "*So what?*" will force you to articulate just how and in what ways that law relates to the facts of the case you are discussing. Once you figure out the relationship, be sure to tell your reader what it is.

A spiffy slogan might help:

Of every fact you write,

Of every law you cite,

Ask "So *what*?"

Well, maybe not.

So ends our discussion of office memos. How do argumentative briefs differ?

Argumentative Briefs

An argumentative writing, if it is directed at an appellate court, is known as a "*brief*"; if it is directed at a trial court judge, it is known as a "*Memorandum of Points and Authorities*." Who knows?

Local court rules will dictate their precise format. Usually, up front, you will be required to list all of the cases, statutes, law review articles and other authorities you discuss to allow the judge to gather them before reading your prose.

A traditional format:

1. Caption
2. Table of Authorities
3. Facts and Procedural Status
4. Summary of Argument
5. Argument

Court of Appeals

Mills,

 Plaintiff/Appellant

  Appellant's Opening Brief

 versus

Wyman,

 Defendant/Respondent

Table of Authorities

Restatement (Second) of Contracts, Section 89a

Webb v. McGowin, 27 Ala. App. 82, 168 So. 196 (1935)

Statement of Facts and Procedural History

Levi Wyman, 25–year-old son of the defendant, fell sick upon his return from a sea voyage. The plaintiff, Charles Mills, cared for the young man for several weeks. Unfortunately, the young man died. Upon hearing of the kindness plaintiff bestowed on his son, the defendant wrote plaintiff, promising to pay the expenses plaintiff incurred in boarding and nursing defendant's son. Later the defendant refused to pay, and plaintiff brought suit. The trial court granted summary judgment to the defendant on the basis that his promise is not enforceable because it neither was supported by current consideration nor fell within the provisions of Restatement Section 89a.

Plaintiff appeals this decision.

Summary of Argument

The defendant's promise to reimburse the plaintiff for the sums expended by the plaintiff in caring for the defendant's son, although not supported by consideration, is enforceable under the theory of past benefit conferred as provided in Restatement (Second) of Contracts 89a. That section provides:

   (1) A promise made in recognition of a benefit previously received by the promisor is binding. . . .

   (2) A promise is not binding under Subsection (1)

      (a) if the benefit was conferred as a gift . . . or

      (b) to the extent that its value is disproportionate to the benefit.

A. The defendant received a "benefit" from the kindness shown by the plaintiff to the defendant's son in that he knows that his son died, not on the street, but well cared for;

B.   The plaintiff did not confer that benefit as a "gift" even though he did not expect payment for it; to define any act done without expectation of payment as a "gift" would mean that no one could ever recover under Section 89a;

C.   The value of the promise made by the defendant, to pay plaintiff's out-of-pockets costs, is not "disproportionate" to the benefit he received.

In the analysis portion of the brief, you will use the above captions to introduce each section. This will allow the judge to skip to the section he or she finds most troublesome.

If yours is the *opening* brief or memorandum, you have a choice as to the order in which you make your points. Here, the order simply tracks the order as set out in the Restatement. If you are *replying* to an opening brief or memorandum, you should adopt the same order as your opponent so that the judge can easily turn to both positions on each point.

To help your reader understand the law, you must always put your legal arguments in context. Don't throw your reader into the middle of things. To illustrate, take a torts case where the plaintiff is suing for battery. The Plaintiff had entered a room, said "I'm going to kill you," and then pointed what was clearly a water gun at the defendant. The defendant thereupon took out his own real gun and shot the plaintiff in the arm. Although the issue will be whether the defendant was acting in self-defense, don't simply jump to it. Put it in context:

> *"The defendant, in shooting the plaintiff, committed a battery. However, he will raise the issue of self-defense. Clearly while a credible statement, "I am going to kill you," would justify self-defense, the issue becomes whether the plaintiff's exhibition of a "water gun" vitiated his threat."*

A variation of the error of failing to put a legal argument in context often occurs in *response briefs*. All arguments should make sense without forcing the judge to refer back to an argument made by your opponent. To illustrate, if you were *responding* to the above brief, your point A might look something like this:

> *A. The plaintiff did not confer a "benefit" on the defendant in that plaintiff's acts only benefitted defendant's adult son. The Restatement language should be interpreted as requiring a direct material benefit which is not present here. If the plaintiff did not confer a benefit on the defendant, then defendant's promise is not enforceable under Section 89a.*

> *The Restatement enforces promises stemming from past benefits conferred only if the "promise was made in recognition of a benefit received by the promisor." In his opening brief, plaintiff argues that the word "benefit" should be interpreted quite broadly, as including the peace of mind a father has in knowing that his son did not die on the street. While this is no doubt a benefit in some sense, it would be improper to interpret the word that broad-*

ly. It would be more consistent with the prior case law, upon which the Restatement rests, to interpret the word as requiring a "direct and material" benefit.

Note that this argument begins by alluding to the plaintiff's position. The judge need not refer back to it.

Note also that legal terms are in quotes, thus assuring the reader that we are discussing legal requirements as opposed to interesting tidbits.

That gives you a good idea of the format of legal briefs. As to the substance, they should address the three main concerns of the judge:

a.   *To do justice between the parties*

This will turn on an effective statement of facts

b.   *To follow controlling cases and statutes*

Cases are rules of law announced in a particular factual context and justified by a certain rationale. Both context and rationale can be used to distinguish a case or to argue that it applies by analogy. Statutes often appear as simple declarations, without legislative rationale. You will have to posit purposes and goals in order to interpret ambiguities.

c.   *To create good precedent for further cases*

This involves arguing policies, slippery slopes, and floodgates.

All of this will be reviewed in the Chapter on Oral Advocacy. Read it before writing an argumentative brief.

CHAPTER 20

EDITING

"God and I both knew what it meant once.

Now God alone knows."

Robert Browning, on an early poem

Put your draft aside for a week or so (or, in the case of a Nutshell, five years or so). When you then read it, you will read it as a *reader*, not as the author. You will spot phrases, sentences, and even paragraphs ready for rewriting. Or for the chopping block. Cutting things out of your first draft will be essential, yet hard. Your intended victims will scream, "No, not me; I'm the crux of the whole thing. Look at that paragraph over there! Why, it's nothing but fluff. Cut it. Leave me. In fact, *expand me!*"

Another effective editing technique is reading your draft out loud, *slowly*. You will pick up careless errors in punctuation and spelling. Problems of style will jump out. If a sentence cannot be read aloud easily, it's not well written. If it cannot be read without gasping for air, it is too long.

Write as you talk. If, reading aloud, it doesn't sound like you, you're in trouble. Few of us are instinctively pompous, or verbose. We write that way because we think that's the way to write. When we talk, on the other hand, we actually want the other person to understand.

George Gross, my prof, says, "Get the sound of your voice in your writing." (When I reread this, I can hear his voice.)

You might consider a three step editing process. In the first, check for essentials—the statement of the issues to be decided, the controlling law, and good transitions. In the second edit, focus on your legal analysis—whether it is explicit and whether you consider both sides. In the final, look for stylistic problems that make your draft cumbersome.

Edit for the Essentials

Highlight your statement of the issues, the controlling law, and the first sentence of each paragraph. That done, go back and reread what you have highlighted, looking for:

1.   *Issues and controlling law*

Do you clearly state the issues your reader must resolve? Do you clearly state the controlling law? Can it be understood by a lawyer who is not 100% on top of the law in the particular area? Do you copy, rather than paraphrase, the key language from statutes, cases or other authorities? Do you come in in the middle of the movie or do you begin with basic propositions of law? Can *you* understand what you have written or does God now stand alone?

For quotes longer than 50 words, indent on both margins and single space.

2. *Transitions*

Check if each is a RILS transition, one which *relates* the new topic to the last, one which *introduces* the subject, and one which tells the reader the *legal significance* of the subject. You do *not* need a RILS transition every time; however, every time, you need a good reason why you don't.

Edit for Good Legal Analysis

Focus, separately, on each of your points or arguments. Stand back and ask yourself, "Is this as clear as I can make it?" "Have I considered both sides?"

Explicitness

There is no room for interesting facts, standing alone; there is no room for brilliant legal analysis, standing alone. Reading your draft, is it clear how each *fact* you discuss relates to the law? How each *legal principle* you discuss relates to the facts of the case? As to each fact you have written, and as to each legal point you make, ask *"So what?"*

Both sides

Even when you are writing an argumentative brief, you must consider, and respond to, your opponent's arguments. Here the saying is, *"Yes, that's true, but...."* Stop after each point you make and ask, "How could I respond to that?"

Order

As part of your legal analysis edit, you might want to make a very quick outline of your points or arguments and then check to see if you have put them in the best order. Beginners often fail to realize that they have considerable choice in the order of the points they make. They tend to begin at the beginning and push through to the bitter end.

The first point you make, and the last, are the most likely to have impact. In argumentative writing, put important arguments first and last; those in the middle tend to be overlooked and forgotten. In office memos, and I think exams as well, I would lead with the most interesting issue and conclude with the least.

Edit for Common Stylistic Errors

Once you are convinced your legal analysis stands up, reread your entire draft, this time looking for common errors: wordiness, pomposity, stop signs and forbidding text.

Wordiness

The less cluttered your work, the more forceful it will be. "Omit needless words," advise Strunk and White, the authors of the classic *Elements of Style*. Omitting needless words does not mean omitting detail or treating subjects in outline form. It means that *each word must tell*.

There are several ways to reduce clutter, and *small savings add up quickly*. If you cut a couple of words per sentence, by the end of twenty pages, you will have saved your reader three pages of garbage. If I had done that, you would have been at the movies by now.

It might be a good idea to go through the draft and *highlight verbs*. This is because verbs often contribute to wordiness. Use the active voice and avoid both verb derivatives and excess verbs.

Active voice. An easy way to delete words is to find sentences written in the passive voice and rewrite them in the active. Compare:

The case was reversed by the Supreme Court. Passive voice, eight words.

The Supreme Court reversed the case. Active voice, six words.

Verb derivatives. Language began with grunts— short, powerful and very much to the point. With civilization came decadence and, still worse, verb derivatives—people no longer *act*, they *take action*; they no longer *decide*, they *make decisions*; they no longer *steal*, they *obtain money through false pretense*. Verb derivatives are weak, wordy, and sinful. Write in grunts.

Excess verbs. Any sentence with *more than one verb* is a target. *Clauses* (a group of words with a verb) can often become *phrases* (a group of words without a verb).

"When the lawyer *was conducting* her cross-examination, the witness got up and left." 14 words.

"During cross-examination, the witness got up and left." 9 words.

Pomposity

People who have to decide, your audience, are not impressed with big words, Latin phrases, or even "party of the first part." They want to know what you know so they can decide. Write to communicate; you are not Lord What's-His–Face nor were meant to be.

Reading for pomposity means looking for big words, long sentences, and the overuse of adjectives, adverbs and intensifiers.

Look for throat-clearing phrases:

At the present time	*now*
In the event of	*if*
In the majority of instances	*usually*
With the exception that	*except*
For the reason that	*because*
In my considered opinion	*I think*

Watch *puffing*. Facts, not volume, convince. The overuse of *intensifiers, adjectives* and *adverbs* is puffing.

The lecture was very boring.

The author is asking us to take her word for it. If the matter is important, she should tell us what *facts* lead to her conclusion. Then we can come to our own conclusion.

During the lecture I went to sleep.

Verbs and nouns tell. Adjectives opine. H.L. Mencken, on writing headlines:

Not: **McGuinnis Lacks Ethical Sense**

Rather: **McGuinnis Steals $1,257,876.25**

Stop Signs

Rereading your prose, be sensitive to constructions that stop the reader mid-sentence such as:

"The promisee will argue that he did not confer the benefit as a gift."

"Who is the promisee here, Mills or Wyman?" Instead:

"The promisee, Mr. Mills, will argue...."

Still your reader stops to think, "Is Mills the father or the guy who helped the son?

"The promisee, Mr. Mills, the man who aided the son, will argue that he did not confer the benefit as a gift."

Good. But what is the benefit we are talking about?

"The promisee, Mr. Mills, the man who aided the son, will argue that he did not confer the benefit, here caring for the son, as a gift."

Write in concrete terms so that the reader will know immediately and without thought whom and what you are talking about.

The plaintiff, the woman injured,....

The respondent, the doctor who filed the false return, ...

Avoid constructions like:

As to the former argument, the plaintiff would argue....

Under Subsection 2a of the Restatement, the promise would not be enforceable.

These constructions *stop* the reader. "Which was the *former* argument?" "What did Subsection 2a provide?" These interruptions are irksome and can be avoided easily. You need not repeat the *entire* former argument; you can usually identify it in two or three words. The same is true in identifying particular subsections.

Under Subsection 2a of the Restatement, dealing with benefits conferred as gifts, the promise would not be enforceable.

Forbidding Text

There is nothing worse than turning a page and seeing nothing but type, type, type. Alice of Wonderland once remarked, "What's the good of a book without pictures?" Unfortunately, in our business, forget pictures.

But still you can make your page visually inviting. White space sells. Indent long quotes. Break up long paragraphs. There is nothing worse than a page full of print and nothing better than an occasional paragraph of one or two sentences. A page with a lot of white is a joy to behold.

'Tis.

CHAPTER 21

ORAL ADVOCACY
(MOOT COURT)

"No, Mommy, please don't send me to my room. I didn't mean to spill it. It slipped. When Ben knocked over his soup, he didn't have to go to his room. Send me to my room only if I'm really bad."

There you have it—the big three, instinctively. Arguing spilt milk in the kitchen or free speech in the Supreme Court, all you have are *facts* (it was an accident), *precedent* (previous leniency toward Ben), and *policy* (the overuse of deterrence). The rest is technique and avoiding passing out.

Just when you get comfortable in law school, they'll spring Moot Court. Assigned to represent one side of an appeal, you'll write a brief and then, as your opponent sits there calmly taking notes, argue for twenty to thirty minutes before, quite likely, a panel of three judges (the original cast of *Men in Black*).

"May it please the Court," you'll begin, building confidence. *"My name is . . . ."* *"Just a minute, Counselor,"* one of judges, the one you thought was the kind one, will interrupt. *"Before you continue, on page 13 of your brief, you cite the*

Myer *case. Now isn't it true that that case is distinguishable because . . ."*

Chaos theory predicts you can't. It proves correct in oral argument. (Of course, it also proves incorrect—that is the nature of paradox). You prepare; you plan; you practice. Finally, it's Opening Night. Then, as you stand before the Court, one question and everything falls apart.

Don't fret. The truth of the matter is that, once we get away from our sterile script and are thrown into the exciting intellectual moment of oral argument, we're better.

An effective legal argument first recognizes that the judges are faced with a difficult legal issue and need your help in coming to a correct solution. This recognition will dictate your technique, the subject of the next chapter. Second, an effective legal argument will address the concerns of the judges. They will likely be concerned with three things: (1) doing justice between the parties (and this usually turns on questions of *fact*), (2) correctly applying existing law, be it statutory or case law (*precedent*), and (3) creating good law (*policy*).

Doing Justice: The Importance of Facts

The statement of facts is "not merely part of the argument, it is more often than not the argument itself. A case well stated is far more than half argued."

Those are the words of John W. Davis, the leading appellate lawyer of his day. One cannot overemphasize the importance of factual perceptions on legal decisions. Judges, bless them, want to do justice, and this often turns on the facts of a given situation.

In litigation, both sides have lived the same basic events. From those events, however, they have come to radically different conclusions. This is because they start with the basic human premise, "I'm right," and then go about viewing the world in a way that supports that premise. The two sides will emphasize different events and will draw different inferences.

Take the case of Edward Charles Davis. He was arrested for shoplifting but never convicted, the charges against him dropped. Thereafter, however, his picture appeared on a flyer showing "active shoplifters," which was distributed by police to local merchants. Davis was not amused; he filed a civil rights action against the police. The United States Supreme Court introduced the case as follows:

Petitioner Paul is the Chief of Police of Louisville, Ky. while petitioner McDaniel occupies the same position in the Jefferson County. They agreed to combine their efforts for the purpose of alerting local area merchants to possible shoplifters who might be operating during the Christmas season. In early December petitioners distributed to approximately 800 merchants in the Louisville metropolitan area a "flyer" [of active shoplifters].

The flyer consisted of five pages of "mug shot" photos, arranged alphabetically. In approximately the center of page 2 there appeared photos and the name of the respondent, Edward Charles Davis III.

Paul v. Davis, 424 U.S. 693.

Who do you think should win this case, Davis or the police?

The case could have been introduced differently, as it was in a law review:

Plaintiff Edward Charles Davis, a photographer for the Louisville Courier–Journal and Times, was arrested in Louisville, Kentucky on a charge of shoplifting. He pled not guilty. The charge was "filed away with leave [to reinstate]," but he was never called upon to face that charge in court. With the onset of the Christmas season defendants McDaniel and Paul, the chiefs of police for Jefferson County and Louisville, jointly prepared a five-page flyer containing the names and mug shots of "Active Shoplifters." Copies of this bulletin were distributed to merchants warning them of possible shoplifters. In fact, the flyer was composed not only of persons actually convicted of shoplifting, but included persons who had been merely arrested. Plaintiff's name and mug shot were included in the flyer.

Who should win this case, Davis or the police?

These two statements, covering much of the same ground, create different impressions. How? Reread them. How to tell a compelling story is a fundamental lawyering skill.

Note that the versions have different protagonists. The Supreme Court version begins with the defendants, both "Chiefs of Police," who were combining efforts to alert local merchants of possible shoplifters. It was, after all, Christmas. The law review version begins with the Mr. Davis, and we immediately learn some sympathetic facts about him: he has an actual job and, although arrested, was never convicted.

As readers we tend to be most sympathetic with the first person we meet, and their viewpoint is apt to become ours. Latecomers usually have an uphill battle in convincing us that we are wrong.

Another thing to note about the two versions is how they deal with unfavorable information. The law review article, up front, stresses that Mr. Davis had not been convicted; the Supreme Court's statement of facts is silent on the issue, at least during the critical first two paragraphs. On the other hand, while the law review article tells us that Mr. Davis's picture was "included in the flyer," only in the Supreme Court version do we learn that Mr. Davis's picture was "in approximately the center of page 2."

Finally note the importance of language. In the law review article, the words "mug shot" are used twice. The Supreme Court does indicate that the flyer contained " 'mug shot' *photos*" but then, when it comes to the actual case of Mr. Davis, states that his "photos" were included.

Jerome Frank, a leading jurist of his day, noted the hypnotic power of words. Why were early common law courts hostile to arbitration clauses in contracts? Because an early judge labeled them an attempt to *"oust"* the jurisdiction of the courts. Well, no one is going to put up with that. Of course, arbitration clauses could have been characterized as *"parties freely choosing an alternative forum"* and, had they been, the emotional charge would flow in the other direction.

Another example of the power of language comes from the Contract doctrine known as the "duty to mitigate." It provides that, if a party continues to perform a contract after the other side has improperly repudiated it, that party cannot claim increased damages. For example, I have a contract with you to paint your house. When I am half way done, you tell me to quit but I go on painting. I cannot sue you for the labor I put in *after* you told me to quit. Professor Williston will tell you that a party cannot *"pile up"* damages and, of course, all right-thinking people would agree with him. However, you could characterize what I was doing was simply *"doing what I promised to do"* and, if this be the characterization, the result might be different.

All of this is not to suggest that either the Supreme Court or the law review author were self-consciously trying to manipulate us by choosing their protagonist, by stressing or downplaying certain facts, or by using certain powerful words. What I am suggesting is that point of view determines in large part what we see. The law review writer "saw" an innocent man getting hurt; it is clear how he or she would have decided the case. Conversely, the majority of the Supreme Court primarily "saw" two government officials doing their jobs in a creative way.

Who's right?

There is a famous gestalt drawing which includes the images of both a young woman and an elderly woman. Some see one, some see the other. *Both are there and no one's right.*

The trick to an effective statement of facts is to get the judges to view the conflict as does your client. Try reading your statement of facts to a nine or ten year old and then asking, "Who should win?" If it isn't your client, redraft!

The danger of trying to tell a convincing story is that you will tend to leave out unfavorable facts. Don't.

How to deal with unfavorable facts? Be honest. The other side will have its say. If you misstate facts or omit important information because it is damaging, the court's sense of sympathy will turn to one of betrayal. If the court trusts you, you are halfway home; if you lose that trust by playing fast and loose with the facts, you might as well stay home.

In a student negotiation role play, one of the "secret" facts we give to the plaintiff's lawyers is that their client, who is claiming substantial personal injuries, has begun to play tennis. Law students tend to (not to put too fine a point on it) lie: "My client is still badly injured." Later, in critique, they will respond, "That wasn't a lie, I didn't say she wasn't playing tennis." Or if they *did* say she wasn't playing tennis, they will argue, "That wasn't a lie; what I meant was that she wasn't playing tennis *right then*."

We had two experienced litigators demonstrate the negotiation. The longtime personal injury lawyer began:

> *"Before we begin, let me tell you something about my client. She is so anxious to overcome the harm inflicted on her by your client that she is even trying to play tennis."*

In practice, when you are asked to either file a lawsuit or take an appeal, think long and hard of the facts and of the law that hurt you. If you cannot somehow turn the facts or distinguish the law, you shouldn't file the lawsuit or take the appeal. The facts and the law won't go away.

Of course, in law school, you can't opt out of Moot Court on the basis that your case is lousy.

If your desire to tell a compelling story may lead you to omit unfavorable facts, your desire to tell a candid story may lead you to include too many: your statement of facts should not read as one long apology. It is perfectly fine to put positive spins on negative facts. And you can omit some negative facts simply on the basis that you cannot include everything. The *test for omission* that I employ: when my opponent brings up the fact, will the court feel a sense of betrayal? Is the fact of such significance that its omission is misleading? Had the Supreme Court never mentioned Davis was not convicted or had the law review writer never mentioned the motivation of the police, I think they would have told essentially misleading stories. Had I heard the original story without being told those facts, I would feel betrayed when I learned them.

Bottom line. In your statement of facts, acknowledge those unfavorable facts that are significant. If possible, as illustrated by the tennis example, try to turn these facts to your advantage. If you can't, still acknowledge them. Trial lawyers attempt to "draw the sting" from unfavorable facts by mentioning them before their opponent does. "Well, if the plaintiff's lawyer brought up this matter of his client playing tennis, it can't be too bad." The same principal applies in oral advocacy.

One final point concerning your statement of facts: use verbs and nouns, not adverbs or adjectives, and stick to the facts rather than resort to pleas for justice. If justice is really on your side, your proclaiming it in a grand sweeping manner won't convince the court. Facts might. Look at the two statements in *Davis*. Neither statement resorted to adjectives or pleas, and yet each convinced the reader of very different positions.

A compelling factual statement motivates the court to rule in your favor; now you must establish a rationale that permits it to do so. You must discuss both the past (precedent) and the future (policy).

Following the Law: Arguing Cases and Statutes

Courts must follow the rules of law announced in prior controlling decisions (those of higher courts in the jurisdiction) unless (1) those decisions are distinguishable or (2) the court is willing to overrule those prior decisions, something courts are loath to do.

Chapter Two describes how one goes about distinguishing cases. To review:

> *The rule of law announced in a case (its holding or black letter) is announced in a specific factual context and is justified by a particular rationale. To distinguish a case (so the rule of law would not apply in the case at hand), you can argue either that the facts are essentially different or that the rationale does not apply. Conversely, you can argue a case should apply by analogy by pointing out that, even though the facts are essentially different, the rationale of the case would apply.*

Given the operation of *stare decisis*, we can conclude:

1. *If precedent is with you, you're favored.* Convince the court the prior cases are indistinguishable and you win—unless, of course, the court is willing to overrule those cases.

Against the overruling of precedent you have several powerful stock arguments:

a. Overruling in *this* instance is a bad idea because people relied on the rule announced in prior decisions. It may open prison doors or subject people to liability for acts that were previously immune.

b. Overruling in *any* instance is a bad idea because it rejects the wisdom of the past and creates uncertainty in the legal order. The more decisions that are reversed, the less any can be relied upon.

2. *If precedent is against you, try harder.* Even if you convince the court that the prior cases are distinguishable, you still are not a winner. All you have done is show the court it *need not* apply the rule to your case. Now you must, citing reasons of policy, convince the court that it *should not*.

Courts must follow controlling *statutes* as well. Often they come as statements of law without a factual context and without a rationale. If the language of the statute is ambiguous, you must posit a legislative purpose and then, given that purpose, interpret the language. I have described this process in greater detail in Chapter 5.

When dealing with a statute, the first choice is to argue that it can be interpreted so as to support your position. Only as a last resort should you argue that a statute be declared unconstitutional and this is for many of the same reasons that your last choice is to argue that a prior case be overruled.

Courts are much more comfortable deciding on narrow grounds. Argue for a case to be overturned, or a statute to be declared unconstitutional, only if you have no other choice. The only exception to this conservative approach is in a case where the cause is more important than the case. *Brown v. Board of Education* involved the schools in Toledo. However, it was vastly more important to get the Supreme Court to reject the notion that "separate can be equal" than it was to integrate the Toledo schools on the basis that they were in violation of the "separate but equal" standard.

One error in arguing controlling law is to forget that the judges will also be interested in doing justice between the parties and in creating good precedent. Even where a statute or case is on your side, don't just cite it and then sit down:

"The rule is X and I win."

You must *motivate the court* to follow rule X; tell the court why rule X is a just rule and why it advances sound public policy.

For example, if you are raising a Statute of Frauds defense to a oral contract, don't just point to the statute, tell the court that it must refuse to enforce the agreement and then, raising your arms, begin your victory lap around the courtroom. Tell the court why refusing to enforce the oral contract is a good idea; tell the court how the Statute of Frauds protects important social interests. Otherwise, who knows? There are exceptions to the Statute of Frauds, and the court is always interested in doing justice.

Creating Good Law: Arguing Policy

Under the doctrine of stare decisis, whatever the court decides will become precedent for future cases. Judges will be concerned not only with doing justice between the parties before them and following prior cases and statutes, but also with creating a good rule of law to guide future judges. The question is not only why your client should win, but also why all persons in the same situation as your client should win.

> *Will the "rule" you ask for produce justice or chaos?*

> *Is the "rule" operational in the sense that juries can understand it, lawyers can work with it, and other legal functionaries can administer it?*

Policy arguments are limited only by the imagination of the lawyers. For example, in a case brought by a cancer patient against a tobacco company, the company's lawyer can argue that it would be good policy to deny recovery on the basis that people should take responsibility for their actions; the lawyer for the patient can argue that it would be good policy to allow recovery as it would send a message as to the dangers of tobacco.

There are two kinds of policy arguments that need to be addressed: *Slippery Slopes* and *Floodgates*.

*"If we invalidate this lease clause which excul-
pates the landlord from liability for negligence,
the next thing you know we'll have all kinds of
tenants in here demanding that we rewrite their
leases, even the amount of rent."*

As I explained in Chapter 4, there are *three* responses to all slippery slope arguments. Write them out—
they will be on the final. (Yeah, but if *they* are on
the final, then *everything* will be on the final.)

1. *All slippery slope arguments are reversible.*
   Knowing this, you can at least make an offensive feint.

   *"If you refuse to invalidate this clause, then
   landlords will insist that you enforce the most
   repugnant of clauses. 'They agreed to forfeit
   their firstborn in the event of late payment; it
   says so in clause 43(F)(iv), and this court
   doesn't rewrite leases!'"* (If *this* point isn't on
   the final, then *nothing* will be on the final.)

2. *Most slopes have dumps*—things to grab on to.
   Here you show how future judges can distinguish the madness you are asking the court to
   pursue.

   *"Your Honor, this exculpatory clause is unique
   in that it relieves the landlord from liability for
   personal injury. There is a strong policy to
   encourage landowners to take reasonable steps
   to avoid such injury. No such policy is involved
   in other lease terms, surely not the amount of
   rent."* (Because the three responses to slippery

slopes are so essential, if they are on the final, nothing else need be.)

3. *Or you can take the slide all the way down.*

   "Your Honor, now that you mention it, that would not be such a bad idea." (Come to think of it, everything *should* be on the final.)

"Opening the floodgates" is a particularly virulent and repugnant form of slippery slope.

   "If we do justice to your client, why then all kinds of ragamuffins will be coming in here to demand justice!"

You now know how to cope.

   "Your Honor, if you refuse to do justice to my client, you will never do justice to anyone." (Reversing the slippery slope.)

   "Your Honor, doing justice for ragamuffins might not be a bad idea." (Sliding all the way down.)

Probably here the best approach is option three: finding a dump to grab.

   "Your Honor, not to worry. Only rich folks know where you are."

To review, your goals in Moot Court are modest: convince the court that fairness between the parties means your client wins, fidelity to precedent means your client wins, and writing great law means your client wins. Simple enough. But how to get from here to there? Turn the page.

CHAPTER 22

MECHANICS OF ORAL ARGUMENT

What's the most important thing? "A sincere and single desire to be helpful to the Court."

John W. Davis, appellate lawyer, extraordinaire

Be helpful to the Court? How can this be? Isn't your job to win? Perhaps Davis winked. Perhaps one should feign "help" as a clever technique but, by all means, close the sale.

In preparing your case, you will have spent a long time sorting out the facts, wrestling with the law and considering the policies at stake. Because you have done so from the perspective of your client, you have come to believe that a careful consideration of those factors should lead the court to rule in your favor. If you don't believe that, with one exception I will discuss momentarily, you shouldn't—at least in real life—be pursuing the case.

Your job is not to force the court to come to your conclusion but to help it see how you came to it. Any case worth its salt will be close. In real life, the Court wants to come to the correct decision and needs your help in sorting out the law and facts.

They will not know the facts nor the law nearly as well as you do. The judges need your guidance through the thickets.

Judges don't need dazzle, mirrors or bullying. And they don't need sophistry, pathos or bathos.

What judges need is (1) candor, (2) focus on the two or three main points which will swing their decision and (3) discussion of the points that concern them, not those that concern you.

Candor

If you are committed to helping the court, you will:

1. Concede the valid points the opponent raises. "Yes, my opponent is correct, the case did hold that. However, we believe that it is distinguishable."

2. Listen to the Court's concerns and respond to them; don't ignore or deny them. "Yes, if you were to hold for my client, certain expectations may be upset. However, we believe that they may not be as extensive as feared because of the following limiting features."

3. Acknowledge the closeness of the contest. "I wish the cases were more clear in this area, but they are not. A fair reading of them, I submit, supports my position because...."

4. Cite and discuss cases and statutes that tend to go against your position, even if your opponent hasn't. The Rules of Professional Con-

duct require citation of adverse "controlling authority." This is a fairly narrow requirement. You should go further. As an officer of the court, you don't want the court to render a judgment upon ignorance. If you don't have good arguments to get around the contrary rulings, *you shouldn't be there.*

5. Admit it if you don't know the answer to a question. If you flounder around trying to invent something, you will just dig a deeper hole, wasting everyone's time. Better to admit you do not know or do not have a good answer and then go on with your argument, thus suggesting that you do not believe the question is determinative.

A caveat on criminal defense. In order to protect the rights of the accused, criminal defense lawyers are allowed much more room to advance arguments that stink. "Your Honor, my client is charged with violating a statute that prohibits 'obtaining money by false pretenses.' I move for a directed verdict as the state has only proved *one* pretense." Enough said.

If you have the wrong attitude, if you are *not* committed to helping the court, if you are selling used cars, you will:

1. Take no prisoners. Deny every point the opposition makes.

2. Attack one's opponent. Personal attacks ("If my worthy opponent bothered to read the cases") are never justified.

Should you argue points you don't believe? No!
But I used to be more sure. Argue a point you don't
believe, and likely your lack of belief will come
across and undermine your overall credibility
("This lawyer doesn't want to help me; this lawyer
wants to make a fool of me"). Further, during oral
argument you don't have much time, and it is
probably best to stick with your winners. If you
can't convince yourself, it is doubtful that you will
convince others. On the other hand, I have seen
courts buy arguments that I thought were foolish
(but, then again, I wasn't the one arguing them).

Focus

Beginners want to cover everything they wrote in
their brief. "That point in footnote twenty-three
sparkles!" Keeping their heads down, talking fast
and dreading interruption, they sprint towards footnote twenty-three!

John W. Davis pointed out that most appeals turn
on two or three main points, some on one. Focus on
them; don't clutter your argument and waste your
time by trying to get in everything you said in your
brief. Note the major difference between written
and oral advocacy. Briefs should cover all the points
while oral presentations should focus on those that
matter.

Davis advised, "going for the jugular." He was
writing in a time when people still ate meat. Today,
while we are enriched with vegetables, we are im-
poverished with metaphors. "Go for the broccoli."

Address the Court's Concerns, Not Yours

When the forward pass was introduced to football, one traditional coach said that of the three possibilities, two are bad. Ditto oral argument.

Keeping your head down, you are earnestly arguing a particular point. The possibilities are:

1. The judges are not convinced of your position and *never* will be; thus you are wasting your time.

2. The judges are *already* convinced of your position; thus you are wasting your time.

3. The judges are *undecided* about your point and *need* further guidance.

How can you make sure it is 3, not 1 or 2?

In an ideal world you could simply stop and ask, "Well, Your Honors, have I convinced you on that one yet? If not, do I have a prayer?" But oral argument is highly stylized, and you can't make this move. Rather, you will have to get the judges asking you questions so that you can address their concerns.

Some judges will pepper you with questions. Others are reticent, too shy to interrupt, too unsure to voice their concerns. So, how do you draw them out?

Invite interruption.

> "I'll discuss the following three issues in the following order. But first, does the Court have any questions?"

"That finishes my discussion of the collateral estoppel issue. Are there any questions before I go on?"

Never tell the judge to shut up.

Seldom do lawyers actually come straight out and do this. They are more subtle:

"Your Honor, I will answer that question in a few minutes. Right now I would like to spend a few minutes throwing interceptions."

Always answer a judge's question when it is asked.

Encourage questions.

When the judges ask you questions, not only will you be able to address their concerns, but also your performance will improve. Watch oral arguments. Lawyers are almost always better when they are responding to questions than when they are giving their speeches. There is movement, creation, engagement. The only time this is not so is when the lawyer hasn't anticipated the question and doesn't have a clue. *Rehearse questions.* You should be able to anticipate many of them: "Your opponent, in his brief, argues that.... and I find that's an interesting point. How do you respond?"

How to encourage questions.

(1) Want them

Judges are people too, and human interaction is a subtle thing. If you fear questions, likely you won't get many. If you rejoice in them, they will come. *To get questions, you have to* want *questions.* Convince yourself that they will make you free and will add life and zip to your presentation.

(2) Maintain eye contact

Sure, the flag does look nice, but only by looking at the judges will you sense what points are important. *Never read* your argument. Have a list of three or four major points and perhaps some citations you want to get right. When preparing your argument, you probably should write it out. Writing slows and focuses the mind. But once you have a draft, reduce it to its essentials and use it as a crib sheet during argument. Dollars to donuts, you won't even need it.

(3) Forget footnote twenty-three

Give up on the notion that you need to cover everything. In real life, there is dispute as to the value of oral argument. Perhaps most cases are won or lost long before, "May it please the Court." But even if oral argument matters, no judge has changed her mind simply because counsel was able to squeeze in one last point, a point which, of course, has already been argued in the brief.

The Structure of Appellate Argument

1. ***Introduce yourself and the client you represent.***

   "May it please the court, my name is D. Vader and I represent Allprovidence Insurance, the

defendant in the action below and petitioner here."

2. **State the nature of the case** (contract, tort, criminal) **and briefly describe its procedural history**.

"This is a suit on a life insurance policy on the life of Mr. Humpty Dumpty, brought by his widow. Our defense is that suit is barred by a suicide clause. At trial, it was our contention that Humpty did not have a 'great fall,' but rather that he took a 'great leap.' After a jury trial, judgment was for the plaintiff. We appeal on the basis that, first, the judge improperly applied the 'plain meaning rule' and, second, improperly excluded the testimony of one of the King's men concerning Humpty's dying declaration."

3. **State the facts of the case**. Remember they are extremely important.

"In order to protect the widows and orphans, the true owners of Allprovidence, and in order to discourage suicide, the Allprovidence Insurance Company routinely includes a suicide clause in its policy, which bars recovery if the decedent took his own life. In this case . . . . "

In stating the facts, remember that the judges have read your brief and thus don't need all the facts recounted. Keep it short and succinct, focusing on the important and determinative facts. Even then, the court will cut you off with, "We are familiar with the facts, proceed with argument." But, given the importance of the statement of facts, don't go up there expecting the court to cut you off or inviting it to: "Does the court want to hear the facts?" Walk to the podium expecting and wanting to tell your story.

4. **State the legal issues and preview the points you intend to argue**. A clear introduction to your legal argument is critical. Otherwise the judges may not follow it.

"It is our contention that the court below erred in applying the Plain Meaning Rule to Nursery Rhymes, thus preventing our argument that 'had a great fall' can be read as meaning 'took a great leap.' Unfortunately, the Yokel below is unfamiliar with Critical Legal Studies and trendy French Literary Criticism which suggests that texts can be read any way one wants.

*"Further, and as an **independent justification for reversal**, we assert the court below improperly excluded, as hearsay, Humpty's remark to one of the King's men, 'Being an egg I never got any respect. So I made myself an omelet.' Although hearsay, we submit that it should have been admitted either as a dying declaration or as state of mind. Which issue do you wish me to address first?"*

5. **Argue the case**. As with your written work, your oral argument will be improved by the effective use of transitions.

Not: *"The next issue concerns the admissibility of Humpty's dying declaration."*

But: *"That concludes my discussion of the Plain Meaning Rule. Unless there are any questions, I would like to now address the matter of Humpty's dying declaration.* **Even if** *this court decides that the court properly applied the Plain Meaning Rule,* **it must reverse** *this case if it finds that the testimony was improperly excluded."*

As more fully described in the chapter on legal writing, *RILS* transitions are best: they *R*elate the new topic to the last; *I*ntroduce it, and show its *L*egal *S*ignificance.

Note that the **relationship** between legal points can be either "and" or "or." That is, the relationship between the plain meaning point and the jury instruction point could either be that the insurance company has to prevail on both to win or, as is the case, on either one. The phrase "even if" captures that relationship in the above example. It is critical, given the law's complexity, to make these relations clear.

Note that you should make clear the **legal significance** of the topic you are introducing. Here you are introducing the matter of the jury instructions and, if you are correct as to this point, the court **must reverse** the lower court. This is so much stronger than just introducing the subject.

The more *explicit* your argument, the more you *tie law and fact* together, and the more *concrete examples* you use, the clearer your argument will be. Consult the chapter on legal writing for further explanation of these hallmarks of clarity.

6.   *Rejoice* if the court asks you questions.

7.   Tell the court what you want it *to do*. Do you want the court to remand the case to the trial court and order a new trial? Do you want an order for some particular relief? It is surprising how often lawyers, about to conclude their argument, cannot answer, "Assuming we agree with your position on the law, what do you want us to do? Let's assume you've won. What should the last paragraph of our opinion say?"

8.   *Conclude and sit down*. In many appellate courts, you are allotted a certain amount of time. There is no requirement, however, that you use it all. If you are done, sit down. Many first-year students do brilliantly until the end. Then, not having not thought of a spiffy ending line, they thrash about aimlessly, repeating bits of prior arguments. Write and rehearse your last line. What do you want to leave the court with?

"Yes, Humpty was a good egg. But courts should not reward despair. Had Humpty realized his widow would not recover, he would still be with us and all the King's men would not have been shown to be incompetent."

Appellate arguments require clear introductions, clear transitions and clear summaries. This means repetition. Repetition is a virtue. As listeners, we can't go back to see how the arguments fit together. Often our minds wander. "What's for lunch?" Repetition is needed. Realize, too, that the judges, no matter how prepared, will not have the same familiarity with the law as you do. Give them a break and don't jump to the heart of your argument, which may turn on a rather fine point of law. Put that argument in context. As with legal writing, *begin with the basics*: "The Plain Meaning Rule basically provides that. . . ." rather than "The Plain Meaning Rule shouldn't apply here because. . . ." The latter construction forces the judges to go back and think, "What is the Plain Meaning Rule?" There is simply no need for them to have to do this. By the way, what is the "latter" construction and what's the problem with the word "latter"?

A Few Pointers on Delivery and on Not Passing Out

1. *Be flexible*. When you move away from your prepared script, you are always a better speaker because you move into the moment. Questions force you to do this. Going second affords great opportunities for spontaneity. Listening to your opponent not only gets your mind off the fact that you are sitting on the *Titanic*, but also allows you to begin your argument with a spontaneous response. The best arguments are a flurry of counterpunches triggered by an opponent's low blow.

2. *Get used to silence.* One of the hardest things to do is to stand before the court, with all eyes on you, trying to collect your thoughts. Two or three seconds *feel* like an eternity. But to everyone else in the room, they feel like two or three seconds. Pauses can highlight. There is *no* need for you to be making noise *all* the time. When asked a question, *don't* immediately reply. Think about your answer. Occasionally, "That's a very good question which I hadn't considered. Let me think a few moments."

3. *Don't assume all questions are hostile.* Judges can ask questions because they need help or *because they want to help you out.* Seldom is their goal to humiliate.

4. *Avoid monotone.* Vary your volume, speed and pitch. Not everything you have to say is of equal status.

5. *A sense of humor helps.* Don't tell jokes but realize that you aren't on the *Titanic.* While it is your only case, no doubt the judges have heard several and, frankly, this stuff gets tedious. You have no idea how welcome a funny line can be.

6. *Don't read long quotes to the court.* If you quote specific language from a statute or opinion, refer to the page in your brief where you quote the language so that the judges can sing along. If specific language is key, for example, in a case interpreting a statute, put

it on a large chart that can be put on an easel during argument.

Coping with nervousness. While sitting there, stop thinking, "Oh no, I'm next!" One way to cope with nervousness is to get your mind off yourself. Concentrate on your opponent's argument while he argues. Listen to what the judges ask him, and watch the judges when he responds. You may want to change your argument in light of what you hear and see. While you argue, concentrate on the argument, not on how you are doing.

Remember to breathe. Nervousness often leads to shallow breathing, which leads to oxygen deficiency, which leads to more nervousness, which leads to death. Take deep breaths; relax your jaw and the back of your neck.

You appear much less nervous than you feel. As for your smug opponent and mighty judges—they are jelly.

Defining and stating your intention. Ultimately the problem of nervousness stems from confusion as to what you are about. In making an oral argument to a court, your goal is not really "don't be the fool," nor is it even to "appear brilliant." Your goal, your intention, should be to convince specific people, the judges, of specific factual or legal conclusions. State your intention to yourself just before you get up there.

"My intention is to help Binder, Boland and Bergman understand why the lower court didn't understand the Plain Meaning Rule. Further,

> *my intention is to get them asking me questions.*"

If you are clear on your intention, then your demeanor, gestures and words will tend to reinforce that intention without conscious effort on your part. Thus you won't have to worry about what you should do with your hands or about talking too softly.

On Teaching Yourself

Anytime you actually do something is a great opportunity for learning. Most of us don't take advantage; we simply go on to our next chore. In the old days, when giants staggered the earth, we would go out for a drink.

After Moot Court, sit down and ask yourself what you have learned from the experience. What have you learned about oral argument? What have you learned about preparation and delivery? What have you learned about getting judges to ask you questions? What have you learned about the adversary process and the law? What have you learned about yourself? And, of course, what have you learned about chaos theory?

A variation on this theme is to list, before your argument, the criteria by which you will evaluate yourself. This will force you to do some serious thinking about the process of argument rather than the substance of your argument.

This is general advice. We all talk about teaching ourselves, but we seldom do anything about it. After your first law school exam, after your first client interview, after your first Supreme Court argument, after you have captured every electoral vote but Maine's, sit down and ask yourself: "What went well and why?" "What went badly and why?"

Now, what have I learned from writing this chapter?

Good question, but, right now, I have get on to the next.

PART FIVE

THE GREAT HEREAFTER

The rush and intensity of the first year become the calm of the second and third. Gone the fear and anxiety born of uncertainty. You will know what is expected both in class and on exams. It will be time for you to take stock.

The first two chapters of this part focus on your second and third years, courses and activities. My main point will be that law school offers you rich opportunities that will not pass your way again: a talented faculty, interested and interesting classmates, and issues that matter. My advice is somewhat biblical: time to put away childish things. For a long time you studied hard to advance yourself, to get into a good college, to get into a good law school. From now on, it is not about yourself, it is about your future clients, those folks who will come to you in times of great need. Be as prepared as you can be.

The last two chapters focus on career choices. In the first, I generally describe choices and considerations. In the second, lawyers from various kinds of practices describe what they do, day in, day out.

CHAPTER 23

THE SECOND AND THIRD YEARS: COURSE SELECTION

So many courses; so little time.

At most law schools, after a rigid first year curriculum, the faculty simply gives up and, with a shrug, sighs "Whatever."

So with your new freedom, what courses should you take in your last two years? First, realize that your legal education does not end with law school. There are bar review courses that help prepare you for the bar and thus lessen the need to take all the "bar" courses in law school. Many state bars require practicing lawyers to take Continuing Legal Education (CLE) courses and thus lessen the need to take every course in law school that you think you will need in practice. And, of course, there will be scads and scads of on-the-job training.

"What does law school offer that bar review courses, CLE programs, and practice don't?"

Let's begin with tough theoretical courses and a war story.

On Theoretical Legal Education

It was the 1960's in the small town of Americus, Georgia. Congress had recently passed the Voting Rights Act, and it was to have an immediate impact. Americus was holding an election for Justice of the Peace and, for the first time since Reconstruction, black citizens were going to vote. In fact, a black woman had decided to run for the office herself.

On the momentous day, when she arrived at the voting place, there were two lines, one marked "Colored." She stood in the "White" line. The deputy sheriff who arrested her was incredulous at being asked why he had done so. He testified, "I ain't completely color blind, you know." I'll never forget that; sitting in the courtroom, I remembered reading in a Supreme Court case, "Our Constitution is color blind."

Between my second and third year in law school, I worked as a summer intern for C.B. King of Albany, Georgia, who was then one of the two black lawyers in the state. C.B. wanted me to research the law to see if we could get a court to throw out the election and make them do it over; make them do it right. I looked up the cases on election irregularities and election fraud (mostly from Chicago).

"C.B., we've had it. You can't challenge the election. The law is clear. Unless the illegalities affected the result, it stands. Given the fact that the incumbent got 83 of the 95 votes, we can't allege that."

C.B. simply sat and stared. Didn't say a word.

I went back to my desk and went into a funk. "Why had I gone to law school? A monkey could have looked up those cases and reported the bad news to C.B. Why had I sat in class for two years, struggling, if I couldn't even try to use the law to do the right thing?"

I went back to the cases. Maybe they could be distinguished. Indeed, maybe there would be language in those cases suggesting that if the controversy wasn't simply about dead people voting, the rule might be different.

I sat and thought and read and reread. And yes, eventually I was able to distinguish those cases and, yes, I even found language to support our position.

I went back to C.B. This time he smiled.

A year later, under federal court order, the small town of Americus had another election. The same guy won, but this time: one line.

———————

Sitting where you are sitting, I thought I was learning the law, and I was often confused and resentful. But I now know I wasn't sitting there to learn the law; I was there to get ready for that hot summer in Georgia.

Push yourself in law school. Take hard courses, for the challenge. Don't run away from tough profs, and don't tune out those "nice" theoretical discussions in law school. They won't be easy, and you won't understand them all. Stay awake. Down the road there will be other hot summers.

Course Selection

Substantive Courses

Like the fact that the sun will eventually blow up, the bar exam is a nagging background concern. Almost all states require a bar exam, which usually is given in late July after you graduate and takes two or three days. Some, in terms of passage rate, are easier than others. Although there is a common core of subjects examined, states vary as to other subjects. The good news is that at the end of your first year, you have already taken the basic bar courses.

Why bring up this unpleasant fact? Isn't it enough to know that the sun is going to blow up? Many students use their time in law school trying to take as many "bar courses" as they can. While these courses are often important in their own right, realize that, after graduation, there will be *bar review courses* that cover the required subjects. As to some subjects, you may wish to pick up the essentials in such courses and devote your law school time to other endeavors.

Other students focus on courses they "know" they will need in the area of law they plan to practice. If you think you know what kind of law you want to practice, surely take some courses in the field to test whether you like it. However, it is foolish to over-specialize during law school. Career interests can and often do change.

There are substantive courses that every "well-rounded" law student should take, if for no other reason than to requite yourself gracefully at cocktail parties (if there are such things anymore). Friends read the paper, and they will ask you basic questions dealing with *Evidence, Corporations, Federal Tax,* and *Constitutional Law.* You wouldn't want to graduate from college, for example, without knowing that at one time not all was well between the states.

Professors

Every law school has a group of truly remarkable teachers. Take as many as you can, not only for their knowledge but also for their style. Some stick closely to the "black letter," while others spin off into the realms of philosophy, economics, and social theory; with some, classes are like boot camp, and, with others, like encounter groups. Sitting there, you are learning more than "Federal Jurisdiction" or "UCC." You are learning how one lawyer approaches and solves problems, uses and communicates knowledge, treats and reacts to people. When it comes your time to do these things, the more models you have, the better.

Take professors you disagree with, the fascists or communists on your faculty. Even without a list, you know who they are. If you take only professors you agree with, you won't be prepared for the ill winds that will surely blow.

Writing Courses

> *"Saturday Night Live" had a mock interview with the extremely prolific author, Steven King. During the interview King typed away, all the time looking at the interviewer and never once at his typewriter. At the end of the interview he was asked, "What are you writing now?"*
>
> *"Let me see," he said, looking down.*

The more you write, the better you will write. Sure, feedback is good, and good feedback is better. However, practice makes perfect.

Most lawyers write for a living, drafting contracts, writing opinion letters and briefs. Even trial lawyers must write trial briefs, and even entertainment lawyers must review contracts. The best way to improve your writing is to write. Take at least one course requiring *extensive research and writing* even if (particularly if) you dread it.

Seminars and Problem Courses

These courses are a refreshing break from the traditional three-cases-and-you're-out courses. They also give you a real sense of lawyering: lawyers don't learn the law, they use the law.

Skills Courses

A recent addition to most law school curriculums are "skills courses," such as trial advocacy, client interviewing, and negotiation. Of the lot, I think the most pressing is trial advocacy, where you do mock trials. Trying a lawsuit gives you a different and more profound understanding of law. This understanding is particularly important if you have vowed never to enter a courtroom as a lawyer.

Approach a simulated skills course with reckless abandon. *Don't Be Yourself.* As Mark Twain once said, "Be yourself" is the worst advice you can give some people.

Do you really know who you are? Who you can be? In skills courses, take a chance and be someone else. If you are shy, yell and pound your shoe on the table. Break out. You never know.

Clinics

Many states have "student practice rules" that allow second or third year students to represent clients in court under the supervision of a fully licensed lawyer. Most law schools take advantage of these rules by having clinical programs. Some are "placement" programs where students work under lawyers at public prosecutors' or defenders' offices. Other schools have "in-house" programs where members of the faculty do the supervision.

I don't think there is a better opportunity to learn ethics and problem-solving than in the clinical setting. Don't leave home without one. But why do in law school what you will do once you graduate? Because of your point of view. Once you graduate and go into practice, the *doing* overwhelms the *questioning*; gone is the time for cool reflection and the challenging of assumptions.

If you take a clinic, consider the role of an anthropologist living with the natives. During the day, do your job, work the pots. At night, sneak off to your tent and get out your pencil:

1. Are lawyers happy?

2. Are they bitterly adverse to each other, or is the practice of law something of a country club affair?

3. Why do some witnesses seem more believable than others? What arguments seem to impress judges?

4. Does the system produce justice? Does it work the way your professors *think* it does?

5. What are the most important skills for a lawyer to have?

Perspective Courses

Often what we learn we take as inevitable. It is only by getting outside of the status quo that we can realize its contingent and political nature. In comparative law courses, in legal history courses, you are not learning about the law of Brazil or the law of the Colonial Period; you are learning about our law, today.

Without contrasts we can't see.

Some Final Thoughts on Legal Education

In my first year Contracts class I gave my students a hypothetical. Seller is continually late in making his deliveries. Buyer, after pleas and much patience, finally cancels the contract. After stating the problem, I asked:

"If you were Seller, what would you say?"

I was looking for a discussion of the various legal theories which throw Buyer into breach for canceling the contract, legal arguments which would allow Seller to crush Buyer.

I looked around the room. As is so often the case with first year students, they were all writing in their notebooks or inspecting their shoes. There was, however, one eager face, that of the eight-year-old son of one of my students. He had been biding his time, drawing pictures. Suddenly he raised his hand. Such behavior, even from an eight-year old, must be rewarded.

"Okay," I said, "What would you say if you were Seller?"

"I'd say, 'I'm sorry'."

———

As Professor William Simon once remarked, legal education presents a caricature of human existence. Plaintiffs want more money and prosecutors want more time; civil defendants want to escape all liability and criminal defendants simply want to escape. In the hundreds and hundreds of case you will read, there are very few heroes.

Holmes once wrote that law students should study the law from the perspective of the "bad man"—the class bully who has no regard for morality and is only interested in what he can get away with. No doubt this is a great learning strategy. But don't confuse either the caricature or the bad man with life.

One of my first clients came to me with a problem with a consumer contract. After the interview, I did some research and, at our next meeting, triumphantly advised:

"You don't have to pay any more on this bill! I have found several legal violations. We can get your money back, you can keep what you bought, and we can sue the store for punitive damages!"

My client looked at me. "But I bought it and I owe the money. I just want you to help work out a payment schedule."

One of our chores as lawyers is to help people say "I'm sorry."

CHAPTER 24

LAW REVIEW, CLERKING, PRO BONO ACTIVITIES AND A SHORT HISTORY OF AMERICAN LEGAL EDUCATION

In this chapter you will learn of many delightful things, of the strange and wondrous institution of law review (and of its stifling prose), of the history of American legal education, and of the marvelous opportunities for you actually to do some good in the universe.

Law schools are rich in opportunities. If yours is part of a university, there will be a variety of cultural events to remind you there is more to life than figuring out who gets a decedent's stuff. And some of you will write for the law review, others will earn money clerking for law firms, and still others will do *pro bono* work, perhaps helping out at legal aid, teaching law-related courses in high schools, or delivering meals-on-wheels to the elderly.

I'll begin with law review.

Law Review

In the sixties, a young mother lay dying in a Washington D.C. hospital. Doctors determined that the only way to save her life was by giving her a blood transfusion. She refused; she was a Jehovah Witness, and her religion prohibited transfusions. Doctors approached Judge Skelly Wright of the United States Court of Appeals. Judge Wright was one of the most respected judges of his time. (He authored the unconscionability case, *Williams v. Walker–Thomas*, which we discussed in Chapter 8.) Judge Wright, after no doubt much anguish, authorized the blood transfusion and thereafter wrote an opinion justifying his decision.

Not long afterward, as a second year law student, in my early twenties, I wrote a law review note on his decision. While I did find some serious flaws with his reasoning and, quite frankly, a few questionable analogies, by and large Judge Wright won my approval.

Other law students, writing for other law reviews, tore him apart.

What's going on here? What qualified us to be Judges of the Universe?

Good grades in Property!

Law reviews present a mind-boggling affront. Law students write articles criticizing (or praising) judges. No one is safe from our razor wit: from intermediate state appellate judges to the Chief Justice of the United States Supreme Court. Talk about the need for blood transfusions. Do second year medical students crowd around operation tables and then fault the procedures of heart-transplant teams? Do budding young scientists trash Einstein?

That beginners can play on the same field as veterans is one of the curious facts about the law. Whether this is a good or bad thing I'll leave to you. It does, however, tend to put the lie to Holmes' famous dictum:

The life of the law is not logic, it is experience.

This routine critique of the judiciary by law review students may be seen as playing an important institutional role. Confronted with the argument that judges can do whatever they like, some academics have defended the judiciary by saying that the fact that judges must write opinions justifying their decisions keeps them intellectually honest. Law reviews are the only institution we have that routinely critiques the work of courts.

There is another institutional role that law reviews play that is more problematic. We all know (some of us better than others) that in the academic world, it is publish or perish. While most academics (English profs) publish in journals refereed by experts in their field (English profs), law professors publish mostly in law reviews. Who decides what gets published? Student editors. Are these editors qualified to pass on the quality and importance of legal scholarship (and hence decide, in at least in some measure, who gets tenure and who doesn't)? Absolutely! They are *third* year.

Even when these editors publish works on important topics (and they frequently do), they insist on the long stylistic tradition of law-review-drab. In 1936, Yale Law Professor Fred Rodell wrote a delightful essay, *"Goodbye to Law Reviews."*

> *There are two things wrong with almost all legal writing. One is style. The other is content. It seems to be a cardinal principle of law review writing and editing that nothing may be said forcefully and nothing may be said amusingly. This, I take it, is in the interest of something called dignity. It does not matter that most people—and even lawyers come into this category—read either to be convinced or to be entertained. It does not matter that even in the comparatively rare instances when people read to be informed, they like a dash of pepper or a dash of salt along with their information. They won't get any seasoning if the law reviews can help it. The law reviews would rather be dignified and ignored.*

If you ever get to be a law review editor, first, my congratulations. Second, lighten up. Otherwise I'll never get published. (One of my early mentors once advised me, "Never change your style, even if it means getting published.")

But I digress.

Most law schools publish law reviews. Several law schools have more than one. It is a honor to be asked to write for law review. Membership is based on good grades or on a writing competition. It is hard work but quite worthwhile. As a second year student, you will be asked to write a note or comment, either on a recent case or on developments in

a particular area of law. Thus you will be involved
in the law's development. Lawyers and judges read
student notes, and your work may influence actual
decisions. Your work will be extensively edited (by a
student editor), and you will come away with a
feeling of how hard it is (and how satisfying) to
produce good work. And, of course, having written
for the review helps come interview time.

Don't make too much about law review. If you
don't make it, realize that most famous lawyers
didn't either. At a UCLA alumni party in a beauti-
ful Malibu home overlooking the Pacific, the owner
walked over to his old Torts Professor, "Good to see
you, Prof. This is what a 'D' in Torts gets you."

Clerking and A Short History of
American Legal Education

Many second and third year law students clerk
for lawyers during school. Generally this involves
legal research. Some professors advise against clerking, as it will surely compete with class work. It also
diminishes the quality of life in the school: with
many law students involved in clerking, there is less
energy for law review, interest clubs, speaker programs and school plays.

My take on it is that it is fine. Many students
need the money. And a good clerkship, just like a
good clinical experience, can be quite educational.

Most lawyers like spunk. If you are going to clerk,
consider negotiating a meaningful clerking experience. The ideal is where you are closely supervised,

where you get feedback, and where the tasks are varied: not *always* arcane memos, sometimes interviewing witnesses, sometimes observing trials, and sometimes depositions.

So what else is there to say about clerking? Not much, except to say that the debate about its propriety reflects a very important division in thinking about legal education: is it better to learn law from books or from working in the vineyards? This debate continues today over the role of clinical legal education. The remainder of this section puts that debate in its historical context.

In the old days, there was *only* clerking; there were no law schools and no LSAT. See, generally, Milton, *Paradise Lost*.

After working several years as an apprentice, the novice took the bar and that was that. When the first law schools were started, they *supplemented* apprenticeship; apprentices worked in law offices in the daytime and gathered at night to hear lectures on legal principles. Slowly law schools took over more turf: eventually they became *alternatives* to apprenticeship, and novices became eligible to take the bar by either route.

The key year in legal education is 1870. Christopher Columbus Langdell became dean of the Harvard Law School. Langdell faced a real problem: how to make law school academically respectable. A lot of traditional academics (English profs) thought that law school did not belong in a university. It was a trade school, devoted to practical knowledge, preparing people to make a living. Nothing theoretical about it. The economist Thorston Veblen once remarked something to the effect, "Law schools belong in the university no more than schools of dance."

That hurt.

How to make law academically respectable? Lawyers may not be cultured, but they're bright. Call law a science. Langdell wrote:

> [L]aw is a science [and] all the available materials of that science are contained in books.... [T]he library is the proper workshop of professors and students alike; it is to us all that the laboratories of the university are to the chemists and physicists, all that the museum of natural history is to the geologists, all that the botanical garden is to the botanists.

Now that law was a science, not a grubby trade, who could keep us out of the tower?

The Harvard model of legal education became the rage. Casebooks (and Langdell wrote the very first one) replaced lectures. Why is your law school *three* years? The correct answer is "c"—because Christopher Columbus Langdell set his up that way.

With law schools safely established in universities and recognized as an alternative to apprenticeship, two more steps had to be taken to establish today's law school. The first was to kill off the competition: apprenticeship. After years of struggle, in a vast majority of states, law school, not apprenticeship, became the *only* way to become a lawyer. The second step was to raise law school admission standards. At first, some college was required, then college graduation, and now, as you are painfully aware, very good grades and a high LSAT score.

Consider the result. Without good academic credentials, you can't attend law school; without graduating from law school, you can't take the bar. The circle closes.

Law professors, in their assault on apprenticeships, marched under the banner of the "public good." Learning law by reading cases, they argued, made for better lawyers than learning law by working with lawyers. Well, perhaps. Cynics smile, seeing simply the imperatives of expansionism.

In any event, the "practical training" of law students was routed. Law school became almost entirely academic. Very few professors ever practiced law. They were hired because they had excelled in academic law schools and then clerked for an appellate court for a year or two.

Beginning in the 1970's, the "practical wing" of legal education counter attacked, marching under the banner of "clinical education." They were met with arguments curiously akin to those raised, over a century before, against Christopher Langdell: "Practical law training is devoid of intellectual vigor." Clinicians today have a solid beach head in the hollowed halls: clinical education is an accepted part of modern legal education, although just how big a part remains open to dispute.

If you are interested in learning more about the fascinating history of the institution you are inhabiting, see Stevens, "Two Cheers for 1870: The American Law School," in *Law in American History* 425 (D. Fleming and B. Bailyn, eds., 1971). For the cynical account, see Auerbach, *Unequal Justice* (1976).

Pro Bono Activities

Every lawyer, regardless of professional prominence or work load, has a responsibility to provide legal services to those unable to pay, and personal involvement in the problems of the disadvantaged can be one of the most rewarding experiences in the life of a lawyer.

—American Bar Association, Model Rules of Professional Conduct

The American Bar Association urges, but does not attempt to require, lawyers to devote fifty hours a year to providing free legal services to the disadvantaged. Do you think this should be mandatory?

Why lawyers and not, say, plumbers? Because lawyers have a monopoly on the legal system, and there has always been a notion that those with monopoly powers have special public service obligations. This is not to say that *pro bono* activities should be mandatory. Indeed, most lawyers probably devote more that fifty hours a year to such activities and, to make them mandatory, tends to diminish their value.

Many law students engage in *pro bono* activities. They are a terrific way to experience your own uniqueness, recognize your own competence, and give something back to a community which has given you so much.

Often volunteer work is legal work, at Legal Aid, Women's Shelters, AIDS clinics, or Public Interest Firms. But a lot of law students volunteer in non-legal capacities. In Washington D.C., law students help prisoners learn to read by tutoring them as they read story books to their children. Elsewhere, law students tutor elementary students as part of "Lawyers for Literacy" programs. Still others deliver "Meals-on-Wheels" to the elderly.

Most law schools have *pro bono* programs. If yours doesn't, don't curse the darkness. Light a candle. Contact the Pro Bono Students of America (pbsa@turing.law.nyu.edu); the American Bar Association Law Student Division (abalsd@abanet.org) or the Pro Bono Director of the Association of American Law Schools (202–296–8851). They can give you pointers on how to organize your own program.

Law school classes can be organized so as to provide a community service. In my AIDS and the Law class, the class wrote "A Guide to the Law of HIV and Agencies That Help." It covered the basic law in the areas that we thought readers would need most: discrimination, access to medical care, living wills, children, dealing with collection agencies and, of course, landlord/tenant. Similar booklets could be written for battered women, for the homeless, for welfare recipients, and, of course, for stock brokers.

One of my favorite *pro bono* activities is teaching in local high schools. Lawyers spend a lot of time addressing groups and a lot of time explaining the law to non-lawyers. High school teaching programs allow you to do both. We have had a program here for years and years, and almost every student who has taken part has said that it was one of his or her best law school experiences.

There can be rewarding and moving occurrences.

Once a law student noticed one of the high school students never said a word. With a stroke of genius, she made her the judge in the trial unit. The girl was transformed; she broke out of her painful self-conscious shell and became an active participant in the class.

Two students once presented the program in a custodial institution for juvenile delinquents. At first the law students were greeted with, "Pigs!" They stayed with it. Ten weeks later, I got letters from the "inmates": "I always thought all the police and lawyers were pigs, out to get me. Now I know that some might actually understand me and help me."

One sociologist studied attitudes toward the law. He found that a major determinant of whether people respected the law and its various institutions was whether their first contacts with the law were positive or negative. Growing up next door to a loud and drunken lawyer tends to poison one's attitude toward the Supreme Court. Teaching in high schools, particularly inner city high schools, you may be the first "lawyer" your students will ever meet. In a very real sense, you become a "drum major" for law.

One great aspect of these programs is that you get to discuss law with people other than law students, law teachers, and bored and resentful companions at cocktail parties.

If you want information on starting such a program, contact "Street Law" at (www.streetlaw.org). It can provide you with materials and information on how to set up a program.

Law-related videos can be used as part of longer programs or as part of one-day high school presentations. A colleague of mine, Andy Silverman, and I have produced a series of them. Each runs about 20 minutes and comes with teaching materials. They don't preach. Rather, they try to educate students as to the legal implications of decisions they might make. They cover such topics as drunk driving, drug abuse, domestic violence and staying in school. I would be happy to send you more information. Hegland@nt.law.arizona.edu.

A Final Word on the Second and Third Years. Don't let the space allocations confuse you. In this chapter I have discussed the condiments of your legal education law review, clerking, and *pro bono* activities. The meat and potatoes of your legal education, or, if you prefer, the bean curd and sprouts, are the traditional courses.

All too soon you will have to make decisions that matter.

CHAPTER 25

CAREER CHOICES

Once upon a time, a student sought a reference. His quest: the large, prestigious law firm of Blah, Blah, and Blah in Gotham City. I asked, "Looking forward to Gotham?"

"No, I hate Gotham. Nothing but traffic and strangers. I would rather go back home, to Hicksville."

"Well, you must like the kind of law they practice at Blah and Blah."

"No, it's mostly corporate. I'd rather work with kids. That's what I did before law school, and that's why I came to law school. I worked at Blah last summer, and I hated it. As I told another summer intern, 'Terence, this is stupid stuff, yet I do my research fast enough.'"

"Then why do you want the job?"

"Because everyone tells me it's a very good one."

Why, in a book designed for first year students, discuss career options? Shouldn't you be frolicking on first year fields, along with Hadley and Baxendale? Shouldn't you be green and golden, singing in your chains, like the sea?

I wish. But reality hits quickly.

You will soon hear, if you haven't already, that only if you are in the top 10% of your class will you be able to get a job. This rumor starts from the fact that usually only large business firms interview second or third year students at the law school. Only these firms can project their needs over the next several years, and often they restrict their hiring to the top of the class. However, smaller firms, and most governmental agencies, hire lawyers only after they graduate and, frequently, only after they have passed the Bar. A little known fact:

Approximately 50% of lawyers were in the bottom 50% of their class.

And not only that. While it is true that great law school success opens the door to certain kinds of law practice, large firm practice and law teaching, once one gets out in the real world *no one cares how well you did in Contracts* or even where you went to school. In practice, success in not measured in bluebooks; it is measured the old-fashioned way, in hard work, honesty, and common sense.

Before continuing, a few other career facts:

70% of lawyers are in private practice, the vast majority in firms of five or less or on their own. Only 5% are in large firms. (By way of comparison, 8.3% of Hollywood actors play lawyers on T.V.)

Only 5% of lawyers defend and prosecute criminals.

It is unlikely that the first job you take after graduation will be your last. Most lawyers change law jobs at least once after law school; some leave law altogether, to govern nations, to make revolutions, or to broadcast the Dodgers.

Studies suggest that there is an inverse relationship between money and job satisfaction. Lawyers with large urban law firms report bigger bucks but less job satisfaction than do lawyers working for the government and public interest firms.

There are very few "hired guns" out there. Most lawyers are convinced they are doing "the Lord's work," be they personal injury lawyers or insurance defense lawyers, prosecutors or criminal defenders, business lawyers or public interest lawyers.

It is worth repeating that in practice success is in large part the product of interpersonal relations and hard work. And common sense.

My first job was with a state-wide program which provided free legal services for the poor. I worked in the Los Angeles office, where my first assignment was to find out whether, if the program opened an office in Delano, California, a business license would be required. Of course my pricey legal education gave me no clue as how I should go about answering that question. Fortunately, a friendly librarian in the county law library got a copy of the City Code of Delano and found the applicable section.

The answer to the question was, "Yes, we'll need a license and it costs $20." In my memo to the boss, did I write, "Yes, we'll need a license and it costs $20" ? No. What I did write, after three or four days of research, was, "Yes, we'll need a license and it costs $20. However, that City Ordinance is unconstitutional as a violation of Free Speech, Equal Protection, and Due Process because...." and I continued for about twenty pages.

My boss was not nearly as impressed with my work as I thought he would be. "If you ever do that again, you're fired."

This chapter will not offer any tips on resume preparation (except don't come off too pompous, as in "Why your firm needs me") nor tips on interview technique (except to appear to *really want* the job that is being offered: enthusiasm routs doubt every time). Rather, I will first discuss influences that can distort your quest, then discuss job attributes that you may want to consider, and, finally, offer some ideas as to what you can do in law school to test your alternatives. But first, we need a goal.

Once I asked a college basketball coach, "Are basketball coaches happy?"

"I don't know about all coaches," he told me. "All I know is that I wake up at 4 o'clock in the morning and realize, 'Great, I get to go to work today.'"

Frankly, I don't know a whole lot of lawyers (or law professors) that feel that way. But why not? Let us, you and me, shoot for the National Championship.

Mulling Things Over

Getting a job is more than getting a job; more than resumes, dressing up, and remaining calm during the interview.

In choosing a job, you are, at least to some degree, choosing what kind of person you will become.

I went to school in Berkeley. One of my radical friends was hired by a commercial firm in Santa Barbara. They told him he would be a Republican in a year. I saw him about a year later.

"They couldn't have been more wrong. It took only six months."

George Orwell had a marvelous insight. When we get a job, we want to conform and hence put on a professional mask. As time wears on, however, our face grows to fit the mask. After twenty years prosecuting criminals, what world view will you have? After a career of advising business, defending insurance companies, or teaching law, whom will you know? What books will you read? Who will you be?

In this life we prepare for things, for moments and events and situations. We worry about things, think about injustices, read what Tolstoy has to say. Then, all of a sudden, the issue is not whether we agree with what we have

*heard and read and studied. This issue is **us**,
and what we have become.*

Robert Coles

Around "interview time," when classmates begin
getting jobs, you will feel an incredible amount of
pressure to land one. And it doesn't help when
friends and family ask, "Well?"

The danger is that you might take a job simply
because "it's there."

I recommend that you take an hour or so now to
write about the kind of job you want. Put the letter
aside and reread it around "interview time." Writing now might help you sort things out; rereading it
then might help you remain calm until you get that
job that wakes you at four o'clock in the morning.

Distorting Influences

A brilliant law school career might not be all it's
cracked up to be.

Many students (maybe you) come to law school
for idealistic reasons: to work with business in
improving the environment, to work with abused
children, or to return to their community to help
those less fortunate. Many of these end up with
Blah, Blah, and Blah, fighting traffic in Gotham
City.

How come?

Many change career goals in law school for good
reasons: learning more about themselves and more

about the choices, they realize that they will be happier doing something they hadn't previously considered. Some of my best friends work for Blah, Blah, and Blah and love it. More power to them.

However, some change goals because they get caught up in law school hype.

Tom Wolfe, in *The Right Stuff*, writes that America's astronauts were not motivated by money, fame, or challenge; they just wanted to get chosen for the most competitive program at the time; they just wanted to prove they were the "right stuff."

There is nothing wrong with this, as long as the "right stuff" is your stuff.

In law school, the "right stuff" is working with ideas rather than with people. This is the implicit lesson. Law school goodies are passed out on the basis of academic performance; compassion, common sense, and, alas, humor, can't be graded and hence don't count for much.

To prove that they are the "right stuff," the "best" students go to large firms. This career path rests on two assumptions, first, that all the "smart lawyers" end up in such firms and, second, that all the interesting legal work is done in them. Both assumptions are false. The two smartest lawyers I know both work for Legal Aid. As to engaging legal work, when I was an appellate lawyer, arguing cases of great moment, I slept soundly. When I was a trial lawyer, doing misdemeanors, I woke up a couple of times a night to jot notes to myself.

Getting caught up in law school hype is one danger to avoid. Another is selling yourself too short. We fear success as well as failure. The psychologist Abraham Maslow calls it "fear of one's own greatness" and "running away from one's own best talents." He asks his students:

> *"Which of you in this class hopes to write the great American novel, or to be a Senator, or Governor, or President? Or a great composer? Or a Saint?"*

His students giggle, blush, and squirm, until he asks, "If not you, then who else?"

This is not to say that you should crave fame or fortune; it is to suggest that you should not run away from your dreams because you fear boldness, because you fear your own best talents.

"Mind-forged manacles"—a phrase of William Blake. "I could *never* do trial work." "I could *never* get a job in Washington." "I could *never* make a living in Hicksville representing kids."

How do you know?

Career Choices

Punt

It is OK to be indecisive. At least, I think it is. After law school, you can take a job that lasts, by definition, only a year or two. This is a good option. These jobs are usually exciting and are of a "once in a lifetime" variety. They provide valuable training and effectively silence those who ask, "Well?"

A *judicial clerkship* is a good choice. Most appellate judges and many trial court judges hire recent graduates as clerks. You get to sit in on either appellate arguments or trials, do legal research, discuss legal matters with your judge, and maybe even get to write an opinion or two. You will learn a great deal about how cases are decided, and most legal employers think a clerkship is a real plus.

Additionally, there are numerous *internships* offered by governmental agencies, public interest groups, and even some law schools.

Clerkships are highly competitive, and the race starts second year. See your Placement Director. Also, you will need recommendations from professors, so best to begin to get to know them now.

Of course, you can stay in school, which is apparently your basic strategy in avoiding growing up. Some law schools offer advanced law degrees in such things as tax. Or you may wish to get another degree in a field which you plan to use in conjunction with law, such as business, finance, real estate, counseling, or ventriloquism.

The hardest part of the "stay-in-school" option, and one which might prove insurmountable, is telling your family.

Non-Legal Careers

Kafka went to law school. He hated it. In fact, it has recently come to light that the first line of his classic, *The Metamorphosis*, has been incorrectly translated. The inaccurate translation reads:

> *Gregor Samsa awoke one morning and found that he had turned into a gigantic cockroach.*

The corrected translation reads:

> *Gregor Samsa woke up one morning and found that he had turned into a rather rotund tax lawyer.*

A surprising number of disgruntled lawyers become novelists (and, no doubt, disgruntled novelists swell our ranks). Others go into business (Kafka wouldn't have liked that either), teaching, politics, and the media. A good friend of mine went into "development" (fund-raising), using his legal knowledge of wills and tax law. Another wanted to get into producing movies. She went to Hollywood, rented an apartment, hung out at the studios, finally, after several months, got a law job, and now, after several years, is producing her own movies.

Karen Waterman, a law school placement specialist, advises that routine want ads can be rich sources of ideas. "Would this job involve the use of legal skills?" Many jobs involve legal skills (such as risk management and compliance work) but traditionally have been filled with non-lawyers.

Show up and surprise everyone.

Of course, it is easier to get a traditional law job. However, maybe the rest of your life is worth a little effort, a little imagination, a little gumption.

Traditional Law Jobs

Your choices are vastly more than big firms versus small firms, prosecuting versus defending.

Public interest Law, Legal Aid

Law reporting (print or TV)

Teaching (in law schools or colleges or community colleges)

Risk management; contract compliance

In-house legal counsel

Legislative counsel, lobbying

Government work (from Washington to Hicksville)

Law librarian (law schools and large firms), law publishing (writing ALR articles)

Law enforcement (FBI)

Military justice

Circus law

Your Placement Office will have tons and tons of information.

Let me alert you to two "hot" substantive areas of the law: *Intellectual Property* and *Elder Law*. Intellectual Property covers the traditional areas of copyright, patent, and trademark, but also how all of these concepts play out in cyberspace. Things are booming, and there is no end in sight. Elder Law is a relatively new speciality but will also be in great demand as Baby-Boomers reach retirement. For a general look at elder law, see Hegland and Bogutz, *Fifty and Beyond: The Law You and Your Parents Need to Know.*

In weighing your alternatives, what factors should you consider?

Ideas versus people. Some people prefer working with ideas, others with people. Some law practices involve mostly legal research and drafting. These jobs offer "nice" theoretical problems, the luxury of extended research and reflection, and the satisfaction that comes in drafting a well written and thorough legal document, be it a brief or contract. Large firms traditionally offer this kind of employment, but so too do many smaller "specialized" law firms, public interest firms, and "appellate departments" of the public defender and of the district attorney.

At the other end of the continuum are those law jobs that involve working closely with people. Great satisfaction can come in helping people solve real-life problems: helping work out a sensible child custody arrangement, helping two friends set up a partnership, helping a client understand a bureaucratic maze. As a general matter, smaller firms and some government agencies offer greater opportunities to work with people.

Responsibility. The larger the firm or agency, the less responsibility you likely will have. Your work will be constantly reviewed. You will work on parts of elephants.

At the other end of the continuum are jobs that throw you directly into the heat of battle. In some small firms and legal aid offices, you interview clients the first day; in some district attorney and defender offices, you try cases your first week.

Responsibility can be exhilarating; after all those years of studying about the real world, you are suddenly part of it. Your decisions count.

Responsibility can be terrifying. Law is quite complex, and, as a beginner, you know so little. Add to that the elusive criteria of good practice: "Have I worked hard enough?" "Have I raised all the points?" "Has my client been well represented?"

Training. It is essential to develop your professional skills. Larger firms and agencies generally offer good training. Your work is almost always reviewed. This is the other side of "lack of responsibility." Generally you will be given time to "do it right," and the standards of the practice will be quite high.

Many smaller firms and smaller public agencies also insist on the highest professional standards. Don't take a job that allows for sloppy work habits.

An aside on solo practice. Some "hang out their own shingle" upon graduation. But times, since Lincoln, have changed.

Without someone to show you the ropes, without someone to discuss your cases with, you will teeter on the edge of malpractice. The most common cause of legal malpractice is missing deadlines. Once you get three or four cases, it gets very difficult to keep track of things. Working with an established firm or lawyer, you will learn the various retrieval systems. Going out on your own, you may not.

Two pieces of advice, assuming you ignore the implicit advice in the last paragraph. First, keep your overhead low. Second, don't take "dog cases," even if it is just to put some short-term bones on the table. In every community, there are folks who were drugged by the CIA and brainwashed by the F.B.I. (Now we know where our tax dollars go.) These unfortunate folks flutter, like moths, around new shingles. They never go away.

Contentiousness. Even if you restrict your practice to adoption law, or some other form of "happy law," there will be days when you find some other lawyer yelling at you. However, in some laws jobs, such as trying lawsuits, you will find almost constant contentiousness. In other law jobs, such as elder law and business planning, generally there is not another lawyer whose job it is to find fault with your work.

Another area of contentiousness is with one's clients. It is said that, in criminal practice, you deal with bad people at their best and, in family practice, with good people at their worst. Interviewing, ask lawyers not only about how they get along with adverse lawyers but with their own clients.

"Alternative Dispute Resolution" is a movement to introduce kinder and gentler methods into our adversary system. Perhaps mediation can replace litigation and problem-solving the zero-sum game (those in which what one side wins, the other must lose). Brave lawyers are entering traditional combative fields with these goals. If you are repelled by the adversary system, consider this route. Even in traditionally combative law jobs, it may be possible to do something other than "chase each other around the table," where the "good" solution leaves both sides sullen but not mutinous.

Income and security. Larger firms start associates at higher salaries than do other law employers; partners in large firms do exceedingly, embarrassingly, well. Some lawyers in smaller firms undoubtedly overtake their fat-cat brethren and occasionally make "megabucks" by getting into business ventures with their clients. Personal injury lawyers can almost retire if they get "the big one" (but, what with TV advertising, the chances of getting "the big one" are about the same as winning the lottery).

Lawyers making a career in governmental agencies often do quite nicely. Gone, of course, the dream of vast wealth, but some government lawyers earn salaries higher than many lawyers in their area, with better benefits and job security.

Travel, adventure. It's possible.

Esprit de corps. Some law jobs involve a strong sense of shared purpose. One of the things I most value about my own days in practice was my relationship with the other lawyers in the office. We knew about each others' cases, we talked about them, argued about them, and shared the moments of joy and despair.

I found this sense of shared purpose and involvement in legal aid and in public defending. I am sure it exists in most prosecuting offices, in most government jobs, and, I am told, in most small law offices. The larger the firm or agency, the less likely the feeling. This lack of *esprit de corps* will not bother some, those who prefer to work alone (perhaps writing Nutshells) and those who simply want a job and will look for a sense of community elsewhere.

Weighing Careers During Law School

A sports agent was discussing how difficult it is for players to readjust after their playing days are over. "I tell them to keep a diary when they are still playing. What do they enjoy doing in their off hours? What are they good at? That way, when the time comes, they will have some idea of what kind of job they may like."

Keep track of what you like and what you do well. Do you enjoy the conflict of Moot Court or Trial Practice? Do you find the verbal encounter in the classroom exciting? Do you love research? Do you rush to your computer to get your thoughts on paper? Do you like close supervision? Do you like working with classmates?

Although law practice is much different from law school, many facets are the same: reading cases and statutes, making arguments, advising on how the law would play out in a given situation. Once you have given law school a fair run, at least a year, and you find you don't like the law, find it too nit-picky, too confining, too boring, consider getting out. Kafka went on to achieve modest success. So did Harry Truman, who had a year of law school. So too Vince Lombardi, who had a semester.

Course Selection

If you are considering a legal specialty, obviously take the courses in it. Consider that there may be courses in other departments of the university that will expose you to the "nuts and bolts" of a particular career. For example, if you are considering something in the media, check the catalogue of the Journalism Department. Better yet, go over and chat with the people there. Another obvious example is Business School. However, *as career goals often change*, it is a mistake to focus too exclusively in the area of law you think you'll practice.

A warning, however, about "subject matter" career selection. Sure, we all love Contracts, but to "practice" contract law may not be as exciting as it is to "study" contract law. Lucy, Lady Duff Gordon, Hadley and Baxendale, Ship Peerless—gone, all gone. Without them, it may be nothing but widgets.

Most law schools offer courses in *trial practice* and have *clinics*. Clinics involve representing real clients either in a law school clinic or in a field placement. These courses are very important, particularly if you are shying away from them. It may be a matter of breaking out of "mind-forged manacles." You may find that you enjoy the hurly-burly of trial and that you find deep satisfaction in helping people solve real life problems. Or you may conclude "Never again." Either way, you win.

Clinical courses are needed by those students planning to work for small firms or on their own. There is the danger of developing sloppy work habits. Law school courses will instill a sense of excellence in practice.

Work for Lawyers

A good way to experience practice is to work for a lawyer. Law firms and agencies often hire second and third year students to do legal research. Doing the research, hanging out at the office and talking to attorneys and staff can give you a good feel for that particular kind of law practice.

Many law professors advise against clerking, arguing that students will learn more by sticking to the books. I disagree and believe that clerking, if approached from the proper perspective, can be a valuable learning experience, both in terms of legal doctrine and in terms of career choice.

If you are to work for a lawyer, what kind of lawyer? Should you take a job with the kind of firm or agency you "think" you would like to eventually work for? Or should you take a job with one of those "I-could-never-work-with-them" firms? There are pros and cons for each. Some students find permanent employment through their clerking. On the other hand, much can be said for testing as many alternatives as possible. Even if you confirm your suspicion that you could never do insurance defense, having clerked with such a firm will make you a better personal injury lawyer.

Ask Lawyers and Professors

Most of us like to give advice (I, apparently, more than others). If you are considering prosecuting, why not go to the prosecutor's office and ask to see one of the attorneys?

I'm not here looking for a job. I'm here because I want some advice. I am thinking about prosecuting when I graduate but I really don't know much about it. Perhaps you can tell me about it; perhaps I could sit in and watch what you do.

Note: This can be turned into a very clever job-getting ploy.

Now, Ms. Banker, I'm not looking for a job working in your legal department. I realize you are probably full. What I would like is some advice on how to go about getting a job in the legal department of a bank.

Of course *I* would never be bold enough simply to show up at a law office, unannounced. The problem is meeting lawyers. One possibility is to get together with some classmates, ask a friendly professor for some names of recent graduates, and throw a party.

We're first year students, and we want to meet some lawyers so we can get some feel for what it's like. Want to come to a party?

You can also infiltrate sections of your local Bar Association; many have student memberships. Another way to meet lawyers is to attend Continuing Legal Education (CLE) programs and go to Bar conventions.

Try to get your professors talking about their practice experiences. Most likely they will be more interesting than the Rule in Shelley's Case.

Go to Court

It takes absolutely no courage to walk quietly into the back of a courtroom and sit through a trial. Again, this experience is probably most needed by those who will "never" step into a courtroom—who knows, perhaps they'll never leave.

Read Books

There are several books about law practice. I recommend, as openers:

The Associates, Jay Osborne (author of *Paper Chase*), deals with life in a Wall Street firm.

Trial and Error, D. Michael Tomkins, is the story of a young lawyer starting off in solo practice.

Confessions of a Criminal Lawyer, Seymour Wishman, presents a criminal defense lawyer reflecting on several years of practice.

These books are relatively short, quite candid, and at places, humorous. They are excellent introductions to various kinds of practice. Ask your professors for other titles.

A Final Word

What does your future hold? Perhaps you will argue cases that shape your times, or perhaps you will be the trusted advisor of powerful groups, huge corporations, or even Presidents. Or perhaps you will never make the front page and will be simply another lawyer in the yellow pages, helping people with everyday problems. There is greatness in that as well.

Finally, don't make too much of your ambition. It's OK even if you don't get your fifteen minutes of fame. In John Bolt's play, *A Man for All Seasons*, Sir Thomas More is discussing careers with the politically ambitious Richard Rich.

> *More: Why not be a teacher? You'd be a fine teacher. Perhaps even a great one.*

> *Rich: And if I was, who would know of it?*

> *More: You, your pupils, your friends, God. Not a bad public that.*

Comforting thought and not a bad place to end all of this.

I hope you enjoyed reading this book half as much as I enjoyed writing it. Frankly, it's hard to say goodbye. Keep in touch. Hegland@nt.law.arizona.edu.

CHAPTER 26

LAWYERS TALK ABOUT THEIR JOBS

My thinking about this chapter has changed. The original intent was to have lawyers write about what they do in order to provide career information. Reading what they have written it strikes me that the real value of the chapter lies elsewhere, in combating cynicism concerning the practice of law. My sense is that law students quickly lose idealism and enthusiasm for their chosen profession. I think this happens because in law school, law practice is presented as something abstract and lifeless, as intellectual game-playing without emotional or ethical content. My hope is that, in reading what these lawyers do, you will realize that yours was a wise decision. The practice of law is neither abstract nor amoral; it is alive, fulfilling, and caring.

The lawyers who write on the following pages are friends, not statistical abstracts. I selected them because they are reflective and insightful. Although I selected lawyers doing different kinds of law jobs, no attempt was made for "balance", either in terms of "type" of practice, age of practitioner, or geography. In describing to them their task I again rejected the goal of balance. I prescribed no format. I simply told them that I was writing a book for first-

372

year law students, students who likely knew little about various legal careers and who likely knew little about what lawyers actually do. Write, I advised, what you think might prove useful.

Some focused on questions of career: how they made their own career decisions, the pros and cons of various kinds of practices, things you might do as a law student to help you prepare. Others focused on what they do as lawyers, describing either a typical day or a typical task. A quick disclaimer. These are *individual statements*. I told the lawyers that they were not writing as "representatives" of their kind of practice and not to worry if what they wrote might be atypical. People experience things differently.

This then is not an encyclopedia of the types of law practice. It is rather a collage of what some lawyers thought important to share with you. I have learned from them; so will you.

THERESA GABALDON

Large Firm; Law Teaching

My sister, who is a romance novelist, has the best job in the world. This is largely because she has self-defined it to involve working at night, getting up very late, and eating chocolates for breakfast.

I, a law professor, have the second best job in the world; if eating chocolates were a necessary part of the job description, it would clearly rival my sister's. As it is, I have enormous flexibility about what I do and, within reasonable bounds, when I do it. The highlights, and only strictly scheduled events of the week are, of course, classroom appearances. I currently teach to an average class size of around 120 students; put a microphone in my hand and I become Oprah Winfrey. Coming up with different ways to cover the material is part of the fun, and if I choose to play a game of "Jeopardy" with corporate law topics, none of my teaching colleagues will object (at least not to my face.) My students are good-natured and appreciate whatever effort is expended in their behalf.

Performing scholarly research and writing is another important part of my task, and it is here that the possibilities for marching to one's own drumbeat are most unlimited. I choose my own topics for inquiry, and simply work on them until I have said what I have to say. My most productive "thinking" time starts at 4:00 a.m. and I try to take advantage of it. This may lead to a lull later in the day, but a quick trip to aerobics class recharges my batteries.

Although the description thus far may suggest that the law professor leads a life that is somewhat distanced from others, this is only true if he or she decrees it. If you display any disposition to listen, as well as to impart, students will be by to chat about a truly breath-taking assortment of subjects. Your colleagues can, if you choose, be your sounding boards, your confidantes, your matchmakers, and, every now and then, your bowling partners.

My immediately prior incarnation was as a partner in a large law firm. As such, I had the third best job in the world. In all honesty, flexibility was not one of the things that commended it. Rather, it was the technical challenge—present also in law teaching—and the sense of command. Frankly, the money wasn't bad, either; in ten years of teaching I have yet to achieve my salary in my last year of practice.

I specialized in corporate and securities law, and these are the areas that have carried over into my teaching and my scholarship. It was, at the time, something of a "glamour" practice. The deals were huge, the pace was fast, and the travel arrangements were luxurious. The pressure, however, was intense, and I can remember the feeling in my chest as I realized that a deadline was approaching and that the legal judgment being brought to bear on a multi-million dollar deal was mine. I have no regrets about having lived that life or about having left it, simply because I have found something I like more.

Because I have truly enjoyed both of my law-related professions, I have to believe that there is something about the law that has "worked" for me. I know that it has not, and does not, "work" for everybody. I enjoy the solving-the-maze aspects and the challenges of communicating my solutions to others. I suspect, however, that I lack the passion for justice, fairness, etc., that motivates some—and that's probably just as well for a corporate lawyer. In fact, from my observations, it is passion of this sort, combined with some type of corporate law-practice, that frequently leads to dissatisfaction with the law. There is fulfillment in serving particular clients well, in teaching, and in being an upstanding citizen and contributing member of society, but it will still leave some people feeling that there should be something more.

RICHARD DAVIS

Mid–Size Firm

I arrive in my office at 7:30 a.m. I look at my calendar and realize that I have to travel to a hospital which our firm represents to meet with the Administrator and Risk Manager. Others will be present. A few days ago a 20–day-old premature baby died at the hospital while on a ventilator. The original account suggests that the machine malfunctioned, preventing the baby from breathing normally.

Immediately after the accident, the Director of the Medical Lab at the hospital wanted to test the ventilator. I advised a delay long enough to notify each of the interested parties and to give them an opportunity to be present. The manufacturer of the ventilator and the parents of the baby were notified.

The test is scheduled to begin at 9:00, but I get there early. This will allow me to become familiar with the machine and interview the hospital's personnel who were on duty when the incident occurred. Arriving at 8:15, I talk to the respiratory technician, the nurse on duty and the medical lab technician who will do the testing. By 8:45 I have a general idea of how the machine works, of the suspected problem and of what happened the day in question. I also learn that the hospital coffee gets old after the second cup.

The first person to arrive for the meeting is an investigator from the County Medical Examiner's Office. The family asked that office to be present and to determine the cause of the baby's death. We exchange pleasantries. I am a little anxious and apprehensive because I really do not know what the tests will reveal. My hidden hope is that the tests will prove my client blameless.

The manufacturer is sending someone from its national headquarters in Texas. It is now 9:00, and we receive a call advising us that the manufacturer's rep will be late. The small talk and anxiousness continue. At 9:30, the manufacturer's representative arrives. There is an immediate disagreement over the tests that should be run and who should run them. After discussion, ground rules are laid and pictures are taken to verify and preserve settings on dowels and pressure gauges. Each test is run carefully and meticulously. The pressure gauge is saved for last because it is the suspected culprit. It proves faulty.

Further tests are necessary to determine why the system failed but that necessitates a breakdown of the unit. Moreover, the necessary equipment is not available. The manufacturer's representative wants to take the machine back to the factory for further testing. I disagree. I feel that the machine should be stored in a place where no one can get to it without my knowledge and prior approval. Besides, there should be no destructive testing without giving every interested party an opportunity to be present along with an expert. I suggest that since the Medical Examiner's Office is involved, it should store the machine at its facility. The Medical Examiner's investigator nixes that idea but recommends that it be placed in the Police Department's storage room. We agree and the police are called.

When I arrive in my office around 3:30, I find thirteen telephone messages, most of which require a return call. I learn that two cases were settled and a person with a 2:30 appointment showed up and left after waiting about one-half hour. My secretary says that she was very angry.

I dictate a memo to the file concerning the test because I am certain that a lawsuit will be filed. I sort through the telephone messages and mail so I can arrange them according to some priority.

At 4:30 I receive a telephone call from a friend who is being investigated by the FBI. He wants my advice. I make an appointment for the next day. Next I receive a call from a representative of Farmers Insurance Group. He has a question concerning the value of a case and what should be paid to settle it. I recommend a figure. I answer a few letters and review tomorrow's schedule. I realize that I have a deposition scheduled at the same time that I set the appointment for my friend. I call him back but there is no answer. My calendar indicates that I have a trial next week and there are some things that I must do to be ready for it. I make a list. It is now 6:10 and it is dark outside. There is still a lot of work to be done but it will have to wait until tomorrow.

GRACE McILVAIN

Mid–Size Firm

When I decided to become a lawyer, it was not because I thought the law would be exciting. I thought it would be boring. I did not expect to like the law, let alone love it the way one is supposed to. I wanted a job that would give me responsibility, a chance to use my brain, a good salary, and a chance to advance, none of which I had as a secretary. Those were my sole reasons for applying to law school.

It is amusing to recall what I expected the practice of law to be like when I was in law school. I expected it to be boring and tedious, so tedious that the hours in the office would drag by. Nothing could be further from the truth. I enjoy at least 90% of the things I must do. Filling out time sheets and preparing bills to send to clients are no fun at all, but litigation is very interesting. I think about my cases all my waking hours and often most of the night. I even dream about them.

The responsibilities and time pressures are, however, very stressful. The matters one handles are extremely important to the clients, and they place a great deal of trust in you. Because of that, and for many other more selfish reasons, there is great pressure to achieve an excellent result in every single case which is, of course, impossible. There is never enough time to be as thoroughly prepared as you would like to be. No matter how well organized and self-disciplined you are, every day is a struggle against time. There are never enough hours in the day. In that respect, law school is good preparation for the practice. But the time pressures in practicing law are much greater than time pressures in law school.

There is so much emphasis on legal theories in law school that you begin to believe that legal knowledge and analytical skill are all you need to be a good attorney. Law school doesn't prepare you for the psychological aspects of practicing law. You must build a good relationship with your client and make him or her have confidence in you. You must make the opposing attorney at least respect you, and it is to your advantage to convince him that you are tough, that you know the law, and that you will persevere no matter what. It is to your advantage to make him afraid of you. Yet sometimes you need his cooperation, so you must know when to be nice to him and when to apply pressure. (I use "him" when referring to the opposing attorney because, in litigation, nine times out of ten your opponent is male. If you are a woman, the difficulties of dealing with him are multiplied because even before he meets you, he has probably decided that you are either a pushover or a bitch, and that whichever you are, you are not a good lawyer.)

You need to convince the judges before whom you appear that you know the law, that there is a good reason behind every statement you make, and that you would never ever mislead them. You must convince juries that you are credible and that deserves their verdict.

There is always room to grow. There are always ways you could have handled a case better, which is one of the reasons you are never bored.

DAN COOPER

Public Defender

The most satisfying part of being a public defender is representing people who are despised by the public, the press and the prosecutors. Most cases remain obscure and create no reaction. On occasion, however, a defendant comes along who stirs the conscience of the community into moral outrage. It is defending this person that makes me proud to be a lawyer.

I recently represented a man who, along with his wife, was charged with child abuse. The facts were grisly. When I first met my client I was somewhat taken aback by his absolute and total lack of guilt. I try not to prejudge my cases. I was, however, aware when I received this case that the evidence was overwhelming against my client. I was perplexed at his total lack of emotion. Throughout the duration of the case he remained stoic in the face of constant hostility. The prosecutor called my client "a monster." The newspapers covered the case extensively and without objectivity. Even some close friends of mine asked how I could represent this man. The trial lasted nearly two weeks and, although I could not honestly say that I had fun, it was an experience I would not trade. The victim in the case, a nine-year-old girl, was found hog-tied in a motel room. She weighed thirty-two pounds and had been beaten. She had a chipped front tooth, bruises on her face and at least twenty scars on the top of her head which, the State alleged, came from a blunt object. A psychiatrist testified that she had never seen a worse case of psychological and emotional child abuse. A pediatrician testified that the child had been systematically starved for at least four years. A radiologist testified that the child's growth would, in all likelihood, be permanently stunted. And the most damaging witness of all was the little girl—tiny, charming, precocious. She broke down in tears as she turned to look at her mother and stepfather. My client stared at her impassively.

Against the advice of some very skilled trial lawyers, I put my client on the stand. The other lawyers felt that my client's testimony would only enrage an already upset jury. But I wanted the jury to see how narrow and rigid was my client's view of the world. His testimony was stilted, rigid, unsmiling and, I felt, demonstrated a myopic, inadequate personality perfectly capable of being unaware that his nine-year-old stepdaughter had been systematically starved and abused. Certainly his testimony would not prove his innocence. But there was an outside chance that the jury would convict of the lesser, non-intentional child abuse charge if they felt my client was rigid, myopic and pathetic. It was a slim chance in an unpopular, highly publicized case. My closing argument to the jury was emotional. I had convinced myself, if no one else, that the lesser offense would be the appropriate verdict. That the jury convicted my client of the greater offense has not changed my mind. But perhaps my feelings today about that child abuse case typify the nature of this job. I am proud that, in the face of overwhelming adverse publicity, against insurmountable evidence, while not able to convince a jury of my client's innocence, that jury knew that the defendant had a lawyer who fought for him.

RANDY STEVENS

Prosecutor

It took just a little more than a year after my graduation from law school for me to realize that private practice wasn't for me—at least not at that time in my life. I wanted more variety, more action, more excitement. I also wanted to be handling cases that had greater significance than just importance to the client. Having watched several excellent trial attorneys perform in court, I knew that courtroom practice was something I had to try, but I also realized it would take years to get any meaningful experience if I stayed in private practice. Telling the people I worked with that I'd be back in a year or two, I left and joined the local prosecutor's office. That was fourteen years ago.

From my perspective, the *total* experience available in prosecution cannot be duplicated elsewhere, especially for an attorney in the first four or five years. It isn't just the legal experience; it is the broader awareness of life, people and society, awareness of aspects of our society that most of us never dreamed existed. While at the same time, prosecution is an accelerated course in all aspects of trial practice.

Prosecution is the perfect opportunity for you to find out if you really want to be a trial attorney. Almost every young attorney experiences some degree of trial resistance—a hesitancy to try a case in front of a jury. There is a fear of making mistakes, of embarrassing oneself, of "freezing up" and not knowing what to do next. In a busy prosecutor's office, this resistance is usually overcome simply because there isn't time to dwell upon it. A heavy caseload doesn't allow for it. It isn't unusual for new prosecutors to find themselves trying several cases a week. If they begin to enjoy what they are doing, and are comfortable in court, it is only a matter of time before they want to begin trying more complicated and more serious cases. But not all attorneys experience this. After six months to a year, and sometimes even sooner, some realize that they aren't enjoying courtroom work, that they don't like the pressure and the demands of trial work, something no one can really know before they've given it a try. Most prosecutor's offices expect this to happen with a percentage of the young attorneys they hire.

It is usually during the fourth and fifth years when trial skills begin to reach a plateau, which means the attorney can try any type of criminal case with a high level of competency. Most trial attorneys will agree: if a person can competently prosecute a lengthy, difficult criminal case, that person can probably try almost any type of civil case. Law firms recruit heavily from prosecuting offices.

Most attorneys who prosecute do so for five to ten years, then they move on to something else. Looking back, asking myself why I've stayed so long in prosecution, the answer really isn't that hard to determine: I've thoroughly enjoyed myself. I've actually looked forward to going to work each morning. The constant flow of different types of cases, the interchange with victims and witnesses; working with every level of law enforcement: all go together to constitute a level of excitement that makes the job more than just enjoyable. It's experiencing life three or four times more than the average person. Along with this is the additional feeling that in some small way, you are doing something positive for society.

LESLIE COHEN

Public Interest

When I decided to go to law school, it was always to become a "peoples" lawyer. I always wanted to fight for individuals' civil rights. However, when I went to law school, I perceived that fight to involve struggling against racism and sexism, and encroachments on first amendment rights. At that time, little did I know that 12 years later I would actually be fighting discrimination, but for a different group of people—one of the last groups to gain civil rights in our society—persons with serious disabilities or mental illness.

For the last three years, I have been working for a public interest law firm which is the recipient of several federal grants to represent persons with disabilities to be free from abuse and neglect, free from discrimination and to promote access to adequate services and programs. No day is a typical day, but any day could include part of the following:

I strategize with an advocate on how to approach a school district's failure to provide a child with traumatic brain injury appropriate services. Under the federal Individuals with Disabilities Education Act, all school districts are required to provide children with special needs a free and appropriate education including any related services they may need. Should we request a hearing to get the school district to pay for the services of a cognitive trainer to help the child? We decide to submit our expert's report and let the school district respond.

I next speak with an attorney in our office about a pending Americans with Disabilities Act case. Her client, who is deaf, has not been provided interpreter services during required training and in-service meetings at his job. The client is frustrated and feels he can't learn how to do his job better or advance because he is not receiving the technical assistance other workers are. We are in negotiations with the employer and discuss whether providing the client with interpreter services in the future will be enough, or should he receive remedial training and/or compensation for being denied an interpreter for so long.

I receive a phone call that a former client, who had been inappropriately institutionalized at the state hospital for many years. Now he might be returned. Evidently, through lack of appropriate care at a local mental health agency, the client has deteriorated and is in need of hospitalization. I dash off a letter to the local mental health agency apprising them of the situation and demanding that they stabilize our client's care so that he can be returned to his community placement.

I then rush off to a meeting of persons discussing proposed legislative changes to the criminal rules concerning the competency to stand trial law. I am concerned that proposed changes may result in incarceration of individuals with mental disability for long periods of time unnecessarily and in contravention of constitutional principles.

There are just a few of the issues I will address on any given day. Representing persons with disabilities involves important civil rights issues. As our jurisprudence begins to address the rights of persons in the United States who have been previously ignored, such as persons with disabilities, gays and lesbians, immigrants, and children, there should be lots of exciting opportunities available for law students to enter public interest law.

ROBERT FLEMING

Elder Law

It seemed to me that most of the students in my law school class were unsure of their ultimate goals. I was different. I knew with absolute certainty why I was in law school, what I would do with my degree and my professional future. As it happened, I was wrong.

Although my plans drifted from environmental law to the more prosaic water and mining law practice, I knew that I would want to utilize my undergraduate degree (chemistry) and my scientific orientation. Two years out of law school I had learned the hard truth: a new lawyer has little control over what cases or clients might appear. There was a softer truth as well: I surprised myself when I found that I enjoyed working with individual clients, and particularly those with mental or physical limitations.

In one regard, my law school predictions were correct. I doubted that I would "fit in" in a corporate or large firm practice, and the passage of time has proven that my doubts were well founded. I have practiced alone, with a single associate, in partnerships of up to four lawyers and in government settings. Each arrangement has had its attractions.

One other thing I correctly predicted in law school was that I would not be drawn to a litigation-based practice. An office practice filled with appointments with real clients is very rewarding and professionally satisfying.

Our firm practices "elder law." We prepare estate plans, advise clients about long-term care costs, and counsel family members on end-of-life issues. The common thread is that our clients tend to be elderly or disabled, or to be the children or parents of elderly or disabled individuals.

Recently I went through an extraordinary personal experience related to the law practice. A young woman had been a long-time client. I had handled the proceeds of a personal injury settlement while she was a minor, and she left the money in trust with our firm after reaching her majority. She was physically disabled and had a shortened life expectancy, but she exhibited personal strength. A few years ago she decided to name me as her agent for health care decisions—not because she distrusted her family, but because she wanted to remove her mother from the agony of making the ultimate decision.

When I received the call from the hospital, I expected to be told that she had become non-communicative. Instead she remained articulate, and was demanding the removal of the breathing machine which kept her alive. Her father objected, hoping for a miracle. Her mother agreed with her decision, but was in agony. Her siblings represented several different views on how she should proceed. Her physician was sure that if he could get her through her current treatment, she could live several more years—though, he acknowledged, she would never be weaned from the breathing machines.

At her bedside I asked her how she felt about the decision. She clearly mouthed the words "I'm tired–let me go." I went to a room filled with the well-intentioned individuals in her life, each of whom was grappling with her wishes in a different way, and argued for her personal autonomy.

The legal principle was never at issue. She was competent, and had the absolute right to direct the removal of the treatment, and the hospital staff knew it without having to hear it from me. I left the hospital with the certain knowledge that by the time of my arrival at the office she would have died—and she did. In a strict sense, I did not practice law that day—but I accomplished something terribly important to me personally, and my faith in the law and the practice of law was reinforced.

Law school was at least an adequate preparation for the legal aspects of the practice of law. It did not, however, prepare us for the medical, social work, financial, personal or emotional components of the practice. It may be that those components are more easily learned in the on-the-job training of the real world. Still, it would have been nice to have some sense of the application of legal principles to real people's lives.

RITA A. MEISER

Large Firm

The practice of law in a "large" law firm varies dramatically depending upon the firm and the city. In many, people hate briefcases and consider lunch at McDonald's a gourmet delight. Each firm has its own personality, which is reflected in many ways, especially the manner in which it deals with associates. As a result, I describe my practice to you as a person who, while content in my role as a practitioner in my particular law firm, might also not be content in a different large law firm. I also write as a person whose initial perception envisioned a happier legal life in a small firm, and who has been pleasantly surprised at where I have ended up.

My primary orientation in becoming an attorney was to maximize my involvement with people. The areas of law in which I am mostly involved reflect this goal. Mostly I practice hospital law. This is one of those areas that you do not know exists when you are in law school. Hospital law encompasses a broad range of legal problems: removing from a hospital staff a physician who does not perform at the proper standard of care; determining what procedures must be followed when a physician decides that life support systems should be removed, and working through the administrative procedures necessary to have a hospital add a department or beds. The work appeals to me because it involves effecting positive, tangible change in a way that is often lacking in the practice of law.

My second area of practice is employment discrimination, primarily from a defense perspective. I find this work intriguing because of the variety of people and areas to which it exposes me. Processing a discrimination charge, I learn the business operations of the client, as well as meet and work with people involved in the world of business. It has not been my experience that practice from the defense posture necessarily mandates advocacy of personally offensive legal positions. Business people are generally fairly practical. If they recognize that a policy or practice is unlawful and will cause them continuing economic harm, they are generally receptive to changing it. The lawyer plays a role in advancing this recognition.

Finally, I represent two adoption agencies on a pro bono basis. The gratifications are obvious and the ability to participate in this type of activity is often a luxury less easily available in a small firm.

As can be seen, there is little correlation among my major areas of practice. Also, my practice in these areas is not to the exclusion of occasional work in other areas. This is an example of a difference in the personality of my law firm as opposed to some others. Large firms place differing emphasis upon the importance of an attorney specializing, how quickly specialization should occur, and how much pressure is placed upon the associate to specialize in a given area. My specialties evolved over the course of three years of exploring numerous legal areas.

A large firm offers a new lawyer diversity, not only in terms of the type of legal practice offered, but in the people themselves. I initially perceived this to be an advantage of a small firm, but I now find it to be one of the greatest attributes of a large firm. I assumed that I would have closer personal relationships and find the working atmosphere more pleasant and intimate in a small firm. I now believe that a large law firm incorporates numerous types of personalities, and its size permits this diversification not to generate conflict. In a small firm, a personality conflict between two members can create tension for the remaining members in a way which does not occur when 70 lawyers are involved. Also, to the extent one specializes, the pool of working relationships narrows, thereby promoting the more intimate working relationships.

There are advantages and disadvantages to large firm practice, and what those factors are is the function of the given firm. The emphasis upon time commitments, responsibility, and client contact are all variables which must be assessed in evaluating the personality of any firm. In my particular firm, client responsibility and contact came quickly; however, this is not true in every large firm. If you are considering work in a large firm, interview carefully, particularly for second year clerkships, and try to select the firm which you think has the personality with which you are most compatible. Use your second year clerkship at that firm not only to verify whether your perceptions were correct, but to develop your ability to analyze the makeup of other firms, so that if you interview at another firm, you will more quickly be able to assess whether it's for you.

MIKE CHIORAZZI

Law Librarian/Legal Information Specialist

To quote a famous 20th century philosopher poet, "Lately it occurs to me, what a long, strange trip it's been."

I entered law school with no real idea exactly what an attorney did, let alone what kind of law I would like to practice. Then, one day in my first year, a light bulb went on. I was being trained in this newfangled thing called Westlaw. I had, what was for me, a profound insight—this computer stuff is going to be big! That was the extent of my vision. I never claimed to be particularly deep.

Talking with law school librarians, I found that several of them had law degrees. As I learned more about what they did, an idea took hold; after law school I would go to library school. At worst, I could delay adulthood for a year; at best, I could find a career. My decision was not well received by my family. They had hoped for another F. Lee Bailey Jr.; they were getting Marian the Librarian.

What do law librarians do? Work in law firms, corporations, legislative libraries, administrative agencies, court libraries, law book publishing houses and law school libraries. The field also offers opportunities to specialize, in areas such as foreign, comparative and international law, collection development (what to buy to meet an institution's needs), special collections (rare books), and web design. There are more law librarians out there than you might think—the American Association of Law Libraries boasts over 5000 members.

I work in an academic setting and have found the work always interesting, varied and challenging. Starting as a reference librarian, I assisted and trained library patrons in the use of library materials. One moment it might be members of the public researching their own legal problems (from barking dogs to Living Wills), the next a professor interested in a comprehensive listing of 19th century contract treatises. I also taught a class on computer assisted legal research.

Now, as the director of a law school library, I teach legal research related courses, supervise a staff of 20, and administer a budget of $1.5 million. I have helped plan and oversee construction of a new law library building, create computer networks, build library collections, hire and occasionally fire staff, serve on University committees, edit a journal and research and write when I can find the time. Best of all, I get to work for and with law students—an eager and intelligent group, and always interesting.

More and more law firms are hiring librarians to supervise their information technology infrastructure and to provide highly specialized expertise in in a wide array of areas of practice (some examples: complex litigation, securities law, environmental law, government contracts and intellectual property).

With the Internet becoming increasing more important, the demand for librarians, and their knowledge of cutting edge technologies, will surely increase. As Clifford Stoll has said, what the Internet needs is a good librarian.

Beginning law school, I never in my wildest dreams imagined a career as a law librarian. It's not for everyone, but since I have thoroughly enjoyed the long, strange trip I've never looked back.

And, after a while, even my family came to agree that I made a great decision.

BARBARA SATTLER

Criminal Defense, Solo Practice

Growing up in the 50's, I used to watch Perry Mason and think about how great it must be to be a criminal defense attorney. At the time it was only a dream because I didn't know any lawyers, no one in my family had ever graduated from college, and all the lawyers I saw on TV were men. By the mid–70's the world had changed considerably. After living through the 60's and earning a BA and MA, I found myself working as a counselor in a state agency feeling extremely frustrated because my efforts to help people seemed fruitless due to bureaucracy and regulations.

At the old age of 29, I revived the long-dormant idea to going to law school. Now fifteen years later, after trying over a hundred cases including murder, terrorism, and dog abuse, I am a sole-practitioner doing criminal defense, and trying to raise a child. To my surprise I often do more counseling than legal work and still butt my head against a system that seems unresponsive, hostile and unconcerned with individual justice. Often my most valuable service to a client is listening or hand-holding, rather than giving legal services.

With all its frustrations, I wouldn't give up criminal defense or private practice.

Criminal defense work is fast-paced and exhilarating. People ask me all the time, "How can you represent those people and sleep at night?" Although sometimes the people I represent are stupid, uneducated, and may have committed a heinous act, the system is so badly skewed, to punish and to expedite, that the majority of the time the punishment so outweighs the crime that representation is easy. Someone once said a criminal defense lawyer sees "bad" people at their best; a divorce lawyer sees "good" people at their worst. What is difficult for me is dealing with prosecutors who seem more concerned with statistics, and judges who seem more concerned with expediting their calendar than with finding what justice is, or trying to solve a real social problem.

At the end of a trial which didn't go well, I may question my performance (perhaps I could have been better, but I never question that my client deserves my best.

On a typical day, before going to the office, I have to figure out with my husband who will take and pick up our son at daycare and arrange for his other daily activities. Because I run a business (and employ a full-time secretary, part-time attorney, and other support staff), often many hours in the day are filled with administrative matters such as paying bills, deciding what books and supplies are needed or can be put off, fighting with the IRS, and my version of billable hours. These are problems neither law school nor my five years as a public defender ever prepared me for.

I usually handle around twenty active cases (not including inactive appeals or cases which are in other stages of waiting) which typically include DUI's, drug cases, child molestation and rape, domestic violence, and murder. On a typical day I talk to clients (this is where the counseling comes in), write motions, write letters begging for, or explaining, why a certain deal or plea bargain should be given, go to court hearings, interview witnesses, do research and speak with other lawyers, probation officers, or police officers. Sometimes I don't have time to eat lunch or make a personal call.

I will never forget the first time I head the words "not guilty," nor the first time I heard "not guilty," in a murder case. I still feel a thrill seeing my name in print or my picture on TV (at least on a good hair day) and, of course, winning a case. However, over time what has provided the most satisfaction and pride is receiving cards from clients who are writing to thank me, not because of the result (which sometimes is not good), but because they know I fought hard, did my best, and, most importantly, cared.

ANDY SILVERMAN

Legal Aid

It is 9 a.m. I arrived at work awhile ago. The waiting room is filling up and it is my day to be "on."

Being "on" in the legal services parlance signifies your day to do intake interviews. It is the first time the client talks to a lawyer. Such days generally amount to 10 to 15 of these encounters ... the real guts of a legal services practice. I know it is a day that I will get no other work done but seeing clients.

The phone rings ... it is the intake worker informing me that my first client is ready. I am now officially "on" and the stream of clients may go on all day, one right after another.

A young woman with a three-year-old tagging along walks into my office. After the introductions, I go for the extra legal pad and colored pens I always have ready and hand them to the child. I know that if the interview is going to be at all meaningful I have to keep the child happy and busy.

The woman tells me that she is two months behind in rent and the landlord has sent her an eviction notice. She has been out-of-work for the past four months and her ex-husband who she cannot find has not paid child support for the past year. Her problems sound overwhelming. Where do I start? Is there anything legally I can do?

Well, being a lawyer, my initial reaction is to think of legal remedies, the law school approach to the problem. Is there a violation of the landlord-tenant law? Is the eviction notice proper? Will she have any defenses to a possible unlawful detainer action? I start going down this road and quickly realize she can no longer afford this apartment and all she wants is time to find suitable but cheaper housing for her and her child. A phone call to the landlord from me, the lawyer, might do it. She tried the day before and failed. I call and the landlord reluctantly agrees. And another call to a friend in the public housing office helps her cut through the bureaucratic maze to find new housing. She leaves a bit relieved.

Before my next client I think about whether I am a lawyer or a social worker. Did my last client need a lawyer? Or did I do for her just what a corporate attorney does for the corporation president: identify the true problem and find the easiest and fastest way to resolve it. Well, it does not matter, I helped someone and that's all that really counts.

No more time to reflect, the next client is standing at the door. He is a man in his 50's who works part-time as a laborer. He had purchased an insurance policy because of a newspaper advertisement that had made generous promises. But when he became ill, the company said his claim was not covered. Sounds like a legal problem and one that another lawyer in the office may be interested in pursuing. She has handled similar problems and is looking for "the" case to litigate. This may be the one. I get the facts and tell the client we will be in contact. I will talk to the other lawyer tomorrow when I am "off" intake.

Legal problems keep flowing in all day. Food stamp cutoffs, car repossessions, housing foreclosures, there is no end. They have one common ingredient: a person in trouble that needs help. That personal side of legal services keeps me going. It is frustrating; it is gratifying; it is being a legal services attorney.

At the end of the day an older woman walks into my office as my final intake of the day. She does not speak English well but gets across that her son is in the county jail. My first reaction is that she has a criminal problem which legal aid lawyers do not handle. In my tired state I think that I may be able to get rid of this problem quickly. But I hear her out and become fascinated. I remain after closing hours talking to her about her son's complaints about the conditions in the jail. I have heard about that "awful jail" for years but now may have a real, live client that wants to do something about it. She tells me that her son and others in the jail would like to talk to a lawyer about such a suit. I promise her I will see her son tomorrow. It all seems worth it.

JAMIE RATNER

Government Attorney

When I was in law school, I did not have any definitive plan for what I was going to do when I got out. I ended up taking a job with the Transportation Section of the Antitrust Division of the U.S. Department of Justice. I did not have a lifelong dream to prosecute, and in fact philosophically I was not inclined to be a prosecutor. But the job was wonderful. It gave me an opportunity to see from the inside how the U.S. government behaves, it gave me a chance to live and work in Washington, D.C. (which is a fascinating place to live for awhile, although not necessarily a place to ultimately settle down), and it gave me a chance to practice law in a setting where the client was only good analysis and the right thing to do.

Practicing law for the government is a unique thing, but in many ways I consider it the only way to practice law. Money is not the issue: getting it right is the issue. If you think something should be done, you do something. If you think something should not be pursued, you recommend dropping it. Sure, it is a little hard on your stomach lining when you are asked to cross-examine a well-known economist during an airline merger hearing at the Civil Aeronautics Board before you have found out whether you passed the bar. True, you spend a lot of nights at the office when a merger of the Southern Pacific and Santa Fe Railroads is dropped in your lap and you and another lawyer are told that the two of you are the two people in the country responsible for making sure that the railroad industry in the western United States remains competitive.

But one great thing about practicing law for the government is that very early on, you get responsibility and great work. If you accept that responsibility and do your work properly, you can accomplish a lot. Your job makes you the adult in charge. You investigate and prosecute pricefixers who are taking money from ordinary consumers. You make sure mergers don't give a firm so much power that there will be significant harm to the economy. You help to develop coherent policies concerning deregulation of the airline industry. You write Senators explaining the economic and legal implications of proposed legislation and you may even help negotiate treaties.

I will never forget the people. Most of us, non-lawyer and lawyer alike, were there because they liked the work and cared about it, and we were all in it together rather than competitors for some mythical status on some hierarchy. Usually we worked in staffs of two or three. We traveled together, investigated together, threw frisbees down the hall shattering everyone's name plates, jointly wrote briefs and memos and stuck our own brand of humor in the footnotes, played softball, fought with the front office and opposing counsel, and spent a lot of time in that strange state which is relaxation and intensity and humor and frustration all combined in the same space at the same time. Some of my colleagues even married each other. Some of the smartest, most capable, and funniest people I have met in my life I had the opportunity to work with at

Justice, and some of them remain my closest friends.

I don't want to lie to you—while I treasured my time in Washington, working for the government in Washington, D.C. can also drive you to the brink. The tourist traffic around the White House gets on your nerves when you are running a grand jury at the federal courthouse and you are a little late. Or you may not have the same political bent as the people in charge. Political appointees who do not have much of a clue can be your supervisors. (What you learn to do in such a situation is to explain everything fully in an effective and persuasive way; I used to feel confident that if I had managed to explain the matter to some of the people in our front office, persuading a commission of experts or a judge would be quite easy by comparison.)

Practicing law for the government offers a large reward. It isn't monetary * * * it is something more lasting. You can get training, you can get experience, you can make it a career if you want, you can get things done, and you have an opportunity to accomplish things that improve the quality of life for others in the world, which is what being a lawyer is really all about.

JIM WEBB

Government Work/Private Practice

Revolving Doors. The first time I saw one—at age five—I knew that the revolving door was an inherently dangerous instrumentality. Nevertheless, I quickly learned the manipulation of the several variables involved in getting in the door and safely out the other side. By the time all the vectors of the problem were resolved: coincidence of speed, angle of attack, heavy-lady-heavily-laden approaching on conflicting courses, I began to forget my instinctive response to the contraption. When years later I heard of the "revolving door" as metaphor for the shift from private to public practice and out again, I had lost my youthful wariness.

The federal government occasionally publishes a document known, in the vernacular, as the "Plum Book." It lists all the many appointed positions in the executive branch of the government; many acceptable, without great corruption of standards, to lawyers. The Book is full of jobs which are, in turn, full of challenge, power and prestige. It's easy to imagine, in reading that book and thinking about your place in an incoming administration, that the public, honoring your Glorious Leader and your stunning performance as administrative assistant to the assistant administrator for administration, will repeal the twenty-second amendment, and that you and your President will go on indefinitely from triumph to triumph. At worst, it appears that you can, following your government service, slip gracefully into a fine job with a firm or industry that is crying out for your important experience and important contacts.

It doesn't always work that way. A revolving door is a good place to get hung out and dried.

Government jobs are often highly specialized and highly specific to government. No matter how much you know about the Endangered Species Act, you are not going to get a job with the Snail Darter Trust or the Furbish Lousewort Corporation.

The ground also shifts rapidly in politically oriented work. The significance of your experience and your contacts can evaporate as easily as an electoral plurality. Air Force procurement policies, for instance, may provide fodder for a hundred good practices. You, poor turkey, may find after you leave government service in that area that there are a hundred and twenty good practitioners already in the field, and that Jane Fonda is the new Secretary of Defense.

A lawyer's highest distinction and greatest solace is competence. The most reliable way to gain competence is to stick to place and to a defined progression of skills and responsibilities. The revolving door breaks progression.

After a few years away from my home jurisdiction, my most confident recollection of the State's law was the color of the annotated statutes. A rather torpid legislature and a stately judiciary had somehow managed to change a lot of that collections' contents and I had somehow managed to forget a lot of what they hadn't changed. Four years of great decisions made on the Potomac had not done a thing for the simple and vital skills of private practice like effective calendaring and timekeeping. Being less apt at some of those skills than a junior associate or, worse, producing less income for the firm than that junior, doesn't do a thing for the ego.

My view now is that every new start in the practice of law is a start from well behind the line of scrimmage.

One who is a thin-ice-skater and an abyss-skirter, one who ardently wishes to benefit, or, at least, to meddle with others on the broadest possible scale, one who can walk with Assistant Secretaries of Commerce and not lose touch with himself or the kids, one who is an exceptionally quick *and* thorough study and is cursed with nomadic instincts, may find a home for his neuroses in the revolving door.

Today, I find that I am not so constituted. Today, I find myself struggling uphill against the problems of the new start and the envy I often feel for my classmate who found a place and stayed in it, quietly honing his skills, peaceably nurturing his friendships, his practice and his portfolio.

DEBORAH BERNINI

Judge—Trial Court

I have only been on the bench for six months, so I begin each morning by asking myself, "Is this the morning I will succumb to 'Black Robe Disease'?" I spent a good deal of my fourteen years as a litigator criticizing the boneheaded, biased, and cowardly decisions of the judges I appeared before. I had no trouble challenging their authority. Now I feel as if I have stepped through the Looking Glass.

I am amazed at how difficult it can be to "do the right thing" and how unclear the answers often are. I often feel like a first year law student, wanting to yell at the professor, "So what's the damn answer?" Evidentiary rulings are easy, as are most legal rulings. It is the questions of fact that make me pause. Decisions regarding credibility, intent, sincerity, remorse, motivation, fear, and anger are what make the courtroom one of my favorite places to be, but are also what make this job so difficult. I realize that decisiveness is one of the most appreciated qualities in a judge, but I am less quick to judge other human beings in my formal role as judge, than I ever have been in my personal life.

My biggest problem is bad lawyers. I do not mean inexperienced, but rather those who are unprepared, ignorant of the law, or some combination of the two. I have lost my patience with three lawyers in my brief tenure, and all three were criminal defense lawyers whose unpreparedness resulted in costly prices paid by their clients. Having spent most of my lawyer years as a public defender, I struggle with my desire to interrupt or intervene when a defense lawyer appears to be blowing it. Perhaps I am simply not aware of what the lawyer's tactics; perhaps my "help" is not welcome. But there are times when I know major mistakes are being made. If I feel that an accused's rights are going down the toilet, I get involved. No lawyer's ego, theory of the case, or reputation is more important to me than the right of a Defendant to get a fair trial.

I wish that lawyers talked less and said more. I cannot believe how many attorneys can talk for over thirty minutes before they tell you why they are there and what they want. I also now understand why judges fall asleep during trials. I have actually drawn blood digging my nails into the palms of my hands in an attempt to appear alert while trial lawyers waxed eloquent to a jury. Everyone in the courtroom appreciates a lawyer who can get to the point: the clerk, the court reporter, the judge, and especially the jury.

Get to the point and watch your reputation. A trial lawyer's reputation is everything. It means more than ability or talent. The best reputation is that you are honest, you quote the law correctly, and you don't play disclosure games with your opponents. Judges talk among themselves and messing up with one judge will quickly be held against you by others. That doesn't mean that you should never challenge a judge. But pick your fights carefully, find some law that backs you up, and always start with the comment: "With all due respect, your honor." It will at least give you limited immunity for any carefully disguised insults you plan.

I have the greatest job in the world. I get to spend my days in the courtroom, my favorite place to be. My goal is to see that justice is done, and sometimes I see that goal reached. I get to work hard, meet interesting people, watch talented lawyers practice their craft (sometimes), and explain to the public how important our system of justice is—and at the end of each day I go home without the worries and burdens of the trial attorney who constantly wonders if some issue was missed, if some deadline was forgotten.

I hope I always remember how hard it is to be a trial attorney. Maybe I don't have to succumb to the Disease.

WILLIAM C. CANBY, JR.

Federal Appeals Judge

My work cycle is monthly, not daily. One week a month I travel to another city to hear appellate arguments. The other three weeks I am home in chambers dealing with the results of those arguments.

An Argument Day

I arrive at the courthouse where I am supplied with a desk. I have read the briefs for today's arguments during the past week, and now review bench memos prepared by my law clerks. The bench memos summarize the facts and analyze the legal issues.

After half an hour I leave for the robing room, where I meet the other two judges assigned to hear cases with me that day. We enter the courtroom and the presiding judge calls the calendar. The first case is a criminal appeal. Was there probable cause for the search that revealed the cocaine? That determination is highly factual, and all three of us ask questions about the evidence presented at the suppression hearing.

The next case came from the National Labor Relations Board. Was there substantial evidence to support the Board's determination that a union steward was fired for union activity? He had been guilty of some unrelated discipline infractions. When there are mixed motives for firing, what is the test to determine whether the firing was permissible?

We continue through the calendar, hearing either 15 or 30 minute arguments per side in each case. I find that I am on edge during the arguments, both because I find arguments exciting and because I don't want to miss what is said or pass up the opportunity to inject my own questions. We continue through the calendar, without stopping to rule or recess. We hear an admiralty case (man overboard), a diversity case (breach of contract), and an antitrust case (vertical conspiracy).

We return to the robing room to discuss the cases. Because I have least seniority, I give my views first. Some cases are quickly disposed of; the search was legal and the conviction can be affirmed in a short memorandum. We disagree about the antitrust case; that one will take a long time, require an opinion, and I may dissent. The presiding judge makes the writing assignments and we all go to lunch. As I relax I am reminded that arguments are the most satisfying but tiring part of my job. I will spend the rest of the afternoon dictating notes of this morning's cases and getting ready for tomorrow's calendar.

A Day in Chambers

I begin by going through the morning mail, good and bad. Some are memos from other judges concurring in opinions I have drafted and circulated, almost invariably with minor suggestions or corrections. One memo from another judge suggests that one of my proposed opinions is seriously off track. I will have to go back through the opinion, read the cases the other judge cites, and either make changes or risk his dissent. Next I review two proposed opinions by judges in cases where I was a member of the panel; they were heard six weeks ago. I assign each to one of my three law clerks for review. Each will come back to me with a memorandum commenting on the draft.

I next work on the pile of proposed opinions that have come back from my clerks with such memoranda. I go through each opinion, read a case or two if crucial, and check my notes from argument against the opinion. I review my clerks' comments. I then draft a memorandum to the other judge, perhaps concurring, including suggestions for change and noting possible problems.

I meet with my secretary and law clerks together to go over the work in the office. How many opinions are in the mill, and how late they are? Clerks are making initial drafts of almost all of them; I am working on one or two from scratch. We review assignments of bench memos for next month's arguments, and set deadlines for them.

Finally, I get to work on an opinion I am writing: Indian law. I have been working on it off and on for six weeks, and find it difficult and challenging. Ideas for it keep coming up when I am doing other things, and I use some of them. Soon I will float it to my colleagues; eventually it will come down, I hope the way I want it to. *The result matters to a lot of people.* Sometimes it is hard to see that fact behind all the paper in the office, but it comes to the surface every so often. And that makes all the matter to me.

BILL BOYD

Law Professor

It's just after noon. The bluebooks will be delivered shortly. I wonder how the students have done. Was the exam too difficult? Too easy? Was it fair? If not, it wasn't for lack of effort.

I don't look forward to grading exams. Not many of us do. As the Dean is fond of quipping, "Exam grading is what we get paid for. The rest is fun." In any event, most of us worry about the grading. We know the process is far from scientific. The goal is to reduce the margin for error—to design a test that measures a student's command of the subject matter as comprehensively as time permits. This is no modest goal.

The exam today is in bankruptcy. Bankruptcy is a two-hour course. Frankly, that is not enough time to cover such a complicated body of substantive law and procedure. But this can be said about most courses. Perhaps I tried to cover too much. I continually ask myself what it is that students need to know so they can begin to deal intelligently with the range of bankruptcy issues they are likely to confront in practice. Realistically, how many of them will have to worry about the role of a 1111(b)(2) election in a "cram down" of a Chapter 11 plan? But then, can any self-respecting course in bankruptcy not expose students to such mystifying concepts?

It's a difficult line to draw. A well-conceived course is one that accommodates the realities of the limits of time and the needs of most students with the crush of information contained in most areas of the law.

Most of us strive to make our exams reflect this accommodation. The exam should test what we have judged to be important. Obviously, it isn't feasible or necessary to test for everything we cover. But a fair cross-section of the material should be implicated. The trick is to weigh the questions commensurately with the time and attention given the particular point or points in class.

Contrary to what students are inclined to believe, the exam isn't intended to "do in" a certain percentage of students. There are no "traps" aimed at tripping up the unwary. Nothing would please us more if all the students did well. After all, their level of performance reflects upon the quality of our teaching.

We are sensitive to the imperfections in the examination process. We labor hard to compensate. We look for clues that reinforce what the "raw scores" suggest is a good, or a bad, performance. We tend to resolve doubts in a student's favor. It isn't unusual for a teacher to overlook an important omission, or even significant mistake, and to assign an A or B grade to an exam that otherwise is exceptionally good. In such cases we attribute the omission or error to test design or exam pressure.

We don't want students to do poorly. Poor performances present perhaps the greatest difficulty. What accounts for the poor performance? Was it the test? Most of us reread the "bad" exams. We don't want to "ding" a student. We examine carefully for "clues." Is there a problem with completeness? Does it appear that the student seriously misallocated his or her time? Is the deficiency in the depth or accuracy of analysis? Has the student missed or mistreated even the most fundamental of issues? Is the performance truly unsatisfactory?

We agonize a good deal in assigning a grade below a C. Some teachers simply refuse to give bad grades. They don't want to defend them. It's easier to pass all the students. Such behavior is unfair. It's unfair to the students who worked hard and earned a passing grade. It's also unfair to those of us who feel that making the hard decisions "goes with the territory."

Well, here they are. Let's see how they've done. Hmm. OK. Not bad. What? You didn't learn that in my class. Oh, that's better. What explains the earlier blunder? Hey, this is not bad at all. Good point. I hadn't thought about it quite that way myself. Whoops. You can't mean that. Did you misread the question? I see what you did. You were assuming the creditor was only partially secured. Too bad. But the analysis is correct given your assumption. Let's see now. You were clearly wrong on the conversion issue. And you misread one part of the question. But you've hit most of the major points. Some interesting analysis. Very respectable bluebook.

CHARLES ARES

Law Professor

Teaching law is hard work. I've been at it since 1961 and keeping up with movements in the law and getting prepared for class seem to take me about as long now as when I started.

But there is another way in which law teaching is hard. The longer I'm in the academic world the more I worry about just what it is that we teach our students. I don't mean "the law" and "the legal method"—we do that better and better all the time. I mean what we teach, mostly implicitly, about the role lawyers are supposed to play. We teach students from the very outset, as we should, that they are to be highly skilled partisans, that they are to be analytical and very skeptical of factual and legal propositions. They learn under our prodding to state the case as strongly in their clients' favor as the credulity of their audience will permit. They may, in fact, learn not only that truth takes many elusive forms but that sometimes it doesn't really exist. Only zealous representation of our client really counts.

I wonder how many students think that the "legal method" involves lying, or at least "massaging" the truth. Many of us who have been in the profession a while don't realize that we may, at least unconsciously, convey the wrong message to neophytes. One of the most heart warming and yet depressing statements I've heard from a law student was recently uttered at the end of my course in Professional Responsibility. On the way out of the classroom, this good and conscientious student said, "I had almost decided I didn't want to be a lawyer because I don't want to lie for people. But now that I've learned we're not supposed to lie for clients, I feel a lot better."

Good people can be good lawyers. It isn't easy, but then preserving one's integrity never is.

*

INDEX

References are to Pages

419